The New Regional Italian Cuisine Cookbook

The New Regional Italian Cuisine Cookbook

Authors: Reinhardt Hess, Cornelia Schinharl, and Sabine Sälzer
Food Photography: FOODPHOTOGRAPHY EISING

Contents

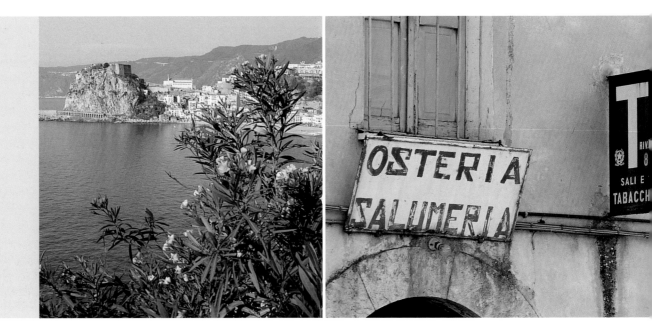

The Beautiful Cuisine

Italy makes us happy. Over and over and always. Even if we have traveled further than the Adriatic Sea or eaten spicier foods than spaghetti all'arrabbiata, or tasted wines from "down under," or enjoyed a Mediterranean afternoon with latte macchiato and ciabatta that have become very popular, nothing seems to have diminished our longing for the original and for our wanting to preserve the flavor of the "authentic" Italian cuisine.

As we began gathering the material for our first cookbook 15 years ago, we wanted above all to pay homage to the culinary traditions of all Italian regions. The richness of details attracted our attention. Which type of pasta is most popular where? Where do Italians cook with butter? Where do they cook with olive oil? Where are the different types of meat, fish, or wild vegetables most common? Beyond pasta, pizza, and risotto, we found an extraordinary variety of dishes that made us realize that one book would not have been enough.

Of course in the meantime, we have seen also that once-regional specialties, such as mozzarella with tomatoes, bruschetta, and/or spaghetti alla carbonara, are prepared all over the world, not just in Italy. And much else has changed since. Our vacations to Italy are no longer just at the beaches or in large cities but also in tiny mountain villages or in locations nestled throughout the southern parts of the Italian boot. Our expectations and our appetites for remarkable and unchangeable dishes have increasingly grown stronger. In this sense, we don't mean the desire of visiting fine restaurants but rather the desire for places where it is still possible to experience an unexpected authentic culinary adventure— a simply set table under a shady tree, a fine dish of pasta superbly prepared, a small glass of wine, and that special Mediterranean mood . . .

And what about the Italian home cooks? They too still honor their ancestors' culinary traditions. They too want to retain a love for the culinary detail while they update and refine the Italian way of cooking. They might prepare osso buco with shanks of lamb instead of veal, or simmer olives in sauces, or use tomatoes in spicy chutneys, or cook tuna on the grill. They might prepare local fish in salt crusts; they might cover casserole specialties with runny polenta layers; they might prepare "risotto" with other types of grains; they might use crostini for delicious appetizer bites. Desserts, too, are evolving: some menus cater to a taste for the light, refreshing, and fruity; others still feature the flavor of coffee or chocolate variations on classics like tiramisù and panna cotta.

Thus, the "New Regional Italian Cuisine." Here are the regions, the people, the ingredients, and the recipes, but presented in a harmonic, authentic, and updated context. Let us share with you what this fascinating cuisine has inspired us to present: 220 new recipes that we hope will inspire you to cook and use good wholesome ingredients.

Furthermore, there is an additional basic idea favorable to this collection of recipes: Today we can truly find almost everything we need to be able to prepare and enjoy authentic Italian food. However, a trip to Italy is still worth your while, even if only to tiny hidden villages behind steep or high mountain peaks.

The Authors and the Publisher

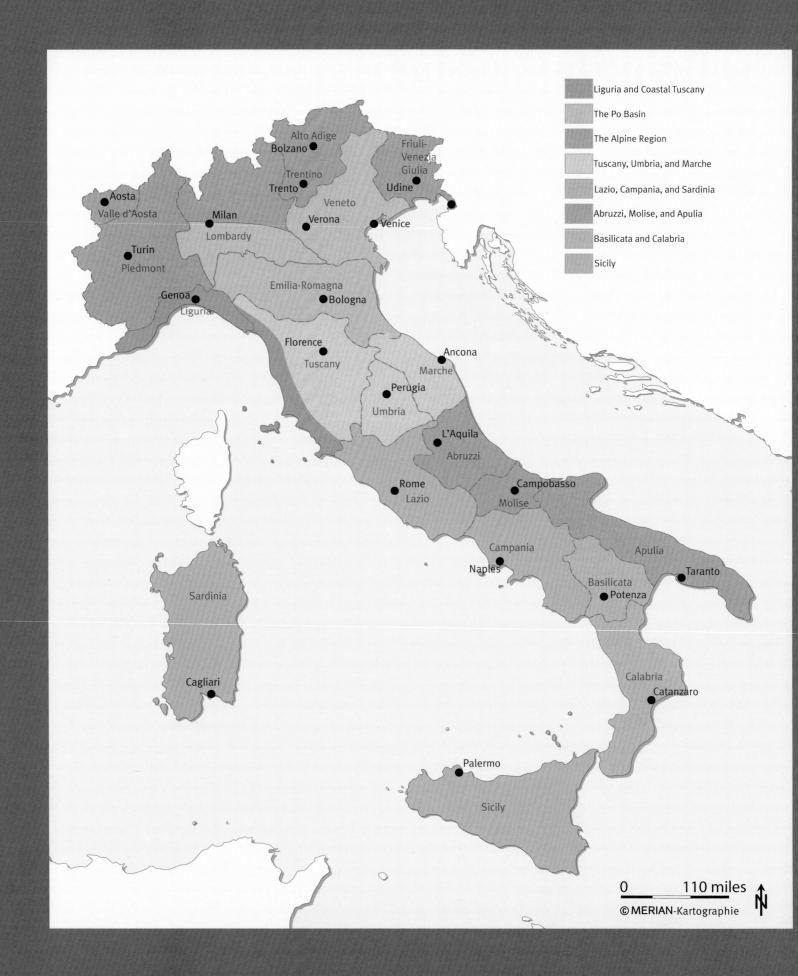

Liguria and Coastal Tuscany

The Po Basin

The Alpine Region

Tuscany, Umbria, and Marche

Lazio, Campania, and Sardinia

Abruzzi, Molise, and Apulia

Basilicata and Calabria

Sicily

Alto Adige
Bolzano

Trentino
Trento

Friuli-
Venezia
Giulia
Udine

Aosta
Valle d'Aosta

Milan
Lombardy

Veneto

Verona

Venice

Turin
Piedmont

Emilia-Romagna

Genoa
Liguria

Bologna

Florence
Tuscany

Ancona
Marche

Perugia
Umbria

L'Aquila
Abruzzi

Rome
Lazio

Campobasso
Molise

Campania

Apulia

Naples

Basilicata
Potenza

Taranto

Sardinia

Calabria
Catanzaro

Cagliari

Palermo

Sicily

0   110 miles

© MERIAN-Kartographie

N

The Culinary Regions

Liguria and Coastal Tuscany

The Ligurian Alps provide shelter from the northern winds, so vegetables, herbs, fruits, olives, and vineyards can thrive here. The cuisine that is brought forth reflects the four seasons. Ancient grains are popular. Herbs are used both as a vegetable and as a flavoring. There is pesto, the fresh basil paste that is ubiquitous in pastas, soups, and casseroles. The fine olive oil from *taggiasca* olives is used for cooking and as a seasoning. Venison, mushrooms, fish, and home-raised rabbits add variety to this cuisine that is simple and at the same time refined.

The Po Basin

The cuisine of this fertile area of Italy reflects abundance: great sausages and cheese products, from mortadella to prosciutto di Parma; Gorgonzola, Asiago, and Parmigiano-Reggiano cheeses are inviting too. In Veneto and Lombardy, rice specialties are often featured as *primi* (first courses); in Emilia-Romagna, pasta is preferably stuffed. Favorite dishes combine diverse vegetables such as pumpkins, mushrooms, spinach, herbs, and radicchio. Geese, chicken, lamb, pork, and beef are of high quality, and the Lagoon of Venice supplies fish and seafood.

The Alpine Region

Featured here are simple, hearty, and nutritious dishes that historically had to provide good nourishment in a cooler climate. They are still marked by the use of pork, mountain cheese, butter, and cream, but they are now prepared according to more updated methods. Traditional dishes and flavors include roasted chestnuts served with new wine; wild mushrooms and truffles loved by many; polenta dishes with bacon and ham; and fish from rivers and lakes.

Tuscany, Umbria, and Marche

The cuisine of central Italy has evolved recently. The wholesome ingredients of its peasant origins, such as legumes, vegetables, herbs, and meats, are served with new ingredients and in new combinations. Chickpeas with seafood, meat with flavorful vegetables, and *antipasti* (appetizers) with zucchini blossoms grace menus and tables, as do dishes like crostini topped with liver spread, appetizers with olive salsas, and desserts topped with chestnuts. Here the regional cuisine caters also to a gourmet palate that appreciates the rich supply of fresh fish and seafood from Marche and the fragrance of truffles from Umbria.

Lazio, Campania, and Sardinia

This cuisine reflects a lively palate and a beautiful climate: Intensely red and flavorful tomatoes, snow-white mozzarellas, and fresh and fragrant lemons are just a few of the main ingredients that mark this regional way of cooking. Beyond classic dishes like tomato and mozzarella salads are pasta topped with mozzarella, risotto with lemon zest and juice, or tender octopus salad enhanced with the addition of apples and celery. From Sardinia come new and simple dishes, while in Lazio, popular specialties such as saltimbocca are prepared with fish.

Abruzzi, Molise, and Apulia

People in the mountainous regions of Abruzzi and Molise love their delicious lamb and free-range, locally raised pork; they cook with hand-picked saffron and, arguably, make Italy's best pasta. Apulia has not only wonderful peppery olive oil but also dishes that include recently "discovered" vegetables such as large beans, small red wild onions, and *cime di rapa* (broccoli rabe). Also superb are the baked goods, especially the bread baked in Altamura. Along the coast, dishes also reflect the abundance of fish that is prepared in many creative ways.

Basilicata and Calabria

Culinary markers of these regions are fresh fish and seafood dishes, and pork. To these main ingredients are usually added dried or fresh legumes and the spicy and ubiquitous *peperoncino* (chili pepper). The red onions of Tropea are renowned; they are eaten either raw or sautéed and prepared in sauces that top homemade noodles. Abundant vegetable harvests during spring and fall are preserved in olive oil and are the typical *antipasto*. Cheeses made from goat's or sheep's milk complement this cuisine that in its simplicity is also very modern.

Sicily

Swordfish, tuna, sardines, and anchovies are the favorite fish of the island's inhabitants. Pungent flavors and aromatic and colorful dishes are popular. Pasta is topped here with either *bottarga* (dried fish roe) or breadcrumbs instead of cheese. Eggplants are included in many specialties; they are featured in appetizers and in *contorni* (side dishes). Tomatoes, peppers, fennel, artichokes, and zucchini also are favorite vegetables. Citrus fruits, capers, and raisins flavor many dishes, and sweet-and-sour flavor combinations reflect the influence of the Arabs, who also introduced here the fruity iced dessert *sorbetto*.

Liguria and Coastal Tuscany

Open to the sea: Rocky and steep coasts, beautiful beaches, and a love of fresh greens

The Region and Its Products

A lot of sea and very little flat land; a mild climate and an abundance of herbs

Shaped like a crescent moon, stretched in the northwest from the French border to the Gulf of La Spezia, Liguria is Italy's northwest region. It offers beautiful beaches and a blue sea. In the south the region reaches to the art monuments of Tuscany and from Carrara to the Maremma to where the isle of Elba hides its many small harbors.

Steep Hills and Small Fields.
Because of the southwest sea winds, the climate here is mild, with not-too-hot summers and not-too-cold winters. This has always lured vacationers. And, where there are guests, there is also fishing, even if the sea does not seem to give as much anymore. Behind the coast that attracts tourists, the land climbs up to touch the chain of the Apennines. Inland from the coastal areas are hidden silent valleys filled with greens and speckled with mountain villages, rocky and remote places where tourists are rarely seen. The villages of Cinque Terre on the west side of La Spezia that reach out to the rocky side of the mountains are the most picturesque.

Since spacious orchards and fields for vegetable cultivation are rare, throughout the centuries the residents have terraced the land to grow basil for pesto, borage and marjoram, sage and rosemary, as well as vegetables and fruits. The effort required to grow and tend vegetables has led to an appreciation of fresh produce. Cabbage, Swiss chard, spinach, and tomatoes are used preferably fresh from the market or directly from the garden or field. Flowers, vineyards, and olive trees also grow along the terraces. Taggiasca olives make a highly valued, light, and delicately flavored olive oil. White beans of Badalucco (north of San Remo) and potatoes grown throughout the Aveto Valley located east of Rapallo are especially good. The small patches of pasture are inhabited by sheep, goats, and occasionally cows, all raised for their milk that is used for cheese; one specialty of the region is a fairly rare cheese, *bruzzu*, made from aged goat ricotta. From this area also come wonderfully fragrant honeys, such as those made from thyme, chestnuts, and lavender.

Evergreen Macchia.
Almost the entire Tuscan coast alternates between sandy beaches and rocky cliffs. Along river estuaries, fine sandy plains are home to such plant species as broom bush and dyer's weed, which can resist the summer droughts. Pinion trees and oaks dominate, and even in winter the intensely green *macchia* or forest can be almost impenetrable. Boar and deer, pheasant and wild geese are abundant here. The plains are home to the Maremma cattle that are hardy and adaptable. Where there are rolling hills, the land is cultivated to grow wheat, vegetables, and grass. Wine is also produced here; large and small winemakers grow a variety of grapes, most notably the Sangiovese variety.

The almost impenetrable bush vegetation of the Maremma gives way to large pinion trees that are rich in cones filled with fragrant pine nuts. The area is under natural resource management protection, and is only accessible to visitors three days per week.

The mighty gray Maremma cattle live outdoors all year round. They are strong and robust with dark and lean meat that is especially suitable for stews and ragùs.

The steep coast of Cinque Terre reaches 1,000 feet high and includes five terraced villages along the Ligurian coast. The retaining dry walls, called *muri a secco*, are set and pointed together without mortar. Several thousand miles long, they are part of the landscape and keep the soil of the area's vineyards in place. In addition to a dry white wine, the area produces a fine sweet wine called Sciacchetrà.

In spite of the sea's vicinity, dried but unsalted cod, called *stoccafisso*, is very important in the cuisine of Tuscany and Liguria. Baccalà, which is cod that has been dried and salted, is an all around favorite. Both have to be soaked for several hours (baccalà a little bit less) before being ready for cooking.

In Liguria, zucchini blossoms seem to be more popular than the vegetable itself. They often garnish pasta sauces, they are served stuffed, or they may be dropped in batter and deep fried.

Waiting for a fish to take the bait can take a while. Liguria and Tuscany's coasts are not rich with fish. Those who catch a bass feel very lucky. More frequently the bait pulls up either sardines or anchovies.

The Cuisine

The most important ingredients are mild olive oil and fresh vegetables

Recipes from Liguria and coastal Tuscany are simple—almost humble—and are typically vegetarian rather than rich in meat. They are based on regional products and on four growing seasons. Even traditional specialties are suitable for a modern, healthful diet without much need of updating.

From the sea. Squid, octopus, and diverse types of mussels are favorites, as well as the fish from the Mediterranean Sea. At times seafood may even be served raw. Otherwise they "swim" in fish soups or in hearty one-pot dishes together with beans and herbs. They may also be deep fried in olive oil until they are crispy.

It must be green. Ligurians have always liked to navigate the seas, and after long voyages they long for fresh greens. They include vegetables and herbs in appetizers, soups, stuffed pasta, and even in tarts. One can hardly find something greener than pesto, the popular herb paste made of basil.

To make pesto, take a good handful of delicate fragrant basil leaves, mince them with sea salt in a mortar or food processor, add pine nuts and young cloves of garlic, and blend until it has the appearance of a thick paste. Mix in either pecorino or parmesan cheese. As a final touch, add olive oil until you obtain a thick, creamy green sauce. Pesto is added to soups, gives flavor to pasta and bread, and to vegetables and sauces.

Noodles, dumplings, cakes, and ice creams made from fresh chestnuts or chestnut flour reflect the dense chestnut forests that once covered the Ligurian region. Later these were replaced by olive groves and fruit orchards, vineyards and vegetable gardens. Lima beans, kale, Swiss chard, cabbage, potatoes for gnocchi and quiches, tomatoes, and the other classic ingredients are grown now, and find their way into pasta, ravioli, and vegetable-based main and side dishes called *contorni*. In the fall, dishes with wild mushrooms, especially prepared with porcini, ovuli, and chanterelle mushrooms, appear on regional menus. The primary legumes are chickpeas (garbanzo beans) that, like in the Middle East, are prepared in many and various ways.

From fields and forests. Not many animals are raised along these coastal regions. Chicken and rabbits are primarily raised for a local and individual necessity. Lamb and goat are reserved for special occasions, and veal is a regional festive favorite. Game animals like deer and boar are still found throughout the forests of Liguria and the Maremma. Game dishes are often prepared with spices, raisins, and chocolate, and can remind us the Saracens and foreign powers that dominated the coasts and the region centuries ago.

a

b

c

d

a Tomatoes, ripened in the sun and served with bread and olive oil, were in the old days the most important meal consumed by farmers during their work in the fields.

b Taggiasca olives were introduced during the Middle Ages by Benedictine monks; they are not only very suitable for the production of olive oil but also for olive canning.

c Delicate basil is almost synonymous with Genoa. It is the basis of pesto that is classically prepared in a mortar with a pestle. The green herb is often cultivated in greenhouses and has lost its strong, astringent flavor.

d Along the coastal areas of Tuscany, legumes, sausages, and dried fish are important and preferred ingredients.

e The small purple-tinged artichokes, called *cimaroli*, can be used whole, including the stem. They appear in many dishes that are prepared as main courses, quiches, or sauces for pasta. When and if they are available they need to be freshly picked and very tender, otherwise they are stringy and taste like straw.

e

The Wines
From simple white wines to expensive super reds

Locally the fruity Ligurian white wines, such as the Vermentino from the western Riviera Ligure di Ponente, are served preferably with fish and seafood; outside the region, however, they are hardly found. The wines from Cinque Terre are rarely exported, as are the white and red wines of Elba Island. The red wines of the Maremma, on the other hand, are world famous. They are known among the classic wines as Super Tuscans.

Indigenous vine varieties.
Liguria's white wines are made from regional vines that are called Albarola, Bosco, Buzzetto, and Pigato that are only to be found here. They taste refreshing and fairly dry with a mellow aftertaste; they are often relatively strong and are of a light yellow color tinged with light green sparkles. The Vermentino vine, which also grows in the Maremma, produces a fruity, almost sparkling, slightly acidic shimmering yellow wine that has a delicate almond flavor and goes very well with appetizers and fish dishes. A Cinque Terre specialty, besides the white wines from Bosco, Albarola, and Vermentino grapes, is the Sciacchetrà, a preciously sweet, golden, and alcohol-rich wine from grapes that were left to dry in the sun before fermentation.

The most important Ligurian red is the Rossese di Dolceacqua that is made throughout the west side of the region near the French border. The Rossese grapes produce dark, cherry-red wines that taste smooth and aromatic. They are usually served with stews, poultry, and roasts.

Maremma's white Bianco di Pitigliano, made principally from Trebbiano grapes, is dry with a delicate scent and at its best while still "new." The Morellino di Scansano, made principally from grapes from the Sangiovese family, has a definite and full-bodied taste and is well suited for aging.

The Bolgheri region, located between the cities of Livorno and Grosseto, has been less renowned for its whites and rosés than for its reds. On the international wine market these reds are called Super Tuscans. When the wine production of the Maremma area was modernized, especially under the patronage of the Antinori family, the French grape varieties Cabernet Sauvignon and Merlot were added to the traditional Sangiovese grape variety; this union brought forth great wines, such as the Ornellaia, Sassicaia, Guada al Tasso and Paleo, that are simply known now as Bolgheri Superiore.

Left: Pitigliano is not only a beautiful small town in the Maremma but also the source of the name of the white wine called Bianco di Pitigliano.
Above: Reowned samples of the region (from left to right)—Il Bruciato, Insoglio del Cinghiale, Scalabrone, Morellino di Scansano, Vermentino.

Regional Recipes

Greens and scented herbs complement Middle Eastern-spiced dishes

The Northwestern cuisine is mainly characterized by natural ingredients and a refined food preparation. Whether it features a stuffed rabbit prepared like a stuffed breast of veal or updated *cappon magro* that translated should be a "healthy capon" but in reality is a fish salad, the specialties are always exciting. Even fried ravioli or the breaded stems of Swiss chard that are called "fish of the mountains" have a lightened sensibility.

Piccolo Cappon Magro
Seafood Salad (Liguria)

INGREDIENTS for 4:

For the vegetables:

½ small cauliflower (about ½ lb)

½ lb green beans

½ lb red potatoes

½ lb carrots

½ lb turnips

3 celery ribs

Salt

For the fish and seafood:

1 lb perch fillet

½ lb peeled and deveined large shrimp

4 large scallops (substitute with 9–10 oz mussels)

Salt and freshly ground pepper

1 Tbsp olive oil

1 Tbsp lemon juice

For the sauce:

3 hard-boiled eggs

2 anchovies (preserved in salt)

1 tsp drained capers

2 fresh parsley sprigs

2 Tbsp pine nuts

4 Tbsp white wine vinegar

⅓ cup olive oil

Salt and freshly ground pepper

4–8 slices stale bread

1 small new head garlic or 1 large clove

PREPARATION TIME: 1½ hours
PER PORTION: about 575 calories

The name of this rich salad from Genoa is somewhat misleading. A *cappone* is a capon, a castrated rooster with rich meat, and *magro* means lean. There is no chicken in this specialty. Since capons were forbidden during Lent, this salad was made with a mixture of fish, seafood, and vegetables, as well as eggs and crisp bread or crackers. This version is no less rich in flavor than the original.

In the beginning, carpasina, a type of twice-baked bread, made with barley was used. This bread is so hard that it requires soaking in water and vinegar before it is ready to serve, usually with garlic, tomatoes, basil, anchovies, and olive oil.

1   Rinse and trim all vegetables. Cut the cauliflower into florets. Peel the potatoes and the turnips and slice them ¼-inch thick. With the peeler, remove all possible strings from the ribs of celery. Cut these in ½-inch long slanted pieces. Prepare a large bowl filled with water and ice cubes. Bring a large pot of water to a boil.

2   Beginning with the light colored vegetable varieties, cook the vegetables, one type at a time, for approximately 10–15 minutes or until still firm to the bite. When they are ready, use a slotted spoon or a perforated strainer to remove the vegetables and drop them into the bowl of ice water. Let the vegetables cool, then drain them.

3   Rinse all seafood and perch. Cut perch into 2½-inch long pieces and the shrimp in halves lengthwise. Cut the scallops in half. Place a steamer basket over the vegetable water (drain some of the water if necessary) and steam the fish and the seafood for 3 to 5 minutes, or until it is opaque. Season with salt and pepper, then drizzle with the olive oil and lemon juice.

4 For the sauce, remove the cooked egg yolk of a hard-boiled egg. Rinse the anchovies and capers; pat them dry and mince them. Rinse and pat dry the parsley; mince the leaves. In food processor or blender, puree or blend the egg yolk, anchovies, capers, parsley, pine nuts, 2 tablespoons of the vinegar, and the olive oil. If necessary, add a few drops of water to obtain a smooth, creamy mixture. Season the sauce with salt and pepper.

5 Place the slices of bread in a dry skillet. Cut the garlic in halves or slice it; add it to the bread. Cook the bread and garlic over medium heat until golden brown. Distribute the bread and garlic on serving dishes and drizzle it with the remaining vinegar.

6 Place the vegetables, fish, and seafood on the slices of roasted bread and garlic; dress everything with the sauce. Peel and slice the remaining eggs to decorate the dish.

Insalatina di Farro e Legumi

Spelt Salad with Legumes (Coastal Tuscany)

INGREDIENTS for 4:

$1/4$ cup dried white beans
(cannellini)

$1/2$ cup spelt

$1/4$ cup lentils

1 carrot or 1 small fennel bulb

1 small green bell pepper

1 small zucchini

1 red onion

1 celery rib

$5^1/2$ Tbsp olive oil

$1/4$ cup pitted black olives

Salt and freshly ground pepper

1 Tbsp white wine vinegar

3 Tbsp aged pecorino cheese

2 Tbsp polenta flour or cornmeal

PREPARATION TIME: 45 minutes
SOAKING TIME: Overnight
COOKING TIME: $1^1/2$ hours
PER PORTION: about 390 calories

1 Soak the beans and the spelt overnight in water to cover (in case you use other spelt kernel products, follow the package directions).

2 Drain and rinse the beans and spelt. Cook them and the lentils separately in clean water until still firm to the bite (the beans and the spelt will require approximately 1–1½ hours cooking time; the lentils approximately 30 minutes). Drain the legumes and kernels and let them cool.

3 Rinse, trim, peel if necessary, and dice the carrot, fennel, pepper, zucchini, onion, and celery (you should find that you will have more or less same quantities of each vegetable).

4 Heat 1 tablespoon of the olive oil in a skillet. Sauté all the vegetables over medium heat; set them aside to cool, and add them to the cooked grains and legumes. Slice the olives thinly and add them to the salad; season with salt, pepper, vinegar, and 4 tablespoons of olive oil.

5 To garnish the dish, grate the cheese after removing the rind. Combine the cheese with the polenta flour. Brush a skillet with the remaining ½ tablespoon of olive oil and heat it well. Distribute a thin layer of polenta and cheese mixture into the skillet; let it fry briefly until the cheese melts and turns golden brown. Loosen it with a spatula and remove it immediately. Set it aside to cool. Break it and use it to garnish the dish.

The mixture dish of legumes and grains, which is often served in Liguria and Tuscany, was created apparently by the women of La Spezia who picked up from the pier-walks whatever fell out of the big sacks that were unloaded at the local port.

Tortino di Patate e Acciughe

Potato and Anchovy Flan (Liguria)

INGREDIENTS for 4:

1 lb plum tomatoes (about 7–8)

2 basil sprigs

6 Tbsp olive oil

1 lb boiling potatoes

2 spring onions

4 anchovies (preserved in salt)

2 garlic cloves

Salt and freshly ground pepper

5 eggs

PREPARATION TIME: 1 hour
BAKING TIME: 25 minutes
PER PORTION: about 345 calories

1 Bring a large pot of water to a boil. Blanch the tomatoes, and rinse them under cold water. Core, peel, seed, and dice them. Place the tomatoes in a colander for 30 minutes to drain all liquid. Remove the basil leaves from the stems. Chop the leaves and combine them with 2 tablespoons of olive oil.

2 Rinse and peel the potatoes; then slice them thinly and cut the slices in thin strips. Trim and thinly slice the onions. Rinse and mince the anchovies.

3 Preheat the oven to 350° F (if convection oven 325° F). Brush a springform pan with 1 tablespoon of olive oil. Heat the remaining 3 tablespoons olive oil in a skillet. Crush the garlic and add it to the oil; let the garlic flavor the oil. Sauté the potato strips over medium heat until golden brown, turning them over periodically with a spatula. Add the onions and anchovies. If necessary, season with salt and distribute the mixture in the springform pan.

4 Whisk the eggs with a pinch of salt and pour them over the potatoes. Bake the flan on the middle oven rack for approximately 25 minutes or until the eggs are set. Set aside to cool.

5 While the flan bakes, puree the tomatoes with the basil-infused oil; season with salt and pepper. To serve, remove the flan from the pan, cut it into wedges, and serve with the pureed tomatoes.

Recommended Wine:
You can also serve the flan with a *gotu*, a glass of wine, such as a Vermentino.

Emmer—Ancestor of Wheat

This ancient grain can claim a 7,000-year-old history

Not long ago, farro was always identified as spelt; however, in recent years we have learned that what some call spelt should actually be called emmer. The ancestor of emmer was a one-kernel cereal called einkorn (*Triticum monococcum*). What we buy today as emmer is actually a hybrid two-kernel wheat variety called *Triticum dicoccum* that has 2 rows of kernels on each side of the head. Emmer, thus, should be included in the family of the hard-wheat species and specifically in the two-kernel row varieties. Soft wheat and spelt are related to it and are of the three-kernel row variety.

Adaptable cereal.
Emmer grows in a variety of soils. It is adaptable to low-temperature climates and is disease resistant, and it is possible to grow it in dry and difficult areas. It served central Europeans, especially from Roman times until the Middle Ages, as a source of food and a bread ingredient until it was replaced by wheat. Wheat offered a richer harvest and a more stable kernel.

Emmer's taste has become popular again and the grain is cultivated more and more. In Italy, it is grown especially along the coast of Tuscany around Garfagnana, where its originality has been protected and labeled IGP (Indicazione Geografica Protetta) as farro della Garfagnana.

Content and flavor.
Two varieties of emmer are offered in Italy, the whole farro (the whole coarse kernel) and farro perlato, which is entirely freed from its bran during the milling process. Farro perlato is lighter in color and requires a shorter cooking time; this is hardly a great advantage if we consider that the whole kernels cook in about 45 minutes, contain more vitamins, and have a more natural organic flavor.

While the bran content of flour made from whole emmer equals that of whole wheat flour, the texture of emmer is finer than that of whole wheat. Noodles and breads made from emmer flour are dark and rich in nutrients but have a finer texture to the palate that those made from whole wheat flour. Also emmer's protein and mineral content is higher.

Easy to prepare.
Emmer's kernels do not need to be soaked in water before cooking. It cooks in about 45 minutes and requires about twice the amount of liquid as grain. Farro is often used in soups and stews with vegetables, served as first course or after it has cooled off, dressed as a salad. It is also prepared with herbs and stewed vegetables or as a side dish with meat or fish. Emmer flour is used to make: focacce, pizzas, breads, and pasta; the hearty, dark pasta goes well with natural and wholesome ingredients such as herbs, olive oil, and small pieces of pecorino cheese. Farro is available in health and natural food stores and Italian delis. Otherwise, why not purchase your own supply directly in Garfagnana?

a For Emmer Salad: Simmer 1 cup of emmer (or spelt) in 2 cups of water for 45 minutes. Cut 10.5 oz of cherry tomatoes in half; and chop finely a small bunch of fresh oregano. Toss with ½ tablespoon of sugar, 2 tablespoons olive oil, salt, and chili powder to taste, and broil in the oven for 10 minutes. Combine with the emmer, then dress everything with additional minced fresh oregano, 1 tablespoon white wine vinegar, and 2 tablespoons of olive oil. Optional: You can top the salad with pecorino cheese shavings.

b The harvest of emmer (farro) is usually not as abundant as that of hard or soft wheat. However, the ancient grain is very adaptable to all kinds of soil and low-temperature climates; as such, emmer can be cultivated easily in rough and difficult mountain terrain. c Farro as well as spelt belong to the wheat family. After being threshed, farro's kernel is still wrapped in a hard hull that is removed during the milling stage. In the case of the farro perlato the outer layer is removed with an additional polishing method. d–f Either as cereal or as flour, farro has again gained popularity in Italy due to its definite aroma and its baking properties.

Ravioli con Zucca e Riso

Pumpkin and Rice Stuffed Ravioli (Liguria)

INGREDIENTS for 4:

For the stuffing:

$1/2$ lb pumpkin meat
(preferably from butternut or
Hokkaido)

$1/4$ cup long-grain rice

Salt and freshly ground pepper

$1/2$ cup ricotta cheese

$1/4$ cup grated parmesan and
pecorino cheese

1 egg

1 Tbsp dried marjoram leaves

For the pasta dough:

3 cups all-purpose or bread flour

3 eggs

Salt

4–6 Tbsp white wine

Flour, to dust work surface

Olive oil, for frying

PREPARATION TIME: $1\frac{1}{2}$ hours
PER PORTION: about 670 calories

1 Preheat the oven to 350° F (if
convection oven 300° F) . Wrap
the pumpkin meat in foil. Bake on
the middle oven rack for about 40
minutes. Meanwhile, cook the rice
in water for about 15 minutes;
drain and set aside to cool in a
colander. Remove the pumpkin
meat from the oven, mash it, and
set it aside to cool. Combine the
pumpkin, rice, ricotta, grated
cheese, egg, marjoram, salt, and
pepper in a bowl. Refrigerate.

2 For the pasta dough, mix the
flour, eggs, salt, and wine in a
large bowl; knead to make a
smooth dough. Cut into pieces
and on a floured work surface, roll
each piece into a very thin sheet.
Cut each sheet in 3 × 2-inch rectangles. Place pumpkin mixture in
the middle of each rectangle; fold
and press each rectangle shut.

3 Heat 1 inch of olive oil in a
skillet and fry the ravioli, until
crispy and golden brown. Drain
them on a layer of paper towels
and serve immediately.

Trenette con Noci e Arance

Trenette with Nuts and Oranges (Liguria)

INGREDIENTS for 4:

$1/4$ cup pine nuts

$1/2$ cup walnuts

1 organic orange

3–4 parsley sprigs

1 small rosemary sprig

2 Tbsp olive oil

3 garlic cloves

Salt and freshly ground pepper

1 lb trenette pasta (substitute with
linguine)

$3/4$ cup heavy cream (or half and
half)

$3\frac{1}{2}$ oz Gorgonzola cheese

Freshly grated nutmeg

3 Tbsp grated parmesan cheese

PREPARATION TIME: 30 minutes
PER PORTION: about 825 calories

1 Chop the pine nuts and walnuts coarsely. Roast them lightly
in a skillet; set aside. Scrub the
orange under hot water and
remove the zest with a grater or
zester, removing as little pith as
possible. Set aside. Rinse the
parsley and rosemary and pat dry;
mince the leaves. Combine with
the orange zest, oil, pine nuts,
walnuts in a small skillet. Peel the
garlic and crush it through the
garlic press into the herb mixture.

2 Bring a large pot of salted
water to a boil. Add the trenette
and cook until al dente, stirring
often. Meanwhile, heat the oil-nut
mixture until the oil simmers gently. Add the cream and simmer for
5 minutes, stirring occasionally.

Trofie Nere Primavera

Black Pasta with Spring Vegetables (Liguria)

3 Mash the Gorgonzola with a fork and add it to the cream sauce, allowing it to simmer and melt. Season the sauce with salt if necessary, pepper, and nutmeg.

4 Drain the trenette and mix with the cheese sauce. Top with parmesan cheese and serve immediately.

The noble mold-cheese Gorgonzola is a variety of *stracchino*, an ancient cheese from the Piedmont and Lombardy regions that migrated very early in time to the Ligurian region. *Stracchino verde* was the original name that referred to the blue-green veins that characterized this noble cheese variety.

INGREDIENTS for 4:

For the pasta dough:

3 cups spelt flour (hard wheat flour)

Flour, to dust work surface

Olive paste (available in delis)

Salt

For the vegetables:

$1/2$ lb asparagus

4 very small zucchini (preferably with the blossoms)

2 spring onions

$1/3$ cup butter

$3/4$ cup green beans (you may substitute with snow peas)

$1/4$–$1/3$ cup vegetable broth

2 Tbsp fresh chopped basil

1 Tbsp each minced fresh thyme, rosemary, and winter savory

Freshly ground pepper

$1/4$ cup grated parmesan cheese

PREPARATION TIME: 1 hour
RESTING TIME: 20 minutes
PER PORTION: about 535 calories

1 Mix the flour, olive paste, and some cold water (about $3/4$ cup) in a large bowl, knead to make a smooth dough. Cover the dough with foil and set it aside to rest for 20 minutes.

2 Punch down the dough and knead it again. Tear small pieces of dough (no larger than a bean) and shape them by hand on a floured work surface to make thin sausage-shaped 1-inch long noodles. Transfer the noodles to a floured dish cloth and let them air dry until you are ready to cook them.

3 Trim (and peel, if thick) the asparagus. Cut off their tips and set them aside. Cut the spears into 1-inch lengths. Trim the zucchini; cut them into matchsticks (or julienne); set aside the zucchini blossoms.

4 Trim the onions; mince the white part. Heat 1 tablespoon of butter in a skillet and sauté the white part of the onion. Add all other vegetables, except the zucchini blossom, and cook for 7 minutes, adding the vegetable broth to moisten everything; stir the mixture periodically.

5 Meanwhile, bring a large pot of salted water to a boil. Drop in the noodles; let them cook until they rise to the surface. When the trofie are ready, remove them from the water with a strainer or slotted spoon and transfer them to a serving platter.

6 Add the remaining butter, herbs, and zucchini blossoms to the sauce. Season the sauce with salt and pepper and pour it over the noodles. Top with parmesan cheese.

Minestra d'Orzo al Basilico

Barley Soup with Basil (Liguria)

INGREDIENTS for 4:

1 cup pearled barley

8 cups vegetable broth

1½ lb unshelled peas (substitute with 1½ cups dry split peas)

1½ lb unshelled beans (substitute with ¾ cup dry baby lima beans)

2 bunches basil

2 garlic cloves

2 Tbsp pine nuts

Salt and freshly ground pepper

2 Tbsp olive oil

PREPARATION TIME: 1 hour
PER PORTION: about 625 calories

1 Rinse the barley under hot water until the water runs clear. Place the barley in a large saucepan, add the broth, and bring to a rolling boil. Reduce the heat, cover, and simmer for 40 minutes.

2 Meanwhile, shell the peas and beans. If necessary, squeeze the peas and beans with your thumb and remove those parts that are hard and leathery.

3 Rinse and pat dry the basil; pull the leaves off the stems. Peel and coarsely chop the garlic. Combine both with the pine nuts and some salt in a mortar with a pestle, and crush or puree in a food processor.

4 Add the peas and the beans to the barley and continue to cook for 5 more minutes. Stir the basil mixture into the soup; season with salt and pepper. Ladle into bowls, drizzle with olive oil, and serve.

Spezzatino di Seppioline

Cuttlefish Stew (Liguria)

INGREDIENTS for 4:

1 lb very small cuttlefish (if they are not available fresh use frozen)

1 lb wide Italian green beans

2 large tomatoes

2 onions

3 garlic cloves

1 celery rib

¼ cup olive oil

1 lb red potatoes

Salt and freshly ground pepper

3 cups fish or vegetable broth

1 bay leaf

1 sprig each fresh basil, parsley, thyme, and oregano

PREPARATION TIME: 30 minutes
COOKING TIME: 1 hour
PER PORTION: about 360 calories

1 Rinse the cuttlefish and pat it dry (if you use frozen, let it thaw first). Rinse the Italian beans; if necessary remove the stringy filaments and cut the beans on an angle into 1-inch pieces.

2 Bring a large pot of water to a rolling boil. Blanch the tomatoes and rinse them in ice water. Core the tomatoes. Drop the cuttlefish in the boiling water; cook for about 1 minute, remove it and place it to drain in a colander. Cut the cuttlefish lengthwise.

3 Peel and mince the onions and garlic. If necessary remove the stringy filaments from the celery and chop finely. Heat the olive oil in a large saucepan. Sauté the onions, garlic, and celery over medium heat for about 10 minutes or until everything is golden brown.

Zuppa di Fagioli e Vongole
Bean Soup with Clams (Coastal Tuscany)

4 Meanwhile, peel and dice the potatoes. Add the cuttlefish to the saucepan and let cook for about 3–4 minutes. Add the beans and stir to coat them with oil. Season with salt and add the potatoes. Sauté everything for a few minutes and add the broth and bay leaf. Season with salt and pepper as necessary; simmer, uncovered, for 20 minutes.

5 Peel the tomatoes and cut them into large pieces. Add the tomatoes to the stew. Continue to simmer for 30 minutes.

6 Just before serving, rinse and pat dry the herbs; chop the leaves coarsely. Add them to the stew. Taste and season with more salt and freshly ground pepper if necessary.

INGREDIENTS for 4:

1 cup dry small white beans (cannellini; substitute with baby lima beans)

1 onion

2 garlic cloves

1 celery rib

1 sprig each fresh rosemary, thyme, mint, and myrtle (substitute with curry herb or bay leaf), and lavender

3 Tbsp olive oil

Salt and freshly ground pepper

1 1/2 lb clams (substitute with mussels)

2 medium tomatoes

2 parsley sprigs

PREPARATION TIME: 20 minutes
SOAKING TIME: Overnight
COOKING TIME: 1 1/2 hours
PER PORTION: about 275 calories

1 Soak the white beans overnight in cold water to cover.

2 Peel and mince the onion and garlic. If necessary remove stringy filaments from the celery and chop finely. Rinse the rosemary, thyme, mint, myrtle, and lavender; pat them dry and with kitchen twine; tie them together like a bouquet.

3 In a saucepan, heat 2 tablespoons of olive oil. Sauté the minced vegetables over medium heat until they are golden. Rinse and add the beans. Add 4 cups of cold water and the bundle of herbs. Bring everything to a rolling boil; reduce the heat and simmer for 1 1/2 hours or until the beans are tender.

4 After 1 hour cooking time, season the beans with salt and pepper. Rinse the clams well, making sure to discard those that are open or damaged.

5 Bring a pot of water to a boil. Blanch the tomatoes; rinse under cold water. Core, peel, halve, and seed them. Rinse and pat dry the parsley; chop the leaves. In a wide saucepan, heat the remaining 1 tablespoon olive oil, sauté the parsley and tomatoes briefly; add the clams. Cook everything over high heat for 3–5 minutes or until clams are open.

6 Remove and discard any clams that have not opened; they can be bad. Remove the bundle of herbs from the soup. Add the clams with their juice to the soup; season with salt and pepper.

Typical for this type of soup:
Use ingredients that are available and in season. On the island of Elba there are all kinds of wild herbs to be found; these give a distinctive taste to the specialty.

Sarde su Bietole

Baked Sardines on Swiss Chard (Liguria)

INGREDIENTS for 4:

1½ lb fresh whole sardines

4 Tbsp coarse sea salt (or kosher salt)

1½ lb Swiss chard

Salt

6 Tbsp olive oil

Freshly ground nutmeg

PREPARATION TIME: 45 minutes
REFRIGERATING TIME: 1 hour
BAKING TIME: 20 minutes
PER PORTION: about 315 calories

Recommended Wine:
A flavorful white wine or, if possible, a light red Pinot Nero from the Friuli Region.

Silver-colored sardines, with their long thin bodies, are more popular in Liguria than in this country; it may be because so many of us are not used to cleaning fish or dealing with fish bones. Do it once, though, and see how easy it is.

For this recipe, buy the smallest and freshest sardines you find; you will be rewarded with the best flavor. If these are not available, look into the frozen fish section and let the sardines thaw before preparing them.

Rubbing the sardines with salt is a way to make the meat firmer and give the fish more flavor. However, this method requires coarse salt because using fine salt will result in too salty sardines.

1 Under running water, remove the scales from the sardines (run a gloved hand against the scales' direction, from tail to head). With the back of a knife carefully scrape off all the remaining scales.

2 Snap off the head of each sardine and pull it down; this will also remove most of the entrails. Cut open the fish at the belly, remove any remaining entrails and the spine. Open the fish like a butterfly and rinse well.

3 With scissors, cut the fish tail. Follow this method for all fish; rinse them well; pat them dry and close them again.

4 Line a shallow baking dish with half of the coarse sea salt. Set the sardines on the layer of salt and cover them with the remaining salt. Refrigerate them, covered, for about 1 hour.

5 Trim and rinse the Swiss chard; cut it into ½-inch wide strips. Bring a large pot of salted water to a rolling boil and blanch the chard for about 5–7 minutes or until the stems are still firm to the bite. Drain the chard in a colander, rinse it with cold water, and set aside to allow it to drain well. Preheat the oven and a baking sheet to 425° F (if convection oven 400°F).

6 Brush 4 large pieces of parchment paper with some olive oil (you may use waxed paper or foil). Divide the Swiss chard among the parchment paper and dust with a little nutmeg. Remove the sardines from the refrigerator; wipe the salt off as well as possible. Place a fish on each layer of Swiss chard; drizzle everything with the remaining olive oil.

7 Fold each portion in the parchment paper and crimp the edges to seal; place each package on the hot baking sheet and bake everything on the middle oven rack for about 20 minutes or until the parchment paper looks golden brown. Place each parchment paper packet on a serving plate. Let each diner open the packet at the table—carefully, as steam may escape.

Orata al Sale

Gilt Head Bream in Salt Crust (Liguria)

INGREDIENTS for 4:

1 large gilt head bream (cleaned, ready-to-cook; about 2½ lb substitute with porgy or sea bass)

Salt and freshly ground pepper

1 basil sprig

4½ lb coarse sea salt (substitute with kosher salt)

5 Tbsp olive oil

1 small lemon

2–3 parsley sprigs

PREPARATION TIME: 1 hour
BAKING TIME: 20–30 minutes
PER PORTION: about 310 calories

1 Cut the sharp spiny fins and spines from the fish with scissors. Rinse the fish well under running water and pat dry. Season the inside of the fish with salt and freshly ground pepper and place the sprig of basil in the cavity.

2 Preheat the oven to 475° F (if convection oven 425° F). Line a baking pan with foil and cover with a ½-inch thick layer of coarse sea salt. Press the fish shut and place it over the layer of salt. Brush the fish with 4 tablespoons of olive oil; cover it with the remaining salt, making sure to press the layer of salt on the fish. Bake the fish on the middle rack for about 20–30 minutes. Turn off the oven, open the oven door slightly, and let the fish bake in the open oven for an additional 10 minutes.

3 With a reamer, extract and collect the lemon juice. Rinse and pat dry the parsley; mince the leaves. Mix both ingredients with salt and enough of the remaining olive oil.

4 Before serving, tap the fish and remove the salt crust. Serve the fish on a platter with the olive oil and lemon juice mixture.

Tonno alla Contadina

Tuna Chowder, Farmer's-Style (Coastal Tuscany)

INGREDIENTS for 4:

1 lb tuna steaks

1 lb tomatoes

1 large onion

2 garlic cloves

¼ cup pitted black olives

2 or 3 sprigs green fennel tops

1 sprig each rosemary, mint, and sage

1½ lb red potatoes

4 Tbsp olive oil

¾ cup fish or vegetable broth

Salt and freshly ground pepper

2 parsley sprigs

PREPARATION TIME: 1¼ hours
PER PORTION: about 545 calories

1 Pat the tuna dry and cut it into 1½-inch cubes; refrigerate. Bring a large pot of water to a boil. Blanch the tomatoes and rinse under cold water. Core, peel, seed, and cut them into cubes.

2 Peel and mince the onion and garlic. Chop the olives. Rinse and pat dry the fennel tops, rosemary, mint, and sage; chop the leaves finely. Peel and rinse the potatoes; cut them into 1½ × 1½-inch cubes.

3 Heat the oil in a large saucepan or Dutch oven. Sauté the onion, garlic, fennel, and herbs until they are translucent but not dark. Add the tomatoes and olives; cook for about 5 minutes. Add the potatoes, broth, and as much water as necessary to cover the potatoes; season with salt and freshly ground pepper. Cook, covered, over medium heat for about 30 minutes or until the potatoes are done.

4 Add the fish; season with salt and cook for 5 more minutes. Remove the pot from the heat

Filetti di Persico in Mantello di Patate

Potato-Covered Ocean Perch (Coastal Tuscany)

and set aside to let the stew rest for 2–3 minutes. Rinse and pat dry the parsley; mince the leaves and sprinkle it over the stew.

INGREDIENTS for 4:

2 large red potatoes

Salt and freshly ground pepper

2 ounces lardo di Colonnata (see Tip)

2 Tbsp olive oil

8 small fillets ocean perch (substitute with sea bass or white mullet)

2 Tbsp lemon juice

2 shallots

2 garlic cloves

4 Tbsp cold butter

¾ cup dry white wine

½ cup fish broth

½ bunch thyme

PREPARATION TIME: 45 minutes
PER PORTION: about 455 calories

1 Peel and rinse the potatoes; slice them thinly. Set aside the end slices. Bring a large pot of salted water to a rolling boil; boil the potatoes for about 1 minute. Drain the slices with a strainer or a slotted spoon; place them on a clean dish cloth and set aside until they are cool.

2 Preheat the oven to 400° F (if convection oven 350° F). Slice the bacon very thinly.

3 Brush a baking sheet with olive oil. Pat the fish dry with paper towel. Season the pieces with salt and pepper. Place the fish on the baking sheet; drizzle the lemon juice over them. Cover the fish with layers of potato and bacon slices as if you were covering them with scales. Season with salt and bake the fish for about 20 minutes or until they appear to be golden brown.

4 Meanwhile, peel and mince the shallots and garlic. Melt 1 tablespoon of butter in a small saucepan. Sauté the vegetables very lightly. Mince 2 tablespoons of the remaining round ends of potatoes and add them to the garlic mixture. Add the broth and wine and let cook on high heat for about 7 minutes or until the liquid has reduced by half. Blend or press this mixture through a cheesecloth-lined sieve and cook it again while whisking in the remaining cold butter.

5 Rinse and pat dry the thyme; remove all small leaves from one sprig. Season the sauce with salt, pepper, and thyme leaves. Place the fish on a serving platter and garnish with the remaining thyme. Serve with the thyme sauce.

Tip: If lardo di Colonnata is not available, use 2 slices of mildly seasoned bacon and place the piece in the freezer until it is ready to be sliced easily. Season the fish and the potato crust only lightly since the bacon is already salted.

31

New Flavors with Wild Herbs

An ancient tradition is rediscovered: Cooking with nature's greens

In the old days, gathering wild plants and herbs was almost a given fact. They were used to flavor meats and fish, prepared as a side dish, and used in savory stuffing, or to fill ravioli. As natural flavors are rediscovered, the importance of these gifts of nature is once again brought forth in this cuisine.

Definite aromas. Wild herbs such as oregano, thyme, bay leaf, and mountain mint, have a stronger aroma than the domesticated varieties. They have always played an important role in the cuisines of Liguria and Elba. The wild greens of the *macchia*, or forest, especially rosemary, juniper, meadow sage, rue, and myrtle, give an extraordinary culinary touch to dishes.

In springtime, when the tender leaves begin to shoot, the wild herbs are a concentrated source of vital nourishment and vitamins. Nettles (called in Italian *ortiche*), with their tender and fine leaves, can be used in place of spinach. They are gathered with gloves; cooking removes their stinging quality. In Liguria, nettles are used to fill superb ravioli; in the Valle d'Aosta, they are prepared in pasta sauce; in Alto Adige, they are used to make flavorful green soups; and in Rome, they are used for dumplings and savory pancakes that are considered a local specialty.

The flavors of the garlic-scented herb ramsons, called *erba orsina*, as well as watercress (*crescione*) and borage (*boraggine*), are increasingly appreciated and used in fish and seafood.

Unusual greens. The young shoots of wild fennel (*finocchio selvatico* or *finocchietto*), frequently found in Liguria and throughout the southern parts of Italy, are harvested in spring; they are a favorite appetizer cooked with lemon juice. They are also prepared in pasta sauces, bean dishes, fish and seafood, and lamb or rabbit recipes. Wild fennel is also used in scrambled eggs and to flavor olive oil. Fennel seeds also flavor olives, breads, cookies, sausages, and pork roasts.

Wild sprouts. Wild asparagus (*asparagi selvatici*) are woody and spinous. Since their shoots are difficult to harvest, they more often are used as a flavoring or an aromatic than as a vegetable. They are not available outside the region and the cultivated asparagus is a poor replacement for these flavorful greens.

Wild arugula sometimes called rucola, ruchetta, or rughetta, is much more flavorful than the cultivated variety. In the old days the herb grew wild everywhere; later it became a popular salad addition. The same happened with dandelion, called *dente di leone* or *catalogna*, and chicony, recognizable by little blue flowers; these plants were also considered weeds. Nevertheless, they are still popular the cuisines of Calabria and Basilicata. Yarrow (*achillea*), with its delicately bitter flavor, is used in Liguria to give flavor to lamb dishes. A wild variety of black garden radish, called *rafano*, is used in Alto Adige to give flavor to green bean dishes. It grows in fields and meadows everywhere.

a Wild fennel grows as a weed throughout Liguria and in the southern regions of Italy. This herb is used to flavor dishes and olive oil. The spindly leaves and tops are very aromatic but are used less frequently because of their spiny quality. Fennel seeds are often used in cooking. The herb can be replaced by fennel greens and seeds that are available in produce and spice sections of supermarkets.

b A blooming myrtle bush on Sardinia. The leaves, like bay leaves, flavor not only dishes such as soups and stews but also ice cream; a bittersweet liqueur called *mirto* is made from its berries.   c Wild thyme and wild sage grow in summer under extreme drought in very difficult terrain. Their aroma is so definite and strong that it remains pronounced even once the herbs are dried. Use them sparingly; these herbs can easily overpower the flavor of a dish.   d Rosemary is also grown as a decorative plant for its beautiful flowers as well as for the fine flavor it adds to grilled specialties.   e Ruchetta or rughetta is the wild arugula that used to grow everywhere in fields and gardens. The wild variety with pointed leaves has more flavor than the cultivated. In this picture it is growing near clusters of blooming and purple great burnet.

Cima di Coniglio
Stuffed Rabbit (Liguria)

INGREDIENTS for 4:

1 saddle of rabbit (with belly flaps; about 1½ lb)

1 thyme sprig

1 heart of Romaine

1 thick slice stale white bread (one day old, without crust)

2–3 Tbsp milk

1½ oz ham

6 pitted black olives

1 egg

1 Tbsp butter, melted

2 Tbsp grated parmesan cheese

Salt and freshly ground pepper

Freshly grated nutmeg

2 Tbsp olive oil

1 bunch mixed vegetables and herbs (3 parsley sprigs, 1 carrot, 1 celery rib)

1 garlic clove

1 cup dry white wine

1 large tomato

5 Tbsp cold butter

PREPARATION TIME: 1¾ hours
PER PORTION: about 540 calories

Recommended Wine:
Fruity, refreshing white wine, such as Vermentino

Stuffed rabbit is a fine variation of the breast of veal as it is prepared throughout the western Ligurian Riviera (around Savona).

Saddle of rabbit is unfortunately not readily and easily available; therefore you will have to either cut it yourself or order it from a butcher. Flatten the saddle on a work surface, making sure that you separate the meat of the belly from the ribs. Beginning by the tail, use a sharp knife to cut, tear, lift, and remove the backbone by making small sharp cuts along the entire body. Open the deboned saddle like a butterfly and remove all remaining fat and cartilage. "Mend" any tears in the saddle with thin slices of prosciutto.

1   Debone the saddle of rabbit to have one large piece of flat meat (see above). Place the rabbit on the work surface meaty side up and the saddle part down; set all the bones aside. Rinse and pat dry the thyme.

2   Bring a large pot of salted water to a boil. Blanch Romaine for 1 minute and drain it. Squeeze the lettuce and chop it finely. Moisten the bread with the milk and rip it in small pieces. Chop the ham, olives, and thyme finely.

3   Mix the lettuce, ham, olives, thyme, egg, the tablespoon of melted butter, and the cheese in a large bowl. Season with salt, pepper, and nutmeg. Place the mixture in the middle of the saddle and fold the belly flaps over it. Season the rabbit with salt and pepper.

4   Brush the rabbit with 1 tablespoon of the olive oil and wrap it first in plastic wrap and then in foil. Bring a large pot of water to a rolling boil and place the rabbit roll in it; reduce the heat and simmer for about 1 hour.

5   For the gravy, chop the bones and mince the parsley, carrot, and celery. In a saucepan, heat the remaining tablespoon of olive oil and brown the bones and vegetables until they are dark golden-brown. Peel and mince the garlic; add it to the gravy and cover everything with water. Cook until the liquid has reduced by half. Pour in the white wine and let simmer again until again reduced to half.

6   Bring a large pot of water to boil. Blanch the tomato and rinse under cold water. Core, peel, seed. Chop the tomato finely. Strain the gravy and return to the saucepan.

7   Remove the rabbit from the simmering water, unwrap, and set aside briefly to cool. Add the juices from the rabbit roll to the gravy. Bring the liquid to a light rolling boil and whisk in the cold butter. Add the tomato. Season the gravy with salt and pepper. Cut the rabbit roll in slices and serve with the gravy.

Petto di Vitello au Zemin

Fried and Stewed Breast of Veal (Liguria)

INGREDIENTS for 4:

1½ lb breast of veal (boneless; cut into two equal pieces)

2–3 medium tomatoes

8 medium shallots or 4 small onions

4 garlic cloves

About 1 cup olive oil

1 thyme sprig

¾ cup dry white wine

Salt and freshly ground pepper

¼ cup pitted black olives

PREPARATION TIME: 30 minutes
COOKING TIME: 1½–2 hours
PER PORTION: about 470 calories

1 Pat the veal dry with paper towels. Bring a large pot of water to a boil. Blanch the tomatoes and rinse under cold water. Core, peel, seed, and dice them. Peel and mince the shallots and garlic.

2 Heat ½ inch of olive oil in a large saucepan. Add the veal and brown on both sides for about 3–4 minutes or until they are crispy. Remove the meat from the oil and drain well. Rinse and pat dry the thyme.

3 Pour out almost all the oil from the saucepan; leave only enough to have a shiny saucepan. Sauté the shallots and garlic until golden brown; add the tomatoes and simmer until they fall apart. Return the meat to the saucepan and add the wine; add the thyme and season with salt and pepper. Bring to rolling boil; reduce the heat, cover, and simmer for 1½–2 hours or until the veal cartilage is tender. Remove the thyme; add the olives and heat everything until ready to serve; taste and correct the seasonings if necessary.

Faraona alla Ligure

Guinea Hen with Raisins, Ligurian-Style (Ligur

INGREDIENTS for 4:

1 large guinea hen (about 2½ lb; substitute with chicken)

2 onions

3 garlic cloves

2 Tbsp raisins

3 Tbsp olive oil

Salt and freshly ground pepper

2 cups dry white wine

1 large boiling potato

2 carrots

1 large zucchini

1 sage sprig

2 Tbsp pine nuts

Olive oil, for frying

PREPARATION TIME: 1¼ hours
PER PORTION: about 535 calories

1 Cut the guinea hen into 6 portions; rinse it and pat it dry. Peel and mince the onions and garlic.

2 Heat 3 Tbsp of oil in a Dutch oven. Brown the guinea hen on all sides, then transfer to a plate. Sauté the onions and garlic until translucent, and add the hen and the raisins; season with salt and pepper. Pour in half of the wine, cover, and cook for about 45 minutes. If necessary, moisten with more wine.

3 Peel the potato and carrots and cut them into matchsticks (julienne). Rinse the zucchini; peel, if desired, and julienne. Wipe the sage leaves clean and julienne; set aside on a paper towel. Put the pine nuts in a dry skillet and toast until golden brown; set them aside.

4 Allow the wine sauce to cook down. Heat the oil for frying in a large saucepan. Fry the vegetables and sage strips until crispy.

Cinghiale in Agrodolce
Sweet-and-Sour Boar (Coastal Tuscany)

Use a strainer or a slotted spoon, to drain them on a paper towel.

5   Season the sauce with salt and pepper. Arrange the guinea hen on a serving platter and add any remaining sauce; garnish with pine nuts, fried vegetables, and fried sage.

INGREDIENTS for 4:

2 lb boneless boar leg

1 bunch mixed vegetables and herbs (3 sprigs of parsley, 1 carrot, 1 rib celery)

5 garlic cloves

2 sprigs each of rosemary, sage, and thyme

3 cups dry red wine

3 carrots

2 celery ribs

2 red onions

4 Tbsp olive oil

$2/3$ cup raisins

1 bay leaf

Salt and freshly ground pepper

3.5 oz Italian *mostarda* (sweet-and-sour preserved fruit; substitute with Pennsylvania-style sweet-and-sour pickled melon rind)

2 Tbsp sugar

2–3 Tbsp red wine vinegar

2 squares unsweetened chocolate

Freshly grated nutmeg

PREPARATION TIME: 45 minutes
MARINATING TIME: Overnight
COOKING TIME: $1^1/_2 - 1^3/_4$ hours
PER PORTION: about 730 calories

1   Pat the boar dry and cut it into 2-inch cubes; set aside in a mixing bowl. Chop the parsley, carrot and celery finely. Peel and mince 2 cloves of the garlic. Rinse 1 spring each of the rosemary, thyme, and sage and pat dry. Add half of these herbs and all of the garlic, parsley, and the chopped vegetable to the boar meat. Pour about $3/_4$ cup of the red wine over, cover, refrigerate overnight.

2   The next day, remove the meat from the marinade and pat dry. Discard the marinade. Trim, peel, and mince the carrots, celery, onions, and the remaining 3 cloves of garlic. Heat 3 tablespoons of olive oil in a large Dutch oven and brown the meat cubes well. Remove the cubes and place them on paper towels to drain.

3   Soak the raisins in $1/_2$ cup of red wine. Pour off the oil from the Dutch oven. Heat the remaining olive oil in the same Dutch oven and sauté the chopped vegetables. Mince the remaining springs of sage, rosemary, and thyme; add the meat, herbs, and bay leaf to the Dutch oven. Pour in some red wine and simmer for about 1 hour. Add more red wine if necessary and cook until the liquid is absorbed and meat is done.

4   Cut the mostarda into small cubes. Sprinkle the sugar over the bottom of a small saucepan and allow the sugar to caramelize lightly. Add the vinegar, the red-wine soaked raisins and the cubed mostarda to the meat. Finely chop the chocolate and stir it in. Simmer everything for an additional 30–45 minutes or until the meat is tender. Season the ragù with salt, pepper, and nutmeg, then serve.

37

Fritto Misto di Mare e Monti

Fried Seafood and Meats (Liguria)

INGREDIENTS for 4:

$^3/_4$ lb small squid

9 oz raw unpeeled shrimp

$10^1/_2$ oz lean lamb (either leg or tenderloin)

$10^1/_2$ oz lean rabbit (boneless saddle; substitute with chicken breast)

4 small zucchini

5 oz fresh white mushrooms

About $^1/_2$ cup of chickpea flour

Salt and freshly ground pepper

2 garlic cloves

About 4 cups olive oil, for frying

2 lemons

PREPARATION TIME: 1 hour
PER PORTION: about 715 calories

Fried seafood is a favorite throughout all Italian regions. In Liguria, however, meat and vegetables are also part of the fritto misto. Sometimes ham, cheese, or mussels are also added on spits. The dish not only looks attractive, but also makes an easy serving of finger food. It must be served piping hot, otherwise it is half as good.

Ligurian cooks often use chickpea flour, which absorbs very little fat when used as a coating. The result? Exceptionally crispy, light fried foods.

Fritto misto is very good served with tartar sauce. Mix mayonnaise with finely chopped pickles, capers, parsley, and basil and serve as a dip.

1 Rinse the squid and trim those parts you wish to remove; cut each squid in $^1/_2$-inch rings. Peel the shrimp, leaving on the tails. With a sharp knife, slit them lengthwise and devein them.

2 Cube the lamb and rabbit and pat it dry with paper towels.

3 Trim the zucchini and quarter lengthwise; cut them into $2^1/_2$-inch pieces. Wipe the mushrooms clean; trim them and cut large ones in half.

4 Season the chickpea flour with salt and pepper. Preheat the oven to 300° F (if convection oven 250° F). Peel the garlic. Heat the olive oil and garlic in a large saucepan. Remove the garlic as soon as it is brown.

5 Dust the squid rings and the shrimp with chickpea flour; working in batches if necessary, fry them in the hot oil until they are golden brown. Remove them with a strainer or slotted spoon and set them aside on a layer of paper towels. Transfer to a heat resistant platter and keep warm on the middle oven rack.

6 Dust the lamb and rabbit with chickpea flour and fry them, also in batches, until they are golden brown. Drain on paper towels and transfer to the oven to keep warm. Dust the zucchini and the mushrooms with chickpea flour; fry them until golden brown.

7 Arrange the fritto misto on a serving platter either on white napkins or parchment paper. Cut the lemons into thin wedges and serve them alongside, drizzling the juice over the seafood.

Condiggion
Raw and Cooked Vegetable Salad (Liguria)

INGREDIENTS for 4:

3 red bell peppers

2 small thin zucchini

4 medium vine-ripened tomatoes

10 pitted black olives

3 anchovies (preserved in salt)

2 Tbsp capers

2 oregano sprigs

Salt and freshly ground pepper

3 Tbsp olive oil

2 hard-boiled eggs

PREPARATION TIME: 45 minutes
PER PORTION: about 185 calories

1   Preheat the oven to the highest temperature. Rinse the peppers, cut them vertically in half, trim the stems, and seed them. Place the peppers, cut-side down, on a baking sheet lined with foil.

2   Roast the peppers on the highest oven rack for about 7–10 minutes or until the peels are almost black. Remove the peppers from the oven and let them cool. Peel them while they are still warm and cut them in vertical strips.

3   Trim the zucchini and cut them into thin slices. Core the tomatoes and cut each into eight wedges. Slice the olives. Rinse the anchovies and pat them dry; mince them together with the capers. Rinse and pat dry the oregano; chop the leaves.

4   Combine all the ingredients in a serving bowl and season with salt and pepper; drizzle with olive oil. Peel the eggs and cut them in quarters; garnish the vegetables with them.

Fagiolini e Patate
Green Beans and Potatoes (Liguria)

INGREDIENTS for 4:

¾ lb red potatoes

1 lb fresh green beans

Salt and freshly ground pepper

2 medium tomatoes

1 garlic clove

2 parsley sprigs

2 Tbsp olive oil

1–2 tsp lemon juice

PREPARATION TIME: 45 minutes
PER PORTION: about 145 calories

1   Bring 2 large pots of salted water to a boil. Scrub the potatoes and boil them in one pot for about 25 minutes. Meanwhile, trim the green beans. Cook the beans in the second pot for about 8–10 minutes or until they are still firm to the bite. Core the tomatoes using a sharp paring knife. With a slotted spoon, hold them briefly in the cooking water.

2   Drain the green beans in a colander and rinse them under cold water; set them aside to drain and cool. Cut the tomatoes in half, seed, and chop them. Drain the potatoes and set them aside to cool. Peel and cut them into 1-inch cubes. Peel the garlic and rinse and pat dry the parsley; mince both.

3   Heat the olive oil in a skillet. Briefly sauté the parsley and garlic. Add the potatoes and green beans; sauté, stirring, then add the remaining and combine. Season with salt, pepper, and lemon juice and serve still warm.

This specialty goes very well with grilled or stewed fish or meat. Don't forget to rinse the cooked green beans under cold water; this will help to retain their vivid color.

Funghi alla Paesana

Wild Mushroom and Potato Casserole,
Peasant-Style (Liguria)

INGREDIENTS for 4:

1½ lb red potatoes

1 lb fresh porcini mushrooms
(cèpes)

Salt

5 Tbsp olive oil + oil for baking
dish

2 sprigs each parsley and oregano

PREPARATION TIME: 25 minutes
COOKING TIME: 20–25 minutes
PER PORTION: about 270 calories

1 Peel the potatoes and slice
them 1/3-inch thick. Preheat the
oven to 400° F (if convection
oven 350° F). Lightly oil a baking
dish or casserole. Bring a large
pot of salted water to rolling boil
and cook the potatoes for about 5
minutes. Drain them and layer
them in the baking dish.

2 Wipe the mushrooms clean;
trim them and rinse them only if
necessary. Cut them in half (slice

the larger ones). Layer these over
the potatoes; season with salt
and drizzle with the olive oil. Bake
on the middle oven rack for about
20–25 minutes. Rinse and pat dry
the herbs; mince the leaves.
Sprinkle them over the mushrooms and potatoes.

This mushroom specialty can
be a main course or can be
served with a light fish or meat
meal. If porcini are not available
you can substitute with white or
cremini mushrooms. If you like,
rub the baking dish with a fresh
garlic clove before layering the
vegetables.

Pesce di Montagna

Fried Swiss Chard Stems (Liguria)

INGREDIENTS for 4:

2 lb wide-stemmed Swiss chard

Salt

2 eggs

¼ cup grated parmesan cheese

1 cup plain dried breadcrumbs

Olive oil, for frying

2 lemons

PREPARATION TIME: 30 minutes
PER PORTION: about 435 calories

1 Cut the stems from the Swiss
chard (reserve the leaves for
another dish); rinse them and cut
them into strips 5 inches long and
1 inch wide. Bring a large pot of
salted water to a rolling boil and
cook the stems for about 3–5
minutes or until still firm to the
bite. Drain them in a colander,
rinse under cold water, pat dry,
and set aside.

2 Whisk together the eggs and
cheese in a large mixing bowl: Put

the breadcrumbs in another bowl.

3 Pour the olive oil into a large
skillet, about 1½ inches deep.
Heat until a stem dropped in the
oil fries with little bubbles.

4 Coat the chard with the egg
mixture and then with the breadcrumbs. Drop a few stems at a
time into the hot oil and fry until
they are golden brown. Drain on
paper towels. Cut the lemons in
wedges. Serve with the wedges of
lemon.

*This Ligurian vegetable spe-
cialty* is classically known as
"mountain fish." The chard stems
resemble the small fried fish that
are commonly prepared along the
coast and are considered a delicacy by the mountain people.

Michette

Raised Bread Rolls (Liguria)

INGREDIENTS for 6:

4 cups bread flour + flour for dusting

$\frac{1}{2}$ cube fresh yeast (0.7 oz)

$\frac{1}{3}$ cup + 1 Tbsp milk + milk for
brushing the rolls

$\frac{1}{4}$ cup sugar + sugar for sprinkling
the rolls

$\frac{1}{3}$ cup + 1 Tbsp olive oil + oil for
the baking sheet

2 eggs

$\frac{1}{2}$ tsp finely grated lemon zest

Pinch salt

PREPARATION TIME: 35 minutes
RESTING TIME: $1\frac{3}{4}$ hours
BAKING TIME: 20 minutes
PER PORTION: about 465 calories

1 Put the flour in a mixing bowl
and make a well in the center;
crumble the yeast into the well.
Combine the milk and sugar and
pour into the well, stirring well.
Set aside, covered, for about 15
minutes.

2 Whisk together the eggs,
lemon zest, and salt in a small
bowl; add this mixture to the flour
sponge and knead to make a
smooth dough. Cover the dough
and let rise for about 1 hour or
until it has doubled in size.

3 Punch down the dough and
knead again; tear the dough in 6
large pieces. On a floured work
surface, roll each piece to a thick
sausage shape. Squeeze and roll
each piece to make four intercon-
nected rolls. Let rise again 30
minutes.

4 Preheat the oven to 400° F (if
convection oven 350° F). Brush a
baking sheet with oil and place
the rolls on it; brush each roll with
milk. Bake on the middle oven
rack for about 20 minutes or until
the rolls are golden brown;
remove them from the oven and
sprinkle them with sugar while
they are still hot.

Crostatina di Mele

Apple Puff Pastry Cake (Liguria)

INGREDIENTS for 4:

Flour, for dusting

2 premade rectangular pieces of
puff pastry (about 5 oz), thawed

2 apples

1 Tbsp lemon juice

$\frac{1}{4}$ cup packed brown sugar

$\frac{1}{2}$ tsp ground cinnamon

2 Tbsp butter

Small strawberries and whipped
cream, to garnish

PREPARATION TIME: 25 minutes
BAKING TIME: 20 minutes
PER PORTION: about 325 calories

1 On a floured work surface,
roll out the puff pastry and cut
them in halves. With a knife or a
very large cookie cutter, cut the
puff pastry into four 6-inch
rounds. Place them on a parchment paper-lined baking sheet.

2 Preheat the oven to 400° F (if
convection oven 350° F). Peel and
core the apples, then cut them
into thin slices. Drizzle them with
the lemon juice.

3 Mix the brown sugar and cinnamon in a small bowl. Sprinkle
some cinnamon sugar on the puff
pastry rounds; layer each with the
apples slices, arranging them in
overlapping circles. Sprinkle with
the remaining cinnamon sugar.

4 Cut the butter into small
pieces and dot on the apple puff
pastry rounds. Bake on the middle oven rack for about 20 minutes or until the pastry borders
are golden brown and the top
sugar layer has slightly
caramelized. Serve them still
warm with strawberries and
whipped cream.

Schiumette

Foam Islands in Pistachio Sauce (Liguria)

INGREDIENTS for 4:

1/3 cup shelled pistachios

2 eggs

1/2 cup sugar

2 cups milk

1 Tbsp cornstarch or arrowroot

2 tsp brown sugar (see Tip)

PREPARATION TIME: 30 minutes
PER PORTION: about 290 calories

1   Finely chop the pistachios in a food processor.

2   Separate the eggs. Combine the egg whites, about 1/3 cup sugar, and the lemon juice in a bowl. Beat until very stiff peaks form. Whisk together about 1/4 cup of the milk, the egg yolks, and the cornstarch or arrowroot.

3   Heat the remaining milk to simmering in a large saucepan and add the pistachios. Use two spoons to scoop out whipped egg white and form into ovals. Drop them gently into the hot milk (be careful not to allow the milk to boil). Partially cover the saucepan; let the islands simmer for about 5 minutes. With a slotted spoon or strainer transfer the islands to a plate; leave the saucepan on the stove.

4   Whisk the egg yolk mixture into the remaining milk and stir it until it thickens to a pudding-like consistency. Pour the sauce over the foam islands and sprinkle them with the brown sugar.

Tip: Fine brown cane sugar is available in health food stores and gourmet supermarkets. However, you can also grind regular brown sugar by using a mortar or a food processor or spice grinder.

Pera Cotta con Salsa

Wine-Poached Pears in Almond Sauce (Liguria)

INGREDIENTS for 4:

4 ripe but firm pears, such as Anjou or Bosc

2 cups dry white wine

1 piece organic lemon zest (about 2–3 inches long)

2 Tbsp sugar

4 Tbsp slivered almonds

1 Tbsp cornstarch or arrowroot

1 Tbsp chopped pistachios

PREPARATION TIME: 40 minutes
COOKING TIME: 20 minutes
PER PORTION: about 280 calories

1   Peel the pears, keeping the stems.

2   Place the pears in a medium saucepan and add the white wine, lemon zest, and sugar. Bring to boil, reduce the heat, and simmer, covered, for about 20 minutes. Remove the pears from the sauce and set them aside to cool.

3   Bring the sauce to a boil and cook until it has reduced by half; remove the lemon zest. In a small skillet, toast the almonds until golden brown; add them to the sauce. Whisk the cornstarch with 1–2 tablespoons cold water and whisk it into the sauce. Whisk the sauce until it thickens; if necessary, puree the sauce to make sure that there are no lumps.

4   Spoon the warm sauce onto dessert plates and place a pear in the middle of each plate; garnish with the chopped pistachios.

The Po Basin

Venice and its lagoons; mountains and hills, lakes, and a fertile basin

The Region and Its Products

Fertile and wealthy: Rice, vegetables, fish, famous cheeses, and pork specialties

Veneto, Emilia-Romagna, and the southern part of Lombardy have much to offer: seafood and fish from the Lagoon of Venice; freshwater fish from Garda and many rivers; and rice, vegetables, and fruits from the Po Basin. Throughout the area, cattle and pigs are raised for the most renowned specialties of the region: Parmigiano-Reggiano cheese and Parma hams, including prosciutto di Parma.

Flavors of the Land. Vegetables grow especially well where there is abundant water. This is particularly true throughout the Po Basin, especially the Lagoon of Venice and the "vegetable island" of Sant'Erasmo. Flavorful small artichokes are famous throughout the area (especially those from Sant' Erasmo, called *castraure*, that are the first fruits of the spring). Bright orange pumpkins and radicchio from the region of Treviso are prized as well. All these vegetables and more are stewed, grilled, or preserved as antipasti, find their way into pasta fillings and sauces, and are used in contorni. Another fine specialty from this area: white asparagus from Bassano del Grappa.

Treasures from the Water. The Lagoon of Venice might not yield as much seafood as in the past. However, there is still a dynamic fish market near Venice's bridge of Rialto where all kinds of unusual and hard-to-find sea creatures are available. The *granceola*, or spider crab, has a delicate flesh; it can be cooked, pickled, or eaten as a simple salad. *Schile* are also very tasty; they are young shrimp, that are often eaten raw, fried, or prepared in tomato sauce over noodles. Inland fish include tench fish from Lake Garda, used in risotto, and char and eels from Emilia. The variety of fish enriches Italian cuisine with light and flavorful possibilities.

Not Always Hearty. Polenta (cornmeal) and rice, stuffed and baked pasta, borlotti beans, and other legumes all seem to be part of a very hearty farmer's way of cooking. Strachy dishes can be refined, however. Polenta in Veneto can be quite elegant. White polenta, made from *biancoperla* corn, is a local specialty that has a fine aromatic and delicate flavor. The fine cornmeal is prepared either with shredded stewed codfish or with soppressa, a local sausage, or with ground or diced meat ragù. Polenta may be served as a mush, or cooled off, cut up, and pan-fried, roasted, or grilled. The risotto rice from the Po Basin, *Vialone*, is among the best; in the Veneto and Lombardy it is typically cooked with vegetables or fish. Borlotti beans (also known as cranberry beans) are prepared with noodles and radicchio in winter and are dressed as a salad with fresh vegetables in summer.

The favorite sights throughout the city of Venice are elegant black gondolas and singing gondolieri. For those who wish to eat and drink well there are several restaurants or, along the city's narrow passages, small taverns called *bacari*.

Frutta e verdure is what the Italian homemaker still today tries to buy fresh daily. Throughout the many markets, Venice has several vegetables such as artichokes and pumpkins that are available in their natural state or prepared and ready-to-cook—fast food for a noble cuisine.

Dolce far niente—the sweet art of doing nothing is even better in front of a historic monument such as a church. Taking it easy with a cup of cappuccino or a glass of Campari is especially relaxing when you can observe at your leisure what happens all around.

Very near to the beautiful wooden bridge Ponte degli Alpini, the historic marker of the picturesque city of Bassano del Grappa, is the Nardini shop whose grappa helped to make the city world famous. The grape-skin brandy is available here as it is in more than 100 distilleries.

The city of Bologna is characterized by its porticoes and arcades. The city is called *La Grassa*—the fat one—a sly reference to its myriad culinary masterpieces.

Emilia-Romagna may feel like heaven to a gourmet, particularly Bologna. Tortellini, Parma ham, and parmesan cheese are only a few examples of the most renowned specialties of this region.

The Cuisine

One can splurge here—from parmesan cheese and homemade pasta to ham

Emilia-Romagna is sometimes called Italy's belly, with the capital Bologna as the navel. (In fact, it was apparently in the shape of Venus's navel that the regional specialty tortellini were created.) But Emilia is not alone in the forefront: Venice and the Veneto, with radicchio, rice, polenta, and the many varieties of fish and seafood from the Lagoon, rival it. And Lombardy is undoubtedly the wealthiest region of Italy.

Alla Bolognese. Just beyond Bologna runs Italy's butter-oil border. Butter and cream flavor the cuisines in the regions north of Bologna, as do cheeses made from cows' milk, like parmesan. Beyond the Apennines toward Tuscany, olive trees grow, and the climate, terrain, and cuisine change.

In spite of its heartiness, Emilia-Romagna's cuisine has remained basic and simple: vegetables cooked with butter and parmesan cheese; homemade pasta, plain or stuffed, but always with an egg in the dough; boiled meat served with several sauces; or the savory stuffed ham hock from Modena called *zampone*, that is simmered in water and served with lentils—all rustic yet classic dishes that have a refinement due to the quality of the ingredients. For culinary innovations no less delicious than classics, try vegetable sauces as a substitute for the famous ragù alla Bolognese that usually tops homemade tagliatelle, or oven-baked lasagne prepared with layers of spinach and pumpkin.

Parmesan cheese could arguably be described as the flavor of Emilia-Romagna; there is almost no dish, spicy or not, that does not call for at least a spoonful of it. But other cheeses play an important role in the cuisines of the region. From Lombardy comes pungent Gorgonzola that enhances fine sauces or crowns the last course of a menu. From the Veneto area, especially from the mountainous and hilly regions, comes Asiago as well as an assortment of lesser-known cheeses, such as *casatella*, a fresh cow's milk cheese not unlike Lombardy's *stracchino*. Another famous cheese of Lombardy, *mascarpone*, is creamy and delicate. It is used not only in popular desserts such as tiramisù but also in savory dishes.

No shortage of vitamins. Please don't be anxious; despite the rich cheeses and hearty sauces throughout the Po Basin, health is not placed on the back burner. Vegetables grow here in great abundance and are prepared and served in many ways and variations. Antipasti typically feature vegetables that are grilled or baked, or *in saor* (a vinegary marinade), or in salads. Primi are enhanced with at least one vegetable or include vegetables as the main ingredients; and most main courses appear on the table with a vegetable or two. During the winter, pumpkins and radicchio are most common; in spring, artichokes and early asparagus make their appearance; and in summer, in Italy as everywhere, it's time for a garden's worth of vegetables, especially tomatoes, zucchini, and a variety of greens.

a

b

a There is hardly a difference today between an elegant *ristorante* and a rather simple *trattoria* or an *osteria*, which in the old days served only wine. If there are locals eating and drinking, you won't be disappointed.

b Tagliatelle are even fit to make a creative cake. It is difficult to choose between fruit tarts or dolci made from mascarpone, chocolate, or nuts.

c Even in the touristy city of Venice one can still find affordable and good *ristoranti*. Away from San Marco or Rialto new places can easily be found.

d Tortellini, whether stuffed with meat, spinach and ricotta, or pumpkin and crushed amaretti, are still a renowned specialty from Emilia-Romagna.

e Emilia-Romagna's best beef and pork are labeled *romagnola*—it's synonymous with quality meat.

The Wines

Refreshing sparkling wines, fruity and light whites, and young but definite reds

Veneto, Emilia-Romagna, and the south of Lombardy—these regions are known for their food, but who wouldn't feel compelled to associate them with Prosecco, Bardolino, Soave, and Valpolicella? But here there is more to discover.

On Veneto's green hills.
Areas around Verona are significant in Italy's wine-growing. Bardolino, Valpolicella, and Amarone are produced, as are Soave, Bianco di Custoza, and Lombardy's Lugana. Bardolino, made from Corvina, Rondinella, and Molinara grapes, is the lightest and the palest red of the region; when labeled Classico or Superiore it tastes grapy and refreshing with a subtle cherry aroma (it is also available as rosé, Chiaretto). From the same type of grapes but mixed differently and from a different area that is a volcanic hill area, come Valpolicella and Amarone. Valpolicella, of which the best are labeled Classico or Superiore, is also a light, refreshing red wine with an aroma of cherries, raspberries, and almonds. For the making of Amarone (same grapes and same area), grapes are dried a few months before pressing them; it is then a heavy and deep red wine with a smooth flavor and rich aroma.

Among white wines, Soave is a medium fruity wine with a smooth acidity that comes mainly from Garganega grapes; look for Soave Classico Superiore. Bianco di Custoza is made from Tocai, Trebbiano, and Garganega grapes; it is refreshing and fruity, but does not age well and is best served young. Lugana from Trebbiano di Lugana (a Verdicchio clone) is dry with a rich bouquet and is considered by many the best white wine of the Po Basin. The Prosecco grape, which lends its name to sparkling and nonsparkling wines, thrives throughout the steep hills between Conegliano and Valdobbiadene. The sparkling wine can vary from dry to sweet and is left to ferment according to tank methods. For this, a very common Prosecco grape wine is produced; then, while the wine is kept in steel tanks, sugar and yeast are added. A second fermentation that creates the bubbles takes place; the yeast drops to the bottom and the sparkling wine is filled in bottles. Prosecco from Conegliano is known as being milder and fruitier than the one from Valdobbiadene; those labeled "superiore di Cartizze" have the reputation of the best.

From southern Lombardy comes Lugana and red wines from the hills DOC Colli Garda Mantovani. *Lambrusco* is originally from Emilia-Romagna. It is both famous and infamous, but it is very well suited to the hearty cuisine of this region. Lambrusco is usually red or rosé and naturally sparkling or bubbly. Less renowned wines include Albana di Romagna, Pagadebit, and Sangiovese di Romagna.

Left: Venice's "streets" are only viable with boats. Wine is transported in this way; for the daily wine consumption large bottles are also fine.
Above: Famous samples of the region (from left to right) – Lambrusco, Amarone, Prosecco, Valpolicella, Lugana.

Regional Recipes

From the coast and from the basin—rice, pasta, vegetables, and creamy desserts

The Po Basin has a lot to offer from the culinary point of view. Modern home cooks and professional chefs have become accustomed to combining old-fashioned ingredients that in the past were never prepared together. The delicate scallops from the Lagoon of Venice are delicious with pureed pumpkins; noodles with anchovy sauce can be served also with fresh peppers, and the traditional boiled meat dish called *bollito misto* may include lamb and boar.

Baccalà Mantecato con Verdure
Pureed Codfish with Vegetables (Veneto)

INGREDIENTS for 4–6:

For the puree:

1 lb baccalà (dried and salted cod-fish)

2 cups milk

2 garlic cloves

About ⅓ cup olive oil

Salt and freshly ground pepper

For the vegetables:

½ each red and yellow bell pepper

2 small zucchini

½ lb large cherry tomatoes

4 thyme sprigs

¼ bunch parsley

1 piece organic lemon zest

¼ cup olive oil

Salt and freshly ground pepper

8–12 slices white Italian bread

PREPARATION TIME: 40 minutes
SOAKING TIME: 1 day
PER PORTION (with 6 servings): about 620 calories

It is peculiar that a dish made from preserved fish has become so famous in a city so closely associated with water. However, it is less unusual if we keep in mind Venice's commercial power. For centuries, ships used to deliver salt to Norway and other northern countries; there the crews became familiar with dried salted fish and took it home. Baccalà, soaked and ready-to-cook, is available today. *Stoccafisso*—unsalted, air-dried cod—was originally used for the puree. Today the dish is usually prepared with baccalà (dried and salted cod), which requires less soaking time and is processed easier.

1   Place the baccalà in a large shallow container and cover it with cold water. Let it soak for 24 hours, changing the water periodically to remove the saltiness.

2   The next day, trim the peppers, zucchini, and tomatoes. Seed the peppers, then cut them in eighths. Slice the zucchini lengthwise ½-inch thick. Cut the tomatoes in half. Put the vegetables on a baking sheet. Rinse and pat dry the parsley and thyme; mince the leaves with the lemon zest. Stir the oil into the minced herbs; season with salt and pepper and drizzle over the vegetables to coat.

3 Drain the fish well and place it in a large saucepan. Pour the milk over the fish and bring to a boil. Reduce the heat and simmer the fish for about 10 minutes. Meanwhile, preheat the broiler. Broil the vegetables about 7 inches away from the heating elements for about 10 minutes, turning them once or twice as necessary.

4 Remove the baccalà from the milk and set it aside to cool; reserve the milk. When the fish is cool, remove the skin and the bones; shred the fish in very small pieces.

5 With a hand mixer, puree the baccalà with about ½ cup of the milk and the olive oil; the puree should be creamy and smooth. Crush the garlic with a garlic press into the puree and season with salt and pepper. Toast the bread slices and spread with the puree. Either serve the vegetables alongside or place a layer of vegetables on the slices of bread and then top with the puree.

Pesce su un Letto d'Insalata

Fish Over a Bed of Red Cabbage (Veneto)

INGREDIENTS for 4:

1 celery rib / 1 onion / 1 sage sprig

1 lemon / 1 orange / Salt and pepper

$\frac{1}{2}$ tsp sugar / 6 Tbsp olive oil

$\frac{1}{2}$ small red cabbage (about $\frac{1}{2}$ lb)

2 cups fish or vegetable broth

2 ocean perch fillets (without skin, about $\frac{1}{2}$ lb)

2 red mullet fillets

8 medium shrimp

PREPARATION TIME: 45 minutes
PER PORTION: about 390 calories

1 Trim and chop the celery. Peel and cut the onion into eighths; rinse and pat dry the sage. Scrub the orange and lemon under hot water; with a grater remove some of the zest from the lemon, then juice it. Use a swivel peeler to remove the peel from half of the orange; cut the peel into thin strips. Juice half of the orange. Whisk together 3 Tbsp of lemon juice, 2 Tbsp orange juice, the lemon and orange zest, and salt and pepper; add 5 tablespoons of olive oil.

2 Trim the red cabbage and slice it very thinly. Heat the remaining oil in a large skillet over medium heat. Sauté the cabbage for about 10 minutes, or until limp; season with salt and pepper.

3 Bring the fish broth to a boil in a large pot. Add the celery, onion, sage, and remaining lemon juice. Cut the perch fillets in half and add them and the red mullet. Peel the shrimp and add to the fish broth. Reduce the heat to low and simmer for 5 minutes.

4 Place the red cabbage on serving plates; remove the fish and the shrimp from the broth and place them over the red cabbage. Garnish with the orange zest. Moisten each portion with some of the fish broth. Serve immediately.

Zucca con Capesante

Pumpkin Puree with Scallops (Veneto)

INGREDIENTS for 4:

2 lbs orange-fleshed pumpkin (such as kabocha pumpkin)

1 onion

2 garlic cloves

4 thyme sprigs

4 Tbsp butter

$\frac{1}{3}$ cup dry white wine, Prosecco, or vegetable broth

About 3 Tbsp balsamic vinegar

1 tsp sugar

4 scallops

Salt and freshly ground pepper

1–2 Tbsp olive oil

PREPARATION TIME: 40 minutes
PER PORTION: about 170 calories

1 Remove the seeds and the filaments from the pumpkin; peel and dice it. Peel and mince the onion and garlic. Rinse and pat dry the thyme; remove the leaves. Heat 1 tablespoon of butter in a skillet over medium heat. Sauté the onion, garlic, and thyme until translucent. Add the pumpkin and let cook briefly; then stir in the wine. Cover and simmer for about 15 minutes.

2 In a small saucepan, combine the balsamic vinegar and sugar. Simmer gently until it has reduced by half.

3 Season the scallops with salt and pepper. Puree the pumpkin with the liquid and whisk half of the remaining butter into it. Season the puree with salt and pepper.

Terrina di Fegatini con Asparagi

Terrine of Chicken Livers with Asparagus (Veneto)

4 Heat the remaining butter in a skillet. Sauté the scallops over medium heat for 1 minute on each side.

5 Spoon the pumpkin puree into a deep preheated serving plate. Place the scallops in the middle. Drizzle with the balsamic vinegar sauce and olive oil.

There are all kinds of pumpkins available on the Venetian market in season. The *suca baruca* (a regional pumpkin species) has an especially flavorful pulp since it grows on a saline soil that is found around the area of Chioggia. This pumpkin is commonly used for dishes such as this puree as well as in risotto and the delicate and small pumpkin gnocchi that are served with melted butter and cheese.

INGREDIENTS for 8–10:
2 garlic cloves
1 organic lemon
2 sprigs each rosemary and sage
2 cups Prosecco or dry white wine
Salt and freshly ground pepper
1 lb asparagus tips
1 lb chicken livers
2–3 envelopes of gelatin
7 Tbsp softened butter
1/4–1/3 pint of heavy cream

PREPARATION TIME: 1 hour
REFRIGERATING TIME: 4 hours
PER PORTION (WITH 10 PEOPLE): about 235 calories

1 Peel and halve the garlic. Scrub the lemon under hot water and use a swivel peeler to remove the peel; extract its juice. Rinse and pat dry the herbs.

2 Combine the garlic, lemon peel, herbs, Prosecco, and salt in a saucepan; bring to a boil. Add the asparagus and simmer over medium heat for about 10 minutes or until still firm to the bite. Remove the asparagus, keeping the liquid at a simmer. Rinse the asparagus under cold water and drain.

3 Clean the chicken livers and remove the membranes. Add them to the white wine liquid and simmer over low heat for about 10 minutes. Remove them from the liquid and set them aside.

4 Whisk the gelatin into cold water and set aside for about 10 minutes. Bring the wine liquid to a boil and let cook down to 1/3 cup; pass this liquid through a fine-meshed sieve and return it to the saucepan.

5 Dice the chicken livers. Combine with the butter in a food processor to a smooth puree. Remove the gelatin from the water and put it in the saucepan over medium heat until it is dissolved. Beat the heavy cream until stiff peaks form.

6 Add the wine liquid and gelatin to the chicken butter; fold in the whipped cream. Season everything with salt, pepper, and 2 teaspoons of lemon juice. Rinse a loaf pan with cold water. Spoon half of the chicken liver mixture into it; arrange the asparagus over this, then carefully spoon in the remaining chicken liver puree.

7 Refrigerate the chicken liver terrine for at least 4 hours before serving it. When it is firm, slice it and serve on small plates with toasted or grilled white bread.

Piadina Ripiena
Stuffed Flatbread (Emilia-Romagna)

INGREDIENTS for 6:

For the dough:

4 cups bread flour + flour, for dusting

1 tsp salt

1 tsp baking powder

$\frac{1}{3}$ cup lard or shortening

For the filling:

$1\frac{1}{2}$ lbs kachoba pumpkin

1 organic lemon

Salt and freshly ground pepper

2 Tbsp olive oil

$1\frac{1}{4}$ bunch each fresh basil, parsley, and arugula

6–12 leaves of romaine lettuce

8–9 oz raveggiolo romagnolo or casatella romagnola cheese (fresh cow milk cheese from Emilia; substitute with *stracchino* or mozzarella)

PREPARATION TIME: 1 hour
PER PORTION: about 585 calories

1 For the dough, combine the flour, salt, and baking powder in a mixing bowl. Cut the lard into small pieces and add it with 5 tablespoons of lukewarm water to the flour. Knead into a soft but not sticky dough.

2 Divide the dough into 6 pieces and shape each into a ball. On a floured work surface roll out each ball to a $\frac{1}{4}$-inch thick round. Puncture each round with a fork. Heat a cast-iron skillet over high heat; cook each round for 2 minutes on each side.

3 For the filling, seed and remove the filaments from the pumpkin; peel it. Cut the pumpkin into $\frac{1}{4}$-inch slices. Use a zester to zest half of the lemon. Mix it with salt, pepper, and oil. Brush the pumpkin slices with the lemon oil and place them on a parchment paper-lined baking sheet.

4 Preheat the broiler. Broil the pumpkin slices 5 inches from the heating element for about 8 minutes, turning them once, until they are golden brown. Remove them from the oven.

5 Rinse, pat dry, and mince the herbs; sprinkle them over the pumpkin. Rinse and pat dry the lettuce; if necessary, slice it open along the thicker part of the rib of the leaves. Split open each flat bread and line the bottom with lettuce; top the lettuce with pumpkin. Thinly slice the cheese and place the slices over the pumpkin; cover this with the flatbread tops.

6 Reduce the oven temperature to 425° F (if convection oven 400° F). Place the piadine on the middle oven rack and heat them for about 5 minutes. Serve warm.

The piadina is the flatbread of the Romagna—it may be served as a side dish or stuffed like a panino, with all sorts of ingredients mixed into the dough. It is always eaten with gusto either warm or cold. Italian cooks bake it on a special round baking surface either made of steel or on a heat-resistant terracotta plate. The best substitute for this method is to use a cast-iron skillet. Tigella, the flatbread from Modena, is made only of wheat flour, water, and salt; it is baked and prepared in the same way.

Torta di Radicchio

Radicchio Tart (Veneto)

INGREDIENTS for 6–8:

For the dough:

3 cups bread flour

1 tsp salt

2/3 cup butter

Oil, for the pie plate

For the topping:

2 small heads radicchio (about 1 lb)

Salt and freshly ground pepper

2 Tbsp olive oil

3 1/2 oz aged Asiago cheese

1 1/3 cups ricotta cheese

2 eggs

PREPARATION TIME: 1 hour
BAKING TIME: 40 minutes
PER PORTION (WITH 8 SERVINGS): about 395 calories

1   For the dough, combine the flour and salt; cube the butter and add it and 4 tablespoons of water to the flour.

2   Knead the dough to a ball; wrap the dough in a clean dish cloth and set it aside while you prepare the topping.

3   Preheat the oven to 350° F (if convection oven 325° F). For the topping, trim and rinse well the radicchio; cut the heads lengthwise in four or eight wedges. Put the radicchio in a baking dish and toss it with salt, pepper, and olive oil. Bake the radicchio for about 15 minutes, turning it over once, or until it is soft. Remove the radicchio from the oven and set it aside to cool.

4   Remove the rind from the Asiago cheese and grate the entire piece; you should have between 3/4 cup and 1 cup. Mix with the ricotta and eggs and season with salt and pepper.

5   Brush a pie plate with the oil. Knead the dough once more and shape it again into a ball. Put the dough between two sheets of plastic wrap and roll it into a circle just larger than the pie plate; line the pie plate with the dough. Stretch the dough around the border to make a thick rim.

6   Top the dough with the radicchio, then spoon in the ricotta mixture. Bake the pie on the middle oven rack for about 40 minutes or until the crust is golden brown. Cool slightly, but serve while still warm.

Try substituting the radicchio with asparagus. Peel the stalks and cut only the lower parts. Bring salted water to a boil and cook the asparagus about 5 minutes then proceed as for the radicchio. For another delicious variation, try Swiss chard and herbs.

Rice—the Spanish legacy

Not only risotto is eaten in Italy, but many varieties of rice are grown

Rice has been grown in Italy, especially throughout the humid wetlands of the Po Basin, since the fifteenth century. Rice cultivation areas include the Piedmont, Lombardy, Emilia-Romagna, Veneto, and even Sardinia. So much rice is produced in Italy that almost half of it can be exported abroad. Cooks have no trouble finding their favorite rice.

Water and warmth.
Rice, originally from Asia, first came to Spain with the Arabs; since the Spaniards were in Lombardy for quite a while, rice and dishes that featured it, such as paella, came and stayed. In paella, round-grain rice is prepared with flavorings and broth in an uncovered pot with constant stirring—which is also the way risotto is made. And rice needs not only liquid for cooking but also for growing. The sprouted rice kernels are planted throughout flooded areas and require enough water during the entire growing season to allow the kernels to grow to full maturity. Piedmont and the Veneto have several water springs that make them ideal for the cultivation of rice. The fields are allowed to dry out only when the rice is mature. Today the once labor-intense harvest is done with huge harvesters. After a drying process, the kernels are freed of their husk and polished until only their white center is left. (For brown rice, the kernels are freed from their husks but are not polished.)

It must be round.
Rice is categorized based on the shape of the kernels: long, medium, and short, or round. In Italy, medium and short rice are preferred because they are more suitable for risotto. Unlike long-grain rice, which typically results in fluffy individual grains, rices grown for risotto are processed to keep a thin layer of starch that ultimately gives the wonderful creaminess to the final dish.

From Arborio to Vialone.
Several strains of rice are used in risotto. Arborio is large and round; good quality varieties have a pale, pearly shimmering center. It cooks in about 25 to 30 minutes. The name Arborio is easily misunderstood as Avorio, which is a steam-processed parboiled rice with smaller kernels that is less preferred. Aaldo rice from Piedmont is a relatively new variety. It has large grains and tends to be mildly sticky but firm to the bite, yet at the same time lends itself to the creaminess that is typical of risotto. It, too, cooks in 25 to 30 minutes. Carnaroli has rather long and large kernels that when cooked remain very firm to the bite; the rice is less sticky than Aaldo. Since it is cultivated less frequently it is usually more expensive. The cooking time of this rice is somewhat shorter: from 20 to 25 minutes. On the other hand, in Veneto where the risotto is softer and prepared with more liquid, a favorite variety is Viaolone nano. This pearl-shaped rice remains firmer to the bite and is less creamy when cooked. It cooks in about 20 minutes. Since the diverse rice varieties have all their different characteristics, the indicated cooking times here should be considered only approximate. As in the case of pasta a reliable cooking time should be tasting for doneness: the rice is cooked when it retains a firm core, that is, when it is still somewhat firm to the bite, without tasting raw.

a For risotto alla Milanese: sauté 1 chopped onion and about 1 lb of your preferred risotto rice in 2 tablespoons of butter. Add about 1/3 cup of dry white wine and let this cook and be absorbed. Ladle simmering broth (out of 4 cups, use $\frac{1}{2}$ cup or so at a time) into the cooking rice, stirring constantly. After 20 to 30 minutes test for doneness. Stir into the rice, with the last ladle of broth, an envelope of saffron, 2 tablespoons of butter, and 4 tablespoons of grated parmesan cheese; season with salt and pepper.

b Favorite varieties of risotto rice, especially Carnaroli, are cultivated throughout Pavia in the Basin between the Po River and the Ticino and Sesia rivers. The small plants require a lot of wetness; for this reason, the fields are surrounded with mud dams and flooded. c In raw rice, the grains are contained in hard strawlike husks that are removed during the milling process. The result is whole rice that still is surrounded by a very fine shell; white rice is obtained by removing it. d There are plenty of different varieties of risotto rice. The first selection occurs based on the size of the grain: riso commune has the smallest and roundest grain; semifino a medium sized; fino the largest. Superfino is the largest rice grain and often describes Arborio and Carnaroli.

Risotto alla Tinca

Tench Risotto (Lombardy)

INGREDIENTS for 4:

2 tench fillets (substitute with whitefish, trout, or char)

1 bunch parsley

1 bunch fresh borage

6–8 spinach leaves

2 garlic cloves

5 Tbsp butter

1 lb risotto rice (about 2 cups)

$\frac{1}{2}$ cup dry white wine

About 4 cups hot vegetable or fish broth

Salt and freshly ground pepper

PREPARATION TIME: 40 minutes
PER PORTION: about 620 calories

1 Remove any bones from the fillets and cut them into bite-sized pieces. Rinse and pat dry the herbs and spinach leaves; remove the stems and chop the leaves. Peel the garlic. Melt 2 tablespoons of the butter in a large saucepan over medium heat, making sure that the butter does not brown. Sauté the fish, the herbs (reserve a few for the garnish), and spinach; press in the garlic; add the rice and stir to coat with fat.

2 Pour in the wine and stir constantly while the liquid is absorbed. Add the broth, $\frac{1}{2}$–1 cup at a time, cook, stirring constantly and waiting until the liquid has been absorbed before adding more. The risotto will simmer for about 20–30 minutes to become creamy yet cooked through.

3 Cut the remaining butter into small pieces and add them and the reserved herbs to the rice. Season the risotto with salt and pepper; serve immediately.

Risotto Gorgonzola e Mele

Apple Risotto with Gorgonzola (Lombardy)

INGREDIENTS for 4:

3 oz pancetta

1 onion

2 large tart apples

4 Tbsp butter

1 lb risotto rice (about 2 cups)

$\frac{1}{2}$ cup dry white wine

About 4 cups hot vegetable broth

2 parsley sprigs

5 oz sharp Gorgonzola (see Tip)

Salt and freshly ground pepper

PREPARATION TIME: 40 minutes
PER PORTION: about 835 calories

1 Cut the pancetta in small cubes. Peel and mince the onion. Core and chop 1 of the apples.

2 Melt 2 tablespoons of the butter in a large saucepan over medium heat, making sure that the butter does not brown. Sauté the pancetta and onion until golden and translucent. Add the chopped apple and the rice and stir until everything is coated with fat.

3 Pour in the wine and stir constantly while the liquid is absorbed. Add the broth, 1/2–1 cup at a time; cook, stirring constantly, and waiting until the liquid is absorbed before adding more. The risotto will simmer for about 20–30 minutes to become creamy yet cooked through.

4 Rinse and pat dry the parsley; mince the leaves. Crumble the Gorgonzola. Peel, core, and slice the remaining apple. Fold 1 tablespoon of the remaining butter, the Gorgonzola, and parsley into the risotto and stir until the butter has melted.

Risotto alla Pilota
Sausage and Cheese Risotto (Lombardy)

5 Melt the remaining tablespoon of butter in a skillet. Sauté the apple slices until golden brown; season with salt and pepper. Season the risotto with salt and pepper and garnish with the apple slices.

Tip: In Lombardy and in Piedmont, cooks differentiate between the very sharp Gorgonzola piccante and Gorgonzola dolce, which has a much milder flavor. Fine supermarkets and delis usually carry both variations. In case you don't find it, ask for the sharpest blue cheese available; do not use the type of Gorgonzola blended with mascarpone.

INGREDIENTS for 4:

3 cups mild beef broth
³⁄₄ lb risotto rice (about 1¹⁄₂ cups)
¹⁄₂ lb mild or sweet Italian sausage (see Tip)
1 small onion
2 Tbsp butter
¹⁄₃ cup dry red wine
5 Tbsp freshly grated parmesan cheese
Salt and freshly ground pepper

PREPARATION TIME: 30 minutes
PER PORTION: about 710 calories

1 Bring the beef broth to a boil in a large saucepan. Add the rice and lower the heat. Simmer, covered, for about 10 to 12 minutes. Turn off the stove and let the rice finish cooking, covered, on the burner.

2 Meanwhile, remove the sausage from its casing and break it into small pieces. Peel and mince the onion. Melt 1 tablespoon of the butter in a large saucepan and brown the sausage and onion over low heat. Stir in the red wine.

3 Cut the remaining butter into small pieces. Stir the butter, sausage, and cheese into the risotto. Season with salt and pepper; serve.

Tip: This is a risotto from Mantova, where it is traditionally prepared during harvest fairs. *Pilota* is the term for the foreman, who was the one who filled the plates for the workers. The *salamelle di Mantova,* fresh sausages from Mantova, have been used for centuries in this dish. Perhaps because meat used to make sausage was of lesser quality—tougher, fattier, or less flavorful—mincing, shredding, and spicing were important. Before being stuffed in the casings, the finely ground meat was seasoned with salt, freshly ground pepper, garlic, and wine. Risotto alla pilota is the only risotto where the rice is cooked in the broth, rather than the broth stirred into the rice.

61

Tortelloni alle Patate e Speck

Tortelloni with Potato and Pancetta Filling (Emilia-Romagna)

INGREDIENTS for 6:

For the pasta dough:

3 cups semolina or bread flour + flour for kneading

2 eggs

1 Tbsp olive oil

For the filling:

2–3 red or Yukon gold potatoes

5 oz pancetta

2 garlic cloves

6 sage leaves

2 thyme sprigs

6–8 arugula leaves

1 Tbsp butter

1 egg

Salt and freshly ground pepper

Freshly grated nutmeg

Furthermore:

1 lb small porcini mushrooms

(you may substitute with either chanterelles or oyster mushrooms)

16 small sage leaves

Salt/freshly ground pepper

4 Tbsp butter

PREPARATION TIME: 2 hours
RESTING TIME: 1–2 hours
PER PORTION: about 425 calories

Tortelloni are a larger version of tortellini, and are usually made with a filling of meat. Pumpkin may also be used. It may be used alone, or enhanced with cheese and egg, or crumbs of a couple of small amaretti which pleasantly bring forth the sweetness of the pumpkin.

A variation of these are *tortelli sulla diastra*. The dough is made only with flour, water, and salt; the filling is made as above but sometimes with pumpkin. The dough is rolled out very thin, cut into rectangles (5 x 7 inches), filled, folded into halves, and pressed together. The tortelli are cooked about 5 minutes in a dry cast-iron pan (the cast-iron pan is called *diastra*; the same used for making *piadina*).

1 For the pasta dough, combine the flour, eggs, about $\frac{1}{3}$ cup of water, the olive oil, and salt in a mixing bowl. Mix and knead to a smooth dough. Wrap the dough in a clean dish cloth and set aside at room temperature for about 30 minutes.

2 For the filling, cook the potatoes in their jacket for 20 minutes or until done; drain them and set them aside. Meanwhile, cut the pancetta in small cubes. Peel and mince the garlic. Rinse and pat dry the herbs; mince the sage. Remove the thyme leaves from the stems. Combine the sage and thyme. Chop the arugula.

3 Melt the butter in a saucepan. Sauté the pancetta, garlic, sage, and thyme over medium heat until the pancetta is translucent. Add the arugula and cook until it is wilted. Peel and rice the potatoes into a large bowl. Stir in the pancetta mixture and egg. Season with salt, pepper, and nutmeg, tasting first as the pancetta is already salty.

4   Divide the dough into pieces; with a rolling pin on a floured work surface or with a pasta machine, roll out each piece as thin as possible. Cut the dough into rounds about 4 inches in diameter using a glass or round cookie cutter. Place about 1 teaspoon of filling in the center of each round.

5   Press each round shut to form half moons, making sure that the edges are pressed firmly shut. Pull and carefully stretch the pointed ends of the pasta pockets; wrap each pocket around your thumb and press the ends together. Set the tortelloni on a clean and well-floured dish cloth for about 1–2 hours.

6   Wipe the mushrooms clean and trim with a paring knife. Depending on their size, cut the mushrooms in half or quarters, or slice them. Rinse and pat dry the sage.

7   Bring a large pot of salted water to a rolling boil. Boil the tortelloni approximately 4 minutes. Meanwhile, melt 3 tablespoons of butter in a skillet. Sauté the mushrooms and sage for about 5 minutes. Stir in the remaining butter; season with salt and pepper. With a slotted spoon or a colander, drain the tortelloni and divide them among serving plates. Spoon the mushroom butter over each portion; serve immediately.

Bigoli in Salsa d'Acciughe
Noodles with Anchovy Sauce (Veneto)

INGREDIENTS for 4:

1 jar (3$^1/_2$ oz) anchovies (pre-served in salt)

2 onions

1 red bell pepper

$^1/_4$ cup olive oil

$^1/_4$ cup dry white wine or Prosecco

1 lb bigoli or whole wheat spaghetti

Salt and freshly ground pepper

$^1/_2$ bunch parsley

PREPARATION TIME: 30 minutes
SOAKING TIME: 1 hour
PER PORTION: about 555 calories

1 Soak the anchovies in water for about 1 hour; periodically change the water. Peel, halve, and thinly slice the onions. Seed and thinly slice the pepper.

2 Heat the oil in a saucepan. Sauté the onions over low heat for 10 minutes, making sure that they don't burn. Add the pepper and wine; let simmer for 10 more minutes.

3 Bring a large pot of salted water to a boil. Cook the bigoli according to package instructions or until they are *al dente* (cooked but still firm to the bite).

4 Remove the anchovies from the soaking water and, if necessary, remove the central bone; crush the fillets with a fork. Rinse and pat dry the parsley; mince the leaves.

5 Add the anchovies and parsley to the onion mixture; season with salt and pepper. Drain the pasta and toss with the anchovy sauce.

Tagliatelle con Ragù
Tagliatelle with Meat Sauce (Emilia-Romagna)

INGREDIENTS for 6:

For the pasta dough:

$^1/_2$ teaspoon saffron

4 cups semolina or bread flour + flour for kneading

Salt and freshly ground pepper

4 eggs

1 Tbsp olive oil

For the ragù:

0.6 oz dried porcini mushrooms

5 oz kabocha or sweet dumpling pumpkin

1 onion

3$^1/_2$ oz mortadella

3 Tbsp butter

1 lb ground pork meat

$^1/_4$ cup dry red wine

$^1/_4$ cup beef broth

2 tsp tomato sauce

Freshly grated nutmeg

$^1/_4$ cup milk

PREPARATION TIME: 50 minutes
RESTING TIME: 3–7 hours
COOKING TIME: 1$^1/_4$ hours
PER PORTION: about 555 calories

1 For the dough, dissolve the saffron in 1 tablespoon of hot water; set aside until the water is deep yellow. Combine the saffron, flour, 1 teaspoon of salt, the eggs, and oil in a mixing bowl. Mix and knead to a smooth dough. Wrap the dough in a clean dish towel and set aside at room temperature for about 30 minutes.

2 Divide the dough into pieces; with a rolling pin on a floured work surface or with a pasta machine, roll out each piece as thin as possible. Let the pasta rest, then cut them into wide strips. Transfer to a clean floured dish cloth and let the tagliatelle dry for 2–6 hours, occasionally turning them over.

3 For the ragù, soak the mushrooms in $^1/_4$ cup of lukewarm water for about 30 minutes. Remove the mushrooms from the water and chop them. Pour the

Strichetti con Asparagi
Strichetti Pasta with Asparagus (Emilia-Romagna)

liquid through a fine-meshed sieve and set it aside.

4   Peel the pumpkin and remove the seeds and filaments; dice it. Peel and mince the onion. Chop the mortadella. Melt the butter in a large skillet. Sauté the mushrooms and pumpkin. Add the ground pork and brown it over medium heat until it crumbles. Add the mortadella and the wine, broth, and mushroom liquid; season with salt, pepper, nutmeg, and tomato sauce. Simmer over low heat for about 45 minutes, stirring occasionally. Stir the milk into the ragù and let the sauce simmer for 30 additional minutes.

5   Bring a large pot of salted water to a rolling boil. Cook the pasta for about 3 minutes or until al dente. Drain the tagliatelle and place on preheated plates; top with the ragù. Serve immediately, with grated parmesan cheese if desired.

INGREDIENTS for 4:

For the pasta dough:

2$\frac{1}{2}$ cups semolina bread flour + flour for kneading

$\frac{1}{4}$ cup grated parmesan cheese

3 eggs + 1 egg yolk

Salt

For the sauce:

1 lb asparagus

3$\frac{1}{2}$ oz ham or prosciutto

1 onion

2 Tbsp butter

$\frac{1}{3}$ cup dry white wine

5 oz mascarpone

Salt and freshly ground pepper

Freshly grated nutmeg

PREPARATION TIME: 1 hour
RESTING TIME: 2 $\frac{1}{2}$ hours
PER PORTION: about 715 calories

1   For the dough, mix the flour, parmesan, eggs, egg yolk, and $\frac{1}{2}$ teaspoon of salt in a mixing bowl.

Knead to form a smooth dough. Wrap the dough in a clean dish towel and set aside at room temperature for about 30 minutes.

2   Knead the dough once more. With a rolling pin on a floured work surface, roll it out about $\frac{1}{3}$-inch thick. Cut the dough into 1 x 2-inch rectangles, turning each rectangle a half turn to shape each piece into bow ties. Set on a clean dish cloth and let pasta dry for about 2 hours; occasionally turn the bow ties over.

3   For the sauce; trim the asparagus; cut the spears on an angle into $\frac{1}{2}$-inch pieces. Cut the ham into thin strips. Peel and chop the onion.

4   Bring a large pot of salted water to a rolling boil. Cook the pasta for about 4 minutes or until

al dente (cooked but still firm to the bite).

5   Meanwhile, melt the butter in a saucepan. Sauté the asparagus, onion, and ham. Add the wine and simmer, covered, over low heat for about 5 minutes. Fold in the mascarpone; season with salt, pepper, and nutmeg. Drain the strichetti and fold them into the sauce; serve on preheated plates, with grated parmesan cheese, if desired.

While they look very much like the commercial farfalle or bow ties, these strichetti are definitely worth making fresh from scratch. Often, dried commercial pasta cooks unevenly in the center and in the thin parts. This does not happen with fresh, homemade strichetti.

Lasagne Verdi
Green Spinach Lasagne (Emilia-Romagna)

INGREDIENTS for 4–6:

$1/_2$ lb asparagus

1 lb fresh spinach

$1/_2$ lb cauliflower

3 zucchini

1 large bunch arugula

6–7 Tbsp butter + butter for greasing the lasagne pan

3 Tbsp flour

3 cups milk

2 tsp tomato paste

Salt and freshly ground pepper

Freshly grated nutmeg

5 oz mozzarella

$51/_2$ oz Gorgonzola

$51/_2$ oz stracchino (Lombardy's soft cow milk cheese; substitute with more mozzarella)

9 oz lasagne noodles

4 Tbsp grated parmesan cheese

PREPARATION TIME: 1 hour
BAKING TIME: 40 minutes
PER PORTION (WITH 6 SERVINGS): about 620 calories

1   Trim the asparagus; cut into $1/_2$-inch pieces. Rinse and clean well the spinach; remove bad leaves and stems. Cut the cauliflower into small florets. Trim and thinly slice the zucchini. Rinse, clean well, and chop the arugula.

2   Melt 4 tablespoons of butter in a saucepan. Add the flour; cook, stirring to make a golden roux. While constantly stirring, add the milk. Simmer over low heat for about 5–10 minutes or until thickened. Continue stirring to prevent the sauce from burning. Season with the tomato paste, salt, pepper, and nutmeg.

3   Meanwhile, with a wet knife, cube the mozzarella, Gorgonzola, and stracchino; combine these cheeses. Bring a large pot of salted water to a boil. Boil the asparagus for 3 minutes; remove

these from the water to drain. Add the cauliflower florets to the water and boil for 2 minutes; remove these also. In the same water blanch the spinach to wilt; remove it and rinse with cold water.

4   Add the lasagne to the boiling water and cook according to package directions. Drain and rinse the pasta sheets in cold water to prevent sticking.

5   Preheat the oven to 350° F (if convection oven 325° F). Grease a rectangular lasagne pan with butter; line it with some of the sauce. Top with alternating layers of pasta, cooked vegetables, arugula, cheese cubes, and more sauce; the top layers should be pasta sheets and sauce. Dust with parmesan cheese and with small pieces of the remaining butter.

Bake the lasagne on the middle oven rack for about 40 minutes or until the top layer is nice golden brown. Let cool slightly before serving; cut into portions and serve.

The cuisine of Emilia-Romagna is famous for its homemade pasta specialties; lasagne alla Bolognese is world famous. Meatless variations are increasingly popular, not only with vegetarians. Here, fine cheeses, including local parmesan cheese, lends itself to an extraordinary experience of flavor.

Gnocchi con Mortadella, Ricotta, e Spinaci

Gnocchi with Mortadella, Ricotta, and Spinach (Emilia-Romagna)

INGREDIENTS for 4:

3¹/₂ oz mortadella

1 bunch borage (substitute with basil or arugula)

1 lb ricotta cheese

2 eggs

Salt and freshly ground pepper

¹/₂ cup grated parmesan cheese

1 cup flour

1 lb fresh spinach

2 garlic cloves

2 Tbsp butter

Finely grated zest of ¹/₂ organic lemon

Freshly grated nutmeg

PREPARATION TIME: 45 minutes
PER PORTION: about 580 calories

1   Dice the mortadella. Rinse and pat dry the borage; mince the leaves. Combine the ricotta, eggs, mortadella, borage, 1 teaspoon of salt, the pepper, parmesan cheese, and flour in a mixing bowl.

2   Bring a large pot of salted water to a boil. Rinse and clean well the spinach; remove the bad leaves and the stems and chop. Peel and thinly slice the garlic.

3   With two spoons or a melon baller, scoop the ricotta mixture, shape into ovals, and drop into the boiling water. Reduce the heat and simmer the dumplings for about 10 minutes. Drain.

4   Meanwhile, melt the butter in a large saucepan. Sauté the garlic. Add the spinach and cook, while stirring constantly, until just wilted. Season with salt, pepper, nutmeg, and lemon zest.

5   Remove the spinach and drain it, reserving the spinach butter. Place the spinach on pre-heated serving plates and top it with the dumplings; pour the spinach butter over the dumplings. The dumplings are best served dusted with parmesan cheese.

Gnudi di ricotta —originally *nudi* meaning naked—is another name for these dumplings.

You should test one dumpling before dropping all of them in the cooking water since ricotta is available in different variations of firmness. If the dumpling stays whole after 1–2 minutes of boiling time, you can add the others; however, if the first falls apart add more flour to the dumpling mixture.

67

Salsicce—Sausages and Salami
From the cartwheel-sized mortadella to the slender salami

Most of the sausages in Italy are made with pork; local specialties may be made with boar, donkey, goose, or horse. Based on their preparation methods, sausages are available made with raw meat, which can be sold fresh or may be aged, or cooked. Mortadella, for example, is made from finely ground meats to which various spices are added before the sausage is cooked.

Fresh sausages. Whether they are made from pork, veal, boar, donkey, or another meat, most commercial sausages are machine made. However, many traditional varieties are still made the old-fashioned way: hand-cut in small pieces with large knives; flavored with spices such as salt, pepper, and garlic, and sometimes with flavorings such as fennel or even white or red wine; and then stuffed into natural casings and twisted into various sized sausages. Fresh sausages are always made with raw meat. Some are eaten raw, others are grilled or fried, in or out of their casings, before finding their way into various dishes. Fresh sausages may be combined with onion, garlic, peperoncino (an Italian chili pepper), herbs, and tomatoes, and served with

pasta or polenta. A simple raw *salsiccia* is the *salamella di Mantova* made with pork, salt, pepper, garlic, and wine. A refined contrast is the *salsiccia di Bra* from Piedmont, which is made with very finely ground veal and lard and seasoned with salt, pepper, nutmeg, cinnamon, and mace. Depending on the manufacturer it can be flavored also with garlic, fennel seeds, leeks, cheese (parmesan, toma, or robiola), and white or sparkling wine. As a classic antipasto they are eaten not only fresh but also raw.

Aged sausages. In addition to fresh sausages, butchers also prepare preserved and aged sausages. In this case, fresh sausages are allowed to dry in rooms with carefully monitored temperature and humidity levels, for a few days or weeks or even for months. Soppressa is famous in the Veneto. A relatively large, soft pork sausage, soppressa is made with relatively large chunks of meat mixed with pepper, salt, nutmeg (sometimes also garlic, cinnamon, cloves, and rosemary), and stuffed in natural casings. The sausage is sliced thinly and eaten as an antipasto, or as a main dish with polenta and vegetables. In Tuscany, *finocchiona* is famous. It too is a rather large sausage, made with finely ground pork, salt, pepper, and fennel seeds. It is sliced not too thin and served as an antipasto.

Cooked sausages. Cotto, or cooked, sausages are made with raw meat, but are cooked before marketing. Mortadella di Bologna, for example, is made with a mixture of meat and cubed lard that is cooked and allowed to cool in its drippings. This is minced and mixed with salt, peppercorns, pistachios, sugar, water, and large cubes of lard. The butcher packs the mixture into natural or synthetic casings, then cooks the sausages for several hours in a special convection oven with dry air at low temperature. Later the sausages are cooled off very fast. Mortadella classica, on the other hand, has very little salt in the "dough" and is seasoned with ground and whole pepper, mace, coriander, and garlic; it is also cooked under very carefully controlled conditions. The temperature is not allowed above 167° F and the sausage is cooked for 24–48 hours.

a Fresh sausages are usually cooked whole on the grill, removed from their casings and crumbled into pasta sauces, or eaten as a savory antipasto. For an antipasto, press the salsicce out of the casing, brown the meat in some olive oil in a skillet with some peperoncino. Moisten and deglaze with red wine and let the wine cook down. Serve with white bread.

b "Enter in this kingdom of gourmets my dear friend, select and sing. Life is still beautiful!!" Whoever is welcomed in that way must take the opportunity!
c Calabria has much to offer when it comes to sausages: the salsiccia di Calabria DOP made with regional pork meat, lard, and spices such as black pepper or chili peppers (peperoncino); the soppressata di Calabria DOP made with medium-large pieces of pork, pepper or peperoncino, and aged at least 45 days; the soppressata from Decollatura or from Presilia prepared with a very spicy peperoncino puree. d In Campania, the sausage aficionado can choose among many varieties of spicy sausages (the specialty salsiccia di polmone or polmonata is prepared with lung and innards) or also a renowned ham (from the small mountain village Pietraroja).

Seppie al Nero
Black Cuttlefish (Veneto)

INGREDIENTS for 4:

1½ lb cuttlefish, cleaned (substitute with squid)

1 onion

2 garlic cloves

4 Tbsp olive oil

1 bay leaf

Pinch ground cloves

¼ cup dry white wine

2 vials squid ink (about 2 oz each)

1 bunch parsley

Juice of 1 lemon

Salt and freshly ground pepper

PREPARATION TIME: 20 minutes
COOKING TIME: 50–60 minutes
PER PORTION: about 260 calories

1   Rinse the cuttlefish and cut it into rings or strips. Peel and mince the onion and garlic.

2   Heat the oil in a large saucepan. Sauté the onion and garlic over medium heat with the bay leaf. Add the cuttlefish; season with the cloves and add the wine. Cover, reduce the heat to low, and simmer for about 20 minutes.

3   Dissolve the squid ink in 1 or 2 tablespoons of lukewarm water; add to the cuttlefish and cook for 30–40 more minutes or until the cuttlefish is tender.

4   Rinse and pat dry the parsley; mince the leaves. Stir the parsley and lemon juice into the cuttlefish. Season with salt and pepper and serve, ideally with polenta.

Salmerino in Padella
Pan-Fried Char (Emilia-Romagna)

INGREDIENTS for 4:

4 garlic cloves

½ bunch parsley

2 rosemary sprigs

4 thyme sprigs

8 oregano sprigs

1 bay leaf

4 juniper berries

1 organic lemon

4 char (about 10½ oz each)

Salt and freshly ground pepper

6 Tbsp butter

PREPARATION TIME: 25 minutes
PER PORTION: about 460 calories

1   Peel and mince the garlic. Rinse and pat dry the herbs; mince the leaves together with the bay leaf and juniper berries. Scrub and rinse the lemon. Use a lemon zester or grater to remove the zest, then juice the lemon.

2   Rinse and pat dry the char; season the cavities with salt and pepper. Combine the garlic, lemon zest, and the herb mixture. Use half of it to season the cavities of the fish.

3   Melt the butter in a large skillet. Working in batches, fry the fish for 5 minutes on each side.

4   When all the fish are cooked, whisk the remaining herb-garlic mixture into the butter. Return the fish to the pan and fry them for 5 more minutes. Drizzle the lemon juice over the fish. Serve immediately, preferably with a mixed salad and oven-fresh bread.

Luccio in Salsa

Sauced Pike (Lombardy)

Recommended Wine:
An aromatic white wine such as Lugana

In the park of Como alle Scale located in the Apennines there are two delicious varieties of delicious char. The *salmerino alpino* is indigenous; the *salmerino fontinalis* was introduced into Emilia around the nineteenth century from North America. The latter has a somewhat brighter colored flesh and comes from colder waters.

Lombardy boasts many rivers and lakes, and this is why there are plenty of recipes for freshwater fish. Besides char, fish like trout, whitefish, and mullets are prepared this way. Another delicious variation: bread the fish before pan-frying it in butter.

INGREDIENTS for 4:

1 pike (about 2–2½ lb)
1 celery rib
1 carrot
1 bulb fennel
1 onion
1 cup dry white wine
1 tsp black peppercorns
Salt
1 organic lemon
2 garlic cloves
¼ bunch parsley
4 anchovies (preserved in oil)
1 tsp fennel seeds
¼ cup olive oil
1 jar (3 oz) nonpareil capers
2 Tbsp white wine vinegar

PREPARATION TIME: 1 hour (excluded cooling time)
MARINATING TIME: Overnight
PER PORTION: about 385 calories

1 Rinse and pat dry the pike. Trim and peel or clean the vegetables; cut them in large chunks. Mix the wine with 3 cups of water and pour the liquid into a large saucepan or fish steamer; add the vegetables. Bring to a simmer and add salt and pepper.

2 Place the pike in the warm liquid; it should not boil and there should be enough to cover the fish. Add more water if necessary. Simmer over very low heat for about 30 minutes, and then turn off the heat and let the fish cool in the liquid.

3 Scrub the lemon under hot water. With a lemon zester or grater remove the zest, then juice the lemon. Peel and mince the garlic. Rinse and pat dry the parsley; mince the leaves. Mince the anchovies and crush the fennel seeds.

4 Remove the pike from the marinade; skin the fillets and use tweezers to remove any bones.

5 Heat the oil in a skillet. Sauté the garlic, lemon zest, parsley, fennel seeds, and anchovies over medium heat. Add the capers, lemon juice, and vinegar; heat this sauce until it thickens slightly.

6 Combine the fish and sauce in a shallow bowl; the fish should be in a single layer. Cover and refrigerate at least overnight. Before serving, let the fish stand at room temperature for about 1 hour.

This specialty from the area of Mantova is especially suitable during summer. Traditional restaurants serve it with grilled or fried sliced polenta. You may also serve this fish as an antipasto with bread.

71

Tacchino all'Uva
Turkey with Grapes (Veneto)

INGREDIENTS for 6–8:

1 young turkey (about 8 lb)

1 organic lemon

1 onion

2 garlic cloves

2 rosemary sprigs

2 bay leaves

Salt and freshly ground pepper

2 Tbsp olive oil

3½ oz thinly sliced pancetta or bacon

2 Tbsp butter

2 cups dry white wine

2 cups red grapes (about 10 oz)

2 pomegranates

PREPARATION TIME: 30 minutes
ROASTING TIME: 3 hours
PER PORTION (WITH 8 SERV-INGS): about 710 calories

1 Rinse and pat dry the turkey inside and outside. Scrub the lemon under hot water. With a lemon zester or grater remove the zest, then juice the lemon. Brush the turkey with the lemon juice.

2 Peel and coarsely chop the onion and garlic. Rinse and pat dry the rosemary and bay leaves. Remove the rosemary needles from the stems. Combine the onion, garlic, and herbs with the lemon zest. Season the cavity of the turkey with salt and pepper and fill it with the onion mixture; seal the cavity with toothpicks.

3 Preheat the oven to 350° F (if convection oven 300° F). Rub the turkey with salt and pepper and brush it with olive oil; place the turkey breast up on a rack in a roasting pan. Cover the breast with slices of pancetta and with small pieces of butter. Pour about half of the wine into the pan. Cover the turkey with foil.

4 Roast the turkey, covered, for about 2 hours. Check the turkey periodically and baste it with more wine and with the pan juices.

5 Rinse the grapes and cut them in half; if necessary remove the seeds with the point of a knife. Cut the pomegranates in half and extract the juice; reserve some seeds for garnish. Brush the turkey with the pomegranate juice; add the grapes to the turkey and let the turkey roast, uncovered, for 1 more hour. The turkey is done when the temperature of the leg or thigh meat registers 180° F.

6 Remove the turkey from the roasting pan and pour the pan juices in a saucepan. Return turkey to the roasting pan and cover loosely to keep warm. Bring the pan juices to a simmer and season with salt and pepper. Cut the turkey in pieces and serve with the gravy.

Christopher Columbus brought the turkey to Italy from his fourth and last voyage to America. During the Renaissance, the bird quickly replaced the peacock that was common throughout Veneto and Emilia on the menus of the rich. Then as now, the fine flavored meat is often served with fruity ingredients. Some chefs prepare the bird exclusively with pomegranate juice and seeds, others like it with lemon and ginger.

Small whole turkeys are not always available; it is best to order them in advance. You can also substitute with a large roasting chicken or a capon.

Ossobuco d'Agnello

Braised Lamb Shanks (Lombardy)

INGREDIENTS for 4:

4 celery ribs

1 large red bell pepper

2 red onions

4 sage sprigs

1 lb cherry tomatoes

4 lamb shanks (each approximately $1\frac{1}{2}$-inch thick and weighing about 9 oz)

Salt and freshly ground pepper

Pinch freshly grated nutmeg

2 Tbsp olive oil

$\frac{1}{4}$ cup dry white wine

2 bay leaves

2 whole cloves

2 juniper berries

1 organic orange

2 garlic cloves

1 bunch basil or arugula

1 apple or pear, or 1 thin slice cantaloupe

1 Tbsp capers

PREPARATION TIME: 35 minutes
STEWING TIME: $1\frac{1}{2}$ hours
PER PORTION: about 465 calories

1 Trim and thinly slice the celery; reserve the leaves. Trim, seed, and dice the pepper. Peel, trim, and thinly slice the onions. Rinse and pat dry the sage; remove the leaves from the stems and slice into thin strips. Rinse the tomatoes and set them aside.

2 With a damp cloth, wipe the lamb shanks, making sure that all possible bone splinters are removed. Season them on both sides with salt, pepper, and nutmeg.

3 Heat the olive oil in a large casserole or Dutch oven. Brown the shanks over high heat, working in batches if necessary; remove the shanks. Sauté the celery, pepper, onions, and sage in the remaining oil. Add the wine and tomatoes. Rinse the bay leaves and add them, the cloves, and juniper berries. Season with salt and pepper. Stir to combine and return the shanks to the pot. Simmer over low heat for about $1\frac{1}{2}$ hours.

4 Before serving, scrub the orange under hot water and use a zester or grater to remove the zest. Peel the garlic. Remove the basil leaves from the stems or rinse and pat dry the arugula. Peel, core, and mince the apple or pear, or mince the cantaloupe. Mince the garlic and basil or arugula. Combine with the lemon zest, capers, and fruit. Season with salt and pepper. Before serving, sprinkle the mixture over the meat. This dish is best served with polenta or, classically, risotto alla Milanese (see page 58).

Recommended Wine:
Serve a light red wine, such as a Valpolicella, or a white wine that has been aged in wood, such as a Soave Superiore.

Ossobuco, braised veal shanks that are served sprinkled with *gremolata,* a mixture of lemon zest, garlic, and parsley, has been a specialty of Lombardy since at least the eighteeth century. It is understandable, therefore, that many variations have evolved since then. The majority of them call for other meats or different spices: One chef might use anchovies in the gremolata, another might substitute the lemon zest and parsley mixture with orange and basil. Here the gremolata is made fruitier with apple, pear, or cantaloupe.

Bollito Misto
Boiled Meat (Emilia-Romagna and Lombardy)

INGREDIENTS for 6:

For the meat:

2 carrots

2 celery ribs

1 large onion

4 garlic cloves

2 sprigs each rosemary, thyme, and sage

$\frac{1}{2}$ bunch parsley

$\frac{1}{2}$ Tbsp black peppercorns

Salt

1 lb boar leg

1 lb leg of lamb

2 legs of rabbits

3–6 raw sausages (such as Italian sausage, about $\frac{1}{2}$ lb)

For tomato sauce:

3–4 large tomatoes

1 onion

1 carrot

2 garlic cloves

1 celery rib

1 rosemary sprig

$\frac{1}{2}$ cup dry red wine

Salt and freshly ground pepper

1 tsp sugar or honey

$\frac{1}{2}$ bunch parsley

1 bunch basil

1 peperoncino (chili pepper)

5 Tbsp olive oil

For the mostarda:

$1\frac{1}{2}$ lb green grapes

1 organic lemon or orange

3 cups dry white wine

$\frac{1}{4}$ cup mustard powder

$\frac{1}{2}$ cup sugar

PREPARATION TIME: 1 hour
COOKING TIME: $3\frac{1}{2}$–4 hours
PER PORTION: about 695 calories

Boiled meat—*bollito misto*—appears on menus and tables throughout northern Italy. In Piedmont, it is served with a green sauce; Emilia-Romagna diners prefer it with mostarda, a syrupy chutney with whole pieces of fruit and sugar, prepared with mustard extract. In Italy, it has become more and more difficult to find authentic mustard extract, once widely available in pharmacies. The synthetic variety is more common, but the flavor is not the same. Unless you find the real thing during a trip to Italy, use less aromatic powdered, or dry, mustard as a substitute. A bollito is best if many varieties of meat boil in the pot and when many different sauces are served alongside. If you see mostarda in an Italian deli, take advantage of your find and buy it either made with fruits or with vegetables. And try boiling the meats with the side dishes like potatoes or other vegetables. Simply boil all the ingredients in the pot together, adding the rabbit toward the end.

1 Peel the carrots and trim the celery. Peel the onion and garlic; rinse and pat dry the herbs. Chop everything coarsely and put into a large saucepan; add the peppercorns. Fill the pot with about 4 quarts water; bring to a boil and add the salt.

2 Add the boar and lamb to the boiling water; reduce the heat and simmer everything for about 2 hours. Add the rabbit and simmer for 30 more minutes. Finally add the sausages and simmer for about 15 minutes.

3 Meanwhile, for the sauce, blanch the tomatoes in another pot of boiling water; rinse under cold water. Core, peel, seed, and dice the tomatoes. Peel and mince the onion, carrot, and garlic. Trim and chop the celery. Rinse and pat dry the rosemary; remove the leaves from the stem.

4 In another large saucepan, combine the tomatoes, onion, carrot, garlic, celery, rosemary, and wine. Season with the salt, pepper, and sugar and bring to a simmer over low heat. Cook uncovered, for about 1 hour, stirring occasionally to prevent burning.

5 Rinse and pat dry the parsley and the basil; mince the leaves. Rinse, trim, and mince the peperoncino. Press the tomato mixture through a fine-meshed sieve and return to the saucepan. Stir in the herbs, peperoncino, and oil; bring to a boil, then let cool.

6 For the mostarda, quarter the grapes and seed them if necessary. Scrub the lemon under hot water. With a zester or grater, remove the zest. Whisk the mustard into the wine. Combine the sugar, grapes, lemon zest, and the mustard wine in a saucepan and bring to a boil. Reduce the heat and simmer for about 45 minutes; set aside to cool.

7 Slice the meats and place them on a serving platter with the sausages. Pour a small amount of broth over the meats and the sausages; serve with the tomato sauce and with mostarda, and pass bread at the table.

Radicchio allo Speck
Radicchio Salad with Bacon (Veneto)

INGREDIENTS for 4:

1 large head radicchio (or use a combination of radicchio di Castelfranco, tardivo, or precoce; see ingredient information on page 78)

4 oz speck bacon or pancetta

Salt and freshly ground pepper

1 Tbsp balsamic vinegar

1 Tbsp shelled walnuts

PREPARATION TIME: 15 minutes
PER PORTION: about 90 calories

1 Rinse, trim, and pat dry the radicchio. If using the radicchio di Castelfranco, shred into bite-sized pieces; cut radicchio tardivo or precoce into 1½-inch wide strips. Combine these in a salad bowl.

2 Dice the speck; fry it in a skillet over heat until translucent; do not allow the bacon to become crispy.

3 Season the bacon with a little salt and pepper and fold it into the radicchio. Distribute the radicchio on the serving plates, drizzle it with balsamic vinegar and garnish with the walnuts.

For generations, bacon grease was the main fat that the poor used in Veneto and throughout the rest of northern Italy. It was used to roast and fry foods, and also to dress salads. Olive oil was rare and expensive.

Radicchio al Forno
Baked Radicchio (Veneto)

INGREDIENTS for 4:

2 small heads pointed radicchio (such as tardivo or precoce)

Salt and freshly ground pepper

2 Tbsp olive oil or butter

3.5 oz Asiago dolce (fresh Asiago, substitute with Montasio)

PREPARATION TIME: 20 minutes
BAKING TIME: 10 minutes
PER PORTION: about 155 calories

1 Preheat the oven to 350° F (if convection oven 325° F). Rinse the radicchio and trim, removing the outer leaves and the root pieces. Cut the tardivo lengthwise into fourths and the precoce into eighths. Place in a baking dish and drizzle with olive oil or top it with curls of butter. Bake the radicchio on the middle oven rack for about 10 minutes.

2 Meanwhile, cut the rind off the cheese and use a swivel peeler to make shavings of cheese.

3 Turn the radicchio over. Top with the cheese shavings and bake 10 more minutes or until the cheese has melted. Serve immediately.

In Veneto, radicchio is rarely served raw but is commonly baked; this gives it an intensely aromatic flavor. It can also be baked without cheese to serve as a side dish or as an appetizer. It is delicious either warm or cold; if serving cold, prepare it using olive oil.

Insalata con Finocchio e Melagrana

Salad with Fennel and Pomegranate

(Veneto)

INGREDIENTS for 4:

1/2 pound mixed greens (such as romaine, radicchio, or arugula)

1 large fennel bulb

1 pomegranate

2 1/2 Tbsp white wine vinegar

Salt and freshly ground pepper

1 tsp honey

5 Tbsp olive oil

2 Tbsp pine nuts

PREPARATION TIME: 20 minutes
PER PORTION: about 155 calories

1 Rinse, trim, and pat dry the greens; shred them into bite-sized pieces. Trim the fennel, reserving the fennel greens. Cut the fennel bulb lengthwise into four wedges; cut out the tough center and slice the rest very thin.

2 Cut open the pomegranate with a knife over a mixing bowl; break it into pieces. Loosen the seeds and let any juice drip into the bowl. Add the vinegar, salt, pepper, and honey to the juice; gradually whisk in the oil.

3 Toast the pine nuts in a dry skillet for 1 minute, stirring constantly, or until they are golden. Toss the greens and fennel with the dressing. Sprinkle with the pomegranate seeds, pine nuts, and some fennel greens.

In Veneto, pomegranate trees are visible everywhere. The bright red seeds are a favorite in salads or in poultry dishes, especially turkey or duck.

Pomodori al Balsamico

Tomatoes with Balsamic Vinegar (Emilia-Romagna)

INGREDIENTS for 4:

1/3 cup balsamic vinegar

1 Tbsp sugar

Salt and freshly ground pepper

2 red onions

3 large tomatoes

2 Tbsp butter

1 Tbsp olive oil

1/2 bunch basil

PREPARATION TIME: 30 minutes
PER PORTION: about 95 calories

1 Bring the vinegar and sugar to a boil in a small saucepan. Let cook and thicken for about 5 minutes; season with salt and pepper.

2 Peel and thinly slice the onions. Bring a large pot of water to a boil. Briefly blanch the tomatoes; rinse them with cold water. Core, peel, and cut them into eighths.

3 Heat the butter and oil in a large saucepan. Sauté the onion slices over low heat for about 8 minutes or until they are still firm to the bite, stirring frequently. Add the tomatoes and simmer for 5 more minutes.

4 Rinse and pat dry the basil. Slice the leaves into thin strips. Stir the basil and balsamic syrup into the tomatoes. Taste and if necessary season with salt and pepper.

These tomatoes are tasty as a side dish served with beef or lamb, and also with *bollito misto.*

Radicchio—Winter's Red Flower

The true radicchio comes from Treviso and the neighboring provinces

Radicchio grows throughout Italy's many regions, but the true, original radicchio is the *tardivo*, with its slender, pointed, and loose leaves. Tardivo thrives well only in the area of Treviso in the Veneto. Here and in the neighboring provinces of Padova and Venice, the plant finds the best water and the necessary climate conditions to grow bright red without becoming bitter.

A plant from the basin.
Radicchio grows especially well in the muddy soil of the triangle area between Castelfranco, Mogliano, and Roncade. It is sown in July but the hard work begins around November and Easter. The plant has to be protected from frost but allowed to be covered with the morning dew, since without these low temperatures the leaves would remain green. The radicchio can be harvested with its roots if it has been exposed to the necessary cold (but not to deep frost). The external leaves are removed right away in the field; then the plants, including the roots, are stacked up in a transparent plastic "cake." Later they are stored in dark rooms for 10 to 20 days with running water circulating around the roots. The temperature of the water must be between 53 and 57° F, exactly the same as the region's temperature. The plants thrive during this bath, and during this time their color grows intensely red with pure white stripes. The constant low temperature and the quality of the water create the conditions for the radicchio to remain the appropriate size and for the plant to develop its balanced and characteristic flavor. After the bath, the plants are stored overnight in sheds and again the outer leaves are removed and the root is peeled. The radicchio rosso tardivo di Treviso—this is its official name—is used raw as a salad green, dressed with a sauce made from borlotti beans, and is also cooked. There are no limits to the ways it is prepared. It can be broiled, baked, and grilled, or stirred into a risotto.

Well protected.
Although most of the radicchio is sold to fulfill demand, not all plants are shipped after the harvest. Some of the plants are set aside for storage by the farmer; (after a first trimming) they are bunched together in bundles. The farmer sets them in softened soil with the roots, covers them with foil, and stores them until March. The plants are not exposed to too much moisture, otherwise they keep on growing. The plants are watered again and allowed to mature only when they are prepared for the market.

Radicchio varieties.
There are four main types of radicchio. The elongated radicchio with wider leaves and a closed head is called radicchio rosso precoce di Treviso (often marketed only as trevisano or radicchio di Treviso). This radicchio's season begins early in September; it is prepared then as a salad or fried, grilled, or stewed. The yellowish-green radicchio with red speckled loose leaves is called radicchio di Castelfranco (named for a small town in the province of Treviso). This variety is available from October on and is the mildest of all radicchios especially used for salads. These two as well as the "father" of all radicchio varieties, the *tardivo*, are labeled as original with the IGP (*indicazione geografica protetta*) original protection label. Radicchio di Chioggia has a round, compact head; it is the most commonly exported variety.

a A radicchio plant has long roots that are harvested with the head since the root is necessary for the proper storage and maturing of the plant. The farmer has to dig deep in the soil if the radicchio is harvested by hand. Modern machines, however, cut open the soil on both sides of the rows of plants and make the work much easier.

b Growing radicchio is labor intensive—the farmer handles the plant several times from sowing to cleaning by hand before the radicchio goes to market; therefore, throughout the province of Treviso it is a family work. It is satisfying labor, but it does not yield big profits.   **C** The external leaves are removed in the field before the plant is either implanted in water or packed carefully under the foil tunnel where it is kept in the soil.   **d** The radicchio roots are rinsed and trimmed before the crop is sent to market. It is pointed and generously cut, otherwise the weight of the root would make up for almost the entire weight. If you find radicchio with roots intact, don't discard them. The root is good to eat, especially if the radicchio is grilled or baked. The flavor is a little bit stronger than the leaves.

Cipolle Fritte al Balsamico

Fried Onions with Balsamic Vinegar (Emilia-Romagna)

INGREDIENTS for 4:

1 pound pearl onions

2 cups olive oil

1 cup balsamic vinegar

1½ Tbsp sugar

Salt and freshly ground pepper

PREPARATION TIME: 35 minutes
PER PORTION: about 180 calories

1 Peel and trim the onions but leave them whole. Heat the oil in a skillet. Working in batches, fry the onions over medium heat for about 4 minutes or until they are golden. Remove them from the oil with a slotted spoon and let them drain on paper towels.

2 Combine the vinegar and sugar in a saucepan. Bring to a boil and cook over high heat for about 5 minutes or until it begins to thicken; season with salt and pepper and stir in the onions; heat again for about 1–2 minutes.

The onions are tasty either warm as a side dish or cold as an antipasto. They are also delicious without the sauce, simply topping a bed of arugula and Romaine lettuce or over other mixed greens.

Polenta al Gorgonzola

Polenta with Gorgonzola (Emilia-Romagna and Veneto)

INGREDIENTS for 4:

2 cups milk

2 cups cornmeal or polenta flour

Salt and freshly ground pepper

5 oz sharp Gorgonzola cheese

1 Tbsp butter

2 Tbsp honey

PREPARATION TIME: 35 minutes
PER PORTION: about 430 calories

1 Bring the milk, and 1½ cups of water to a boil in a saucepan; add a pinch of salt. Reduce the heat and gradually whisk in the cornmeal. Stirring constantly with a wooden spoon or whisking, cook the polenta about 30 minutes. If necessary add a little more water.

2 Dice the Gorgonzola and butter; fold them and the honey into the polenta. Season with salt and pepper.

This savory Polenta is delicious with braised meat such as ossobuco. Polenta made a little bit soupier can also be served as a primo.

Fagioli ai Porcini

Braised Beans with Porcini Mushrooms (Veneto)

INGREDIENTS for 4:

1 1/4 cups dried borlotti beans (substitute with red kidney beans or pinto beans)
1 celery rib
1 carrot
2 onions
2 sprigs sage
1 bay leaf
1.5 oz dried porcini mushrooms
4 Tbsp butter
Salt and freshly ground pepper

PREPARATION TIME: 20 minutes
SOAKING TIME: Overnight
COOKING TIME: 1 hour
PER PORTION: about 285 calories

1   Soak the dried beans overnight in cold water to cover.

2   The next day, drain the beans and put them in a large saucepan

or Dutch oven. Trim the celery, peel the carrot and 1 of the onions; coarsely chop the vegetables and add to the beans. Rinse 1 sprig of sage and add to the beans with the bay leaf. Pour in water to cover the beans; bring to a boil. Cook the beans, partially covered, for about 1 hour; don't overcook them or they will become too soft.

3   Meanwhile, soak the mushrooms in lukewarm water for about 30 minutes.

4   Rinse and pat dry the remaining sage and cut the leaves in strips. Peel and thinly slice the remaining onion. Drain the mushrooms, reserving the soaking water. Chop or thinly slice the mushrooms.

5   Melt the butter in a large saucepan. Sauté the onion until golden and translucent; don't let it become brown. Add the mushrooms and sage and sauté.

6   Strain the soaking liquid through a coffee filter or a fine-meshed sieve and add it to the mushrooms. Drain the beans in a colander and remove the vegetables. Stir the beans into the mushrooms. Cover and cook for about 10 minutes; season with salt and pepper.

The red speckled borlotti beans lose some color during cooking; they are still considered Italy's best beans. Especially in Veneto, cooks are familiar with a whole assortment of this variety. The thick *pavoni* are used in salads; the small *stregoni*, also known as *lamon*, are usually prepared in pasta e fagioli. Lamon beans, originally from the area surrounding the town of the same name, have become such favorites as to have acquired a protected denomination of origin and cost more than double the regular borlotti.

81

Crostata di Mele alla Crema di Mascarpone
Apple Pie with Mascarpone Cream (Lombardy)

Mascarpone, a rich Italian triple-cream cheese, is perhaps best known as an ingredient in *tiramisù*. Although this dessert was first made in Veneto, and was perfected in Treviso, the mascarpone used originates in Lombardy in the areas of Lodi and Abbiategrasso. Mascarpone is more like a buttery cream than a cheese. No wonder—it is made with heavy cream.

Today mascarpone is not only used in Lombardy but throughout the entire Po Basin as a basis for a dessert or for a pasta sauce.

INGREDIENTS for 8–10:

For the crust:
2½ cups all-purpose flour + flour for kneading
Pinch salt
¼ cup sugar
1 tps vanilla sugar
½ cup cold butter
1 egg
1 egg yolk
1 Tbsp melted butter

For the filling:
5 medium tart apples
½ cup sugar
1 tsp grated lemon zest
Pinch ground cinnamon

For the mascarpone cream:
2 very fresh eggs
3 Tbsp sugar
1 Tbsp lemon juice
8–9 oz mascarpone

PREPARATION TIME: 20 minutes
REFRIGERATING TIME: 1 hour
BAKING TIME: 45 minutes
PER PORTION (WITH 10 SERVINGS): about 470 calories

Recommended Wine:
Dry Prosecco

Crostate, crumbly and flat pies, are typically prepared with a filling of fruit or cream. This fruit variation is somewhat special if enhanced with a spoonful of mascarpone cream.

1 For the dough, combine the flour, salt, sugar, and vanilla sugar. Dice the butter and add it, the egg and yolk to the flour. Knead to make a smooth dough. Gather the dough into a ball, wrap in foil, and refrigerate for 1 hour.

2 For the filling, peel, core, and slice the apples lengthwise. Combine the apples, sugar, lemon juice, and the cinnamon in a saucepan. Simmer, covered, over low heat for about 5 minutes; set aside to cool.

3 Preheat the oven to 350° F (if convection oven 325° F). On a floured work surface, knead the dough. Roll about two-thirds of the dough into a circle approximately 13 inches in diameter. Line a pie plate with the dough, keeping a wide rim around the border. Roll out the remaining dough and cut it into strips for a lattice.

4 Line the pie dough with the apples. Top with the dough strips; weaving them into a lattice. Brush the lattice with the melted butter. Bake the crostata on the middle oven rack for 45 minutes or until it is golden brown. Cool to room temperature.

5 Meanwhile, for the mascarpone cream, separate the eggs. Beat the egg yolks and sugar in a large bowl until fluffy and pale. Fold in the mascarpone and lemon juice. In a separate bowl, beat the egg whites until stiff peaks form and fold them into the mascarpone cream.

6 Cut the crostata into 8–10 wedges and serve with a generous scoop of mascarpone cream. If desired, dust each serving with confectioners' sugar.

Semifreddo al Torrone

Nougat Honey Semi-Iced Cream (Lombardy)

INGREDIENTS for 6:

½ cup each peeled almonds and hazelnuts

½ cup honey

2 very fresh eggs

2 Tbsp sugar

½ pint heavy cream

3.5 oz dark chocolate

2 Tbsp milk

Pinch ground cinnamon

PREPARATION TIME: 30 minutes
REFRIGERATING TIME: 1 hour
PER PORTION: about 395 calories

1 Finely chop the almonds and hazelnuts. Place the honey in a metal bowl and beat it over simmering water for 10–15 minutes or until it becomes dark in color. Fold the nuts into the honey and remove from the heat, stirring occasionally as it cools.

2 Separate the eggs. Beat the egg yolks and sugar in a large bowl until fluffy and pale. Fold in the nuts. In separate bowls beat the heavy cream and egg whites until stiff peaks form; fold each into the nuts. Spoon the mixture into six 5–7-oz custard cups or glass dessert cups and freeze for about 1 hour.

3 Break the chocolate into small pieces and combine it with the milk in the top of a double boiler. Melt the chocolate over simmering water. Add the cinnamon and stir well. Drizzle some of the chocolate over the iced cream; if desired, invert the cups and unmold onto dessert plates. Serve immediately with the remaining chocolate on the side.

Torrone is a sweet candy made with egg white, sugar, honey, and almonds or hazelnuts. This dessert is made with very similar ingredients.

Tiramisù alla Pesca

Peach Tiramisù (Veneto)

INGREDIENTS for 8–10:

5 medium peaches

1 vanilla bean

¾ cup sugar

¼ cup lemon juice

4 very fresh eggs

16 oz mascarpone

5–6 oz lady finger cookies (about 22–24 cookies)

6 Tbsp mixed nuts

2 Tbsp butter

Cocoa powder, for dusting

PREPARATION TIME: 30 minutes
REFRIGERATION TIME: 8 hours
PER PORTION (WITH 10 SERVINGS): about 480 calories

1 Bring a large pot of water to a boil. Blanch the peaches and rinse under cold water. Peel, pit, and slice them into thin wedges. With a sharp knife, cut open the vanilla bean and scrape out the seeds. Combine the peaches, ¼ cup of the sugar, the vanilla seeds, and the lemon juice in a large saucepan. Simmer over medium heat for 5 minutes; set the mixture aside to cool.

2 Separate the eggs and beat the egg whites until stiff peaks form. Beat the yolks with another ¼ cup of sugar until fluffy and pale; fold in the mascarpone then fold in the egg whites.

3 Line a square baking pan with a layer of lady finger cookies and cover the cookies with some of the peaches. Spread this layer with some of the mascarpone cream; layer with the remaining lady fingers and peaches, then top with the remaining mascarpone cream.

Semifreddo al Mascarpone con Ciliege

Mascarpone Semi-Iced Cream with Cherries (Emilia-Romagna)

4 Refrigerate the tiramisù for about 8 hours to allow it to set.

5 Before serving, finely chop the nuts. Melt the butter and remaining ¼ cup sugar in a small saucepan and cook until the mixture becomes slightly brown. Add the nuts and cook, stirring constantly, about 2–3 minutes until the nuts brown. Cool slightly, then pour over the tiramisù; dust with cocoa powder and serve.

Authentic tiramisù is prepared by dipping the lady fingers in either coffee or espresso. With this fruity variation, serve the espresso in small cups with the dessert.

INGREDIENTS for 6–8:

For the iced cream:

7 oz amarettini (tiny amaretti)

6 Tbsp cold espresso coffee

3 very fresh eggs

6 Tbsp sugar

1 tsp vanilla sugar

16 oz mascarpone

Cocoa powder and confectioners' sugar, for dusting

For the cherries:

1 lb sweet cherries

¼ cup dry red wine

⅓ cup balsamic vinegar

3 Tbsp of honey

PREPARATION TIME: 45 minutes
REFRIGERATING TIME: 4 hours
THAWING TIME: 2 hours
PER PORTION (WITH 8 SERVINGS): about 535 calories

1 Place the amarettini in a strong plastic bag and crush them with the rolling pin to make medium-coarse crumbs. Mix the crumbs with the espresso.

2 Separate the eggs. Beat the egg yolks, sugar, and vanilla sugar until fluffy and pale; fold in the mascarpone. Beat the egg whites until stiff peaks form and fold them into the mascarpone mixture. Pour the mixture into a 9 × 5-inch loaf pan and freeze for about 4 hours. Two hours before serving, remove the semifreddo from the freezer and thaw in the refrigerator for 2 hours.

3 Meanwhile, pit the cherries. Bring the red wine, vinegar, and honey to a rolling boil in a sauce pan. Cook for about 10 minutes or until it thickens. Add the cherries and simmer over medium heat for 3–4 minutes. Allow the cherries to cool off in the juice.

4 Briefly set the loaf pan with the semifreddo in very hot water. Invert it onto a plate and unmold; cut it into slices. Serve the slices on small plates surrounded by the cherries. Dust with cocoa powder and confectioners' sugar. Serve immediately.

The Alpine Region

Northern Diversity: Mountains, Alpine Meadows, and Plenty of New Cooking Styles

The Region and Its Products

Apples and wine thrive at the foothills of high mountains

Like a gigantic wall of castles, Alpine peaks surround Italy's northern regions: the Valle d'Aosta, Piedmont, the northern part of Lombardy, Alto Adige, Trentino, and the small region with a long name that is Friuli-Venezia Giulia, which borders Austria and the Balkans. In the lowlands, apples, vegetables, and grapes that become wine are big crops, in contrast to the traditional mountain economy.

Long Winters. It takes a while throughout the mountains for the winter snow to disappear and for the spring grass to return; these are not optimal conditions for growing vegetables and fruits. The mountain farmer is left with raising animals that thrive in high altitude, and cheese made from their milk is a staple. With the addition of rennet, milk coagulates, and is then drained, pressed into molds, and may be aged to become cheese. Cheese is, ultimately, preserved milk, and it needs to be brought to town only occasionally. Each mountain region and often each valley has its own cheese varieties: Valle d'Aosta has fontina; the Piedmont has Castelmagno and Gorgonzola; Lombardy has bitto and casera; Alto Adige or South Tyrol and Trentino boast various high-pasture cheeses as well as Grana del Trentino; and Friuli-Venezia has Giulia Montasio.

The Storage of Staples Is a Must. In the past, the remoteness of the high mountain valleys made storing staples a necessity of survival. Today's refined and modern methods for the preservation of milk, meat, and bread originated in areas like this. Hard cheeses, smoked and aged ham and bacon, smoked goose liver and goose sausages, and the dried flat rye bread wheels originally from Alto Adige kept longer than their fresh counterparts, and allowed for a varied diet until warm weather allowed fresh food—or shopping opportunities.

Abounding Grass. The landscape changes throughout the wide valleys and the plains at the foot of the Alps. Here the green of vineyards, apple orchards, and vegetable gardens takes over, and oak forests, which harbor not only the precious truffles and mushrooms but also the deer and game that provide meat for venison and other dishes, dominate. In this region, large lakes such as the Lake Maggiore, Lake Como, and Lake Garda provide trout and other freshwater fish. Piedmont's hazelnuts are as famous as Aldo Adige's chestnuts, which are served during fall's Törggelen events. In Friuli, asparagus and corn for polenta are widely cultivated. In these mountain regions, fertile soil, sunny days, and cool nights combine to facilitate the growth of hardy fruits and vegetables, such as potatoes, cabbage, radicchio, and other greens that taste especially flavorful when touched with frost. Sweet berries, mushrooms, fish, and venison are to be found throughout the area.

In the glacial areas of Piedmont, lakes such as Lake Maggiore and Lake d'Orta with the Isola Giulia, are not only tourist attractions but also a source of freshwater fish such as trout, whitefish, and carp.

Raising pigs is a very important part of the local economy, used for the production of hams, bacon, and sausages. Farmers' expert knowledge of breeding ensures a flavorful and aromatic meat and the right fat content.

Nebbiolo vineyards throughout the hilly terrains of Serralunga d'Alba, the heart of the Barolo region in Piedmont, are the grapes used in the region's best—and best-known—red wines. If the wines produced here are not signature wines with a special denomination of origin, wine producers of this region often call their wines by the municipality's original name, *Barolo Serralunga*.

Thousands of families living at altitudes of nearly 3,300 feet live off the cultivation of fruits and maintain their small gardens and farms. The climate is ideal for growing apples; it is mild, with the sunny days and cool fall nights necessary to enhance the fruits' flavor and quality.

Funghi porcini, or cèpes (as they are known in France), are the favorite mushrooms during fall throughout the Alpine regions; they are prepared raw in salads, broiled, stewed, fried, or dried for storage.

Chestnuts, also called castagne or marroni, are conveniently ready for harvest when the new wine needs to be tasted; roasted chestnuts are then a must during the "Törggelen" that is Aldo Adige's autumnal wine-tasting celebration.

The Cuisine

From the heartiness of Alpine cooking to a lighter Mediterranean culinary creativity

In the old days, life in the mountain regions was made of heavy work and hearty meals. Meals were of necessity heavy and filling; chunky soups, thick stews, and fried or fatty foods gave people the energy they needed. With better living conditions, technological innovations, and even tourism, more refined recipes made it into the local kitchens.

All butter. The Alps are not an impenetrable barrier between Italy and countries to the north; the mountains are interspersed with valleys, through which people of other regions and countries have passed since ancient times. To the west, Italy borders with France and Switzerland; in the east with Austria and Slovenia; all have left their marks. Even with diverse influences, the basics of the Alpine cuisine are similar throughout the entire area. For example, butter is used rather than olive oil; cream and rich creamy cheese are beloved; and polenta, potatoes, and rice are the predominant starches. These foods typically are mildly spiced and hearty; meat is slow-cooked, usually braised or stewed rather than grilled or roasted. Traditional specialties are updated with creativity, and regional ingredients are combined in new ways; overall the area boasts a subtly innovative way of cooking rather than a revolutionary cuisine.

Meals with bread. Appetizers today feature ham, pancetta or speck (the best is from Aldo Adige and Arnad), and a marinated raw beef called *carne salata*. Their culinary forebears were the snacks of meat and bread people would put together as breaks in their work day. Homemade noodles and gnocchi, the fluffy potato dumplings, still play a main role here in the regional assortment of pasta specialties; among the main sources of protein are lake fish, quail, roasted suckling pig, and hearty meat specialties such as the traditional *bollito misto* (an assortment of boiled meat cooked in one pot) and *trippa* (tripe).

Earthly treasures. One regional passion that originates here is also extremely expensive. Truffles, the rare and subterranean *funghi*, are prized. These aromatic and flavorful morsels elevate even the humblest appetizers and main dishes to fine specialties. One might deduce that aroma is an important marker for all Alpine regions, since nowhere else produces more aroma-rich cheeses.

Sweets. Desserts in the Alpine regions remain classic. Domestic fruits such as apples, peaches, and wild berries are served with cheese and nuts, a combination inherited from the cuisines of Austria and Hungary. The love for sweets dates back to a time when hard work was the main fact of life. Sugar was easy to store and hard to spoil, so it was a very important source of energy in the past. Desserts today are served with wines or with grappa, the spirit distilled from grapes that has evolved from a simple farmers' moonshine to a fine *digestivo*.

c

d

e

a The mowing of the steep Alpine meadows is labor-intensive work that still today is done by hand. During winter, the hay is brought down in the valley by sledge.

b Lettuce, herbs, and spring onions thrive in the Piedmont region, which remain protected from Nordic winds by the Alps.

c Grana cheese is produced from cow's milk around the Piedmontese Castelmagno area. The cows feed only on grass that is grown around the lean sand terrains of the surrounding areas; this lends a typical sharper flavor to milk and cheese.

d In Piedmont and the Valle d'Aosta, sharp and aromatic cheeses, called *toma* or *tuma*, are made with cow's milk, with a combination of cow's milk and goat's milk, or with sheep's milk. *Tomini* are the small variations marinated in olive oil with peperoncino and parsley.

e Tradition and hospitality were especially important for survival in the Alpine regions. These virtues are still entrenched today; however, in the kitchens often blow new and amazing breezes.

The Wines

Light white wines, excellent sparkling wines, and superb red wines

The regions at the foot of the Alps keep several secrets. A variety of grapes are grown, but the most prized is the Nebbiolo vine, which is used in many wines: Barolo and Barbaresco, Donnas (also called Donnaz), and Gattinara, Sassella, and Grumello.

Thick skin and long aging time. Nebbiolo grapes ripen slowly and thrive best in Piedmont, along mountain terraces that can stand fog that in October extends into the valleys. The grapes' thick skins protect them from rot, and produce a high content of substances that facilitate the fermentation; this is the reason why these wines require long aging time in barrels and/or bottles before reaching maturity and being ready for consumption. Wines such as Barolo do not cater to impatient people and wine beginners. Easier red wines from the same vine include Langhe Nebbiolo, Nebbiolo d'Alba, or Donnaz, a Nebbiolo variety that originates in the Valle d'Aosta.

Red wines made from grape variety Barbera are hearty and definite: Barbera d'Asti, Barbera d'Alba, and Barbera del Monferrato, are just a few. Although many of these wines are good, you'll find others that are not so good. The determining factor is whether the wine maker reduces the output. One specialty from Friuli is a red wine with a difficult name: the Refosco del Peduncolo Rosso, which is full-bodied with definite and aromatic flavor. Among the other favorite red wines of the Northern Italian regions are the Teroldego from the plain of Rotaliano in the Trentino area, and the South Tyrolean wines made with Schiava grapes such as the Santa Maddalena (St. Magdalener), the Meraner (Merano), and the Kalterersee (Lago di Caldaro).

White wines are not as prevalent here, with the exception of Gavi, from the province of Alexandria. It is sold as Gavi di Gavi. Roero Arneis is a crisp, fruity white wine from the Barolo area that recently gained popularity. Worth seeking out as well are a whole assortment of wines made from Chardonnay grapes, and Gewürztraminer wines that have a good and aromatic flavor.

Sparkling. Northern Italy boasts several sparkling wines, such as Asti Spumante and a similar wine called Moscato d'Asti. These are fruity and sweet sparkling wines that are perfect for serving with desserts. The finest of these sparkling wines are those that originate in the area of Franciacorta in the northern part of Lombardy, which are simply named Franciacorta DOCG. Produced according to traditional methods, these wines are bottle fermented and taste smooth, crisp, and full, even if they are labeled "Brut" (very dry).

Left: Winter can be extremely cold at the foot of the Alps in spite of the proximity to the Mediterranean Sea.
Above: Famous samples of the Region (from left to right) – Teroldego Rotaliano, Refosco, Barolo, South Tyrolean St. Magdalener, Barbera d'Alba.

Regional Recipes

A new breeze blows throughout the kitchen windows

Alpine cooks are slow to devise new and different dishes; this might be due to the region's inherent tendency to maintain traditions at all costs. New recipes and specialties might employ new techniques, but they typically keep basic, locally grown ingredients.

Polpo con Fagioli
Octopus with Beans (Friuli)

INGREDIENTS for 4:

2 lb small octopus or squid

Coarse or kosher salt

1 egg white

Salt and freshly ground pepper

5 Tbsp olive oil

1 lb fresh large beans in the pods
(substitute with lima beans or
baby lima beans)

1 bunch basil

1 garlic clove

1 tsp lemon juice

PREPARATION TIME: 40 minutes
COOKING TIME: 30 minutes
COOLING TIME: 2½ hours
PER PORTION: about 575 calories

This may be the ultimate example of the new cuisine of Friuli: simple, genuine ingredients, enhanced with new culinary ideas—the tentacles of the octopus bound together like a sausage.

Simply cleaned, cut into strips, sautéed with chopped onion, and tossed with beans in a light dressing, the whole creates a new dish.

The pureed beans (look for them at farmers' markets in late spring) are similar to pesto in appearance; however, the taste is totally different. A similar puree is made in Umbria, but the flavor is enhanced with fennel greens.

Recommended Wine:
A flavorful and elegant white wine, such as a Chardonnay from the Friuli region.

1   Bring a large pot of water to a boil. With a very sharp knife, cut the tentacles off the octopus below the head. Rub the tentacles vigorously with coarse sea salt to remove as much of the dark skin as possible. Blanch the tentacles in boiling water for about 1 minute and drain.

2   Beat the egg white and a pinch of salt until soft peaks form; add the tentacles and toss to coat well. Brush a large piece of foil with 1 Tbsp of oil, leaving a 1–2 inch border. Place the tentacles on the foil and make a sausage-shaped roll, alternating long and short tentacles and arranging to make a 3½-inch wide log. Wrap the tentacles in the foil, sealing the edges and pressing shut the ends.

3   Wrap the roll in another layer of foil; make sure that the ends are well sealed. Set the roll in a large pot of cold water and bring to a simmer. Cook, covered, for 30 minutes over low heat. Turn off the heat and allow the octopus "sausage" to cool in the water for about 2 hours. Remove the sausage from the water and let cool in the freezer for 30 more minutes.

4 Meanwhile, hull the beans from their pods and blanch them in boiling water; remove the skins and, if necessary, remove any stringy parts from the beans. Cook the beans in a large pot of boiling water for about 5 minutes.

5 Rinse and pat dry the basil. Remove the leaves from the stems and set the top leaves aside for later use. Drain the beans and puree with the basil leaves in a food processor. Peel the garlic, and pulse it into the puree.

6 Puree the beans again so they are very fine and then blend in the olive oil. The sauce should be very smooth; if necessary pass the sauce through a fine-meshed sieve. Season with salt, pepper, and lemon juice.

7 Remove the octopus sausage from both layers of foil and slice it very thin using a very sharp knife. Arrange the slices on a serving platter and let them thaw until they reach room temperature. Garnish with the bean puree and the basil leaves.

Vinschger Tostato

Toasted Venosta Valley Sandwich (Aldo Adige)

INGREDIENTS for 4:

4 small Vinschger or ciabatta rolls (about 5–6 inches in diameter)

3 oz thinly sliced pancetta or prosciutto

3 oz thinly sliced mortadella

3 oz thinly sliced Genoa salami

8 thin slices South Tyrolean mountain cheese (substitute with Muenster cheese)

4 small pickles

PREPARATION TIME: 10 minutes
BAKING TIME: 10 minutes
PER PORTION: about 635 calories

1   Preheat the oven to 400° F (if convection oven 350° F). Slice open the rolls and layer the bottom of the roll with the pancetta, mortadella, and salami.

2   If necessary, remove the rind from the cheese slices; cover the cold cuts with cheese and top with the other half of the roll. Bake on the middle rack of the oven for about 10 minutes or until the bread is crispy and the cheese has melted.

In the Venosta Valley, these sandwiches are served by wine makers during the Törgellen season; usually the sandwiches are prepared with larger flat Vinschger loaves that are thinner than the smaller Vinschger Paarl. Should the rolls not be available in your area, substitute for them with your favorite rye bread roll or with Italian ciabatta.

Crostini con Tartufo

Truffle Crostini (Alto Adige)

INGREDIENTS for 4:

1 oz white truffles

1 garlic clove

4 Tbsp butter

2 Tbsp grated Grana Padano cheese (substitute with parmesan cheese)

$1/4$–$1/2$ cup vegetable broth

2 tsp lemon juice

Pinch finely grated lemon zest

Salt and freshly ground pepper

4 thick slices white bread

PREPARATION TIME: 20 minutes
PER PORTION: about 210 calories

1   Clean the truffles with a fine brush and warm water. Pat the truffles dry and shave them thin; set a few truffle shavings aside to use as a garnish. Peel and mince the garlic.

2   Melt the butter in a skillet. Sauté the garlic; add the truffles and briefly heat everything. Add the cheese and allow it to melt; stir in enough broth to make a creamy spread.

3   Remove the truffle mixture from the heat and stir in the lemon juice and zest; season with salt and pepper. Toast the bread slices. Spread the toasted bread with the truffle mixture and garnish with the reserved truffle shavings. Serve still warm.

Besides using the extremely expensive white truffles that are available during the winter, you may also use the Italian *bianchetto* truffles that are available during spring and summer. Don't toss the truffle rinds, but dry them and use them to infuse mild olive oil.

Liptauer

Gorgonzola-Mascarpone Cheese Spread (Friuli)

INGREDIENTS for 4:

7–8 oz gorgonzola cheese

3–4 oz mascarpone

1 small onion

1 spring onion

2 anchovies (preserved in salt)

1 Tbsp nonpareil capers (preserved in salt)

$\frac{1}{2}$ tsp caraway seeds

1 tsp paprika

$\frac{1}{2}$ tsp mustard powder

Salt and freshly ground pepper

PREPARATION TIME: 20 minutes
PER PORTION: about 310 calories

1   Crush the gorgonzola in a bowl with a fork. Mix in the mascarpone. Peel, trim, and mince the onion and spring onion; fold into the cheese cream.

2   Rinse, drain, and mince the anchovies and capers. Grind or crush the caraway seeds in a spice grinder or a mortar with the pestle. Add the caraway, paprika, mustard, salt, and pepper to the cheese, mixing to obtain a smooth spread. Refrigerate until ready to serve; accompany with radishes and white bread.

Cheese spreads have been popular since the days of ancient Rome. However, the name of this specialty comes from Hungary, where they call sheep cheese liptauer. This recipe came to Northern Italy via Austria, and is also popular in the eastern parts of Germany.

Involtini di Bresaola

Dried Meat Rolls (Lombardy)

INGREDIENTS for 4:

3 oz thinly sliced bresaola

4 oz Gorgonzola cheese or other aged sharp blue cheese

4 oz caprino cheese (hard goat cheese) or robiola (cream cheese made from goat or sheep milk)

2 Tbsp soft butter

1–2 Tbsp heavy cream

Salt and freshly ground pepper

2 sprigs parsley

1 Tbsp lemon juice

3 Tbsp olive oil

PREPARATION TIME: 20 minutes
PER PORTION: about 350 calories

1   Roll out the bresaola slices on a work surface. Crush and crumble the cheeses into a medium bowl. Mix in the butter and enough heavy cream to make a soft spread; season with salt and pepper.

2   Rinse, pat dry, and mince the parsley. Spread the cheese over the bresaola slices and roll them up; dip the ends in the minced parsley. Place the roll-ups on the serving plates.

3   Whisk salt and pepper into the lemon juice and gradually whisk in the olive oil; drizzle over the rolls. Serve with fresh white bread.

Bresaola from Valtellina is an air-dried, salted beef tenderloin, made in a manner not unlike ham. Throughout Italy, this is a favorite antipasto; it is served either drizzled with lemon juice and olive oil or filled with cheese as it is in this recipe.

97

Truffles—Precious Funghi from Oak Forests

Rarely found without special truffle dogs and pigs: Underground truffles

Only well trained dogs (in France pigs are trained to find them) can smell the presence of these underground delicacies, but they aren't the only creatures who are drawn to truffles. If it is too concentrated the intense aroma may be too off-putting, but if used in small quantities, these precious members of the tuber family can lend an unequaled aroma and flavor.

Black or white. Truffles are the most expensive mushrooms, if not the costliest food. This is not only due to the labor involved in harvesting them but also to their environmental requirements. These rare mushrooms do not easily tolerate a standard way of farming. The two most commonly found are black or white truffles. White truffles come from Alba (Piedmont); they are also called *tartufo bianco* and are at their most aromatic between November and February and have acquired almost a cult status. Alba's truffle market (open on Saturdays from the end of October until the beginning of December) is especially crowded with tourist buyers; professional and commercial truffle dealers go other ways (especially away from the internal revenue service

building). White truffles that grow underground throughout oak woods have a stronger aroma than those of other forests. Those growing under oak trees also have a caramel color, while those growing under other trees are pinkish on the inside. (From the outside they all look the same.) White truffles release a stronger scent when they are shaved very thin and used uncooked over warm dishes. Black and summer truffles, on the other hand, release their best flavor and aroma when cooked in butter or olive oil.

Black truffles. Black truffles (*tartufo nero*) grow in Norcia and Spoleto (Umbria) and are available on the market from December to the middle of March. It coincides with the season that takes place throughout the French region of Périgord. Black truffles thrive under oak and walnut trees; they have wrinkled black skins and a purplish-black inside with a whitish marbling. Black truffles have a more versatile flavoring function according to truffle aficionados; they can lend a strong truffle flavor to sauces and patés. Bagnoli truffles, a variety from Campania, have a gray flesh with white marbling and have a somewhat tar-like aroma that makes them less sought out than other types.

More truffles. After the middle of November black winter truffles (*uncinato*) are available in Umbria. They have a hard, black-brown, bumpy and pear-like outside, a caramel colored, lightly marbled flesh, and a strong flavor that is especially pronounced when sautéed in butter. Black summer truffles (*scorzone*), which also releases their best aroma with heat, are in season from May to November. In springtime the white March truffle (*bianchetto*) is available. For all species the basic rule is: use them as soon as possible while they are freshest. Truffles easily become moldy. To store them, use paper towels or raw rice kernels (in the latter the rice will have a slight scent of truffles). Before using them brush them lightly under running water; peel them to remove the hard skin, and shave them thinly with a truffle slicer.

a The easiest truffle specialty: Cook flat egg noodles in abundant salted water until al dente. Melt 4 Tbsp of butter. Clean and peel 1 black truffle (*tartufo nero* or *d'inverno*); shave the truffle and add it to the melted butter, letting it cook over very low heat. Drain the noodles, pour the truffle butter over them, and toss; serve immediately.

b Truffles have a hard, dark-black, bumpy skin in which sand particles can remain hidden. Before using them, clean them with a fine brush and peel them, removing as little flesh as possible. Preserve the skin in olive oil, which will absorb the truffles' aroma.   C   The black winter truffle, *tartufo nero*, is available on the truffle market from the middle of November to the middle of March. It has a pleasantly aromatic scent; its best flavor is released if the mushroom is not shaved too thin and it is briefly sautéed in fat.   d   The black summer truffle, *scorzone*, is to be found from May to the end of November; it too has a dark, bumpy skin. The flesh, also called *gleba*, is hazelnut brown yellow. Its flavor is reminiscent of porcini mushrooms.

Carne Salata
Marinated Raw Beef with Mushrooms (Trentino)

INGREDIENTS for 8:

For the salata:

1½ lb lean beef (top round)

3 garlic cloves

3 bay leaves

1 tsp dried rosemary needles

1 tsp dried sage leaves

1 Tbsp salt

2 tsp coarsely ground pepper

For the mushrooms:

1 lb small fresh porcini mushrooms (substitute with white or
cremini mushrooms)

2 garlic cloves

3–4 sprigs parsley

Salt

⅓ cup walnut oil

For serving:

About 5 oz mixed spring greens
(such as escarole, radicchio, and
arugula)

Salt and freshly ground pepper

3 Tbsp white wine vinegar

½ cup olive oil

½ bunch mixed fresh herbs (such
as parsley, chives, and thyme)

PREPARATION TIME: 45 minutes
MARINATING TIME: 1 week
PER PORTION: about 355 calories

In the old days, beef was preserved in salt and spices as a winter staple, especially throughout the areas around Arco and around the upper area of the Lake Garda. In time, with the development of modern preservation methods including refrigeration, this method of preserving meat was almost forgotten. Rediscovered as a favorite appetizer, *carne salata* is sliced very thin, dressed with vinegar, olive oil, and black pepper, and is an easy and delicious dish. As a main dish, the slices are cut thicker and grilled, and may be served with brown beans cooked in olive oil with sliced onions. Refrigerated, the meat will keep for up to 3 weeks.

Recommended Wine:
Fruity mild white wine,
such as Trentino's pinot
bianco

1 For the salata, remove all the fatty and tough parts from the meat and pat it dry with paper towels. Peel and slice the garlic. Crush the bay leaves, rosemary, and sage into a small bowl; mix these herbs with salt.

2 Place the meat in a deep dish and sprinkle with the salt mixture; turn the meat over once to coat thoroughly. Cover the dish with foil and refrigerate on the bottom shelf of the refrigerator for about a week; occasionally turn the meat over.

3 When ready to serve, trim the mushrooms, removing any undesirable parts. Clean the mushrooms with a damp paper towel or with a fine brush. Cut or slice the mushrooms in halves or in quarters and place them in a skillet.

4 Peel and mince the garlic. Rinse and pat dry the parsley; mince the leaves. Sprinkle both over the mushrooms. Season with salt and drizzle the walnut oil over the mushrooms. Heat gently and sauté over low heat for about 20 minutes. Let the mushrooms cool in the skillet.

5 Meanwhile, remove the meat from the salt marinade; wipe it dry with paper towels and slice it along the grain in thin strips. (Freezing the meat for about 30 minutes prior to slicing will make it easier).

6 Clean, rinse, and pat dry the salad greens; shred them in bite-sized pieces and arrange them on a platter. Remove the mushrooms from the oil and arrange them over the salad. Loosely top everything with the strips of meat.

7 Season the meat strips with salt and pepper; drizzle with the vinegar and olive oil. Rinse, pat dry, and mince the fresh herbs and sprinkle these over the dish; serve with toasted white bread.

Insalata di Fagioli con Prugne Valligiane

Bean Salad with Bacon and Prunes (Val d'Aosta)

INGREDIENTS for 4:

$^1/_2$ pound dry white beans (about $1^1/_3$ cups)

1 fresh sage sprig

Salt and freshly ground pepper

1 white onion

2 thyme sprigs

3 Tbsp white wine vinegar

$^1/_4$ cup olive oil

12 pitted prunes

2 Tbsp white wine

12 peeled almonds

6 thin slices *lardo* (substitute with pancetta or bacon)

PREPARATION TIME: 35 minutes
SOAKING TIME: Overnight
COOKING TIME: 1 hour and 25 minutes
MARINATING TIME: 30 minutes
PER PORTION: about 650 calories

1 Soak the beans overnight in cold water to cover. Drain the beans and cook them in fresh water with the sage (if you wish you may remove the sage tops and or the flowers for later use) for about 1 hour. Season the beans with salt and remove them from the heat; let them cool in their water for 15 minutes.

2 Drain the beans, rinse them under cold water, and place them in a colander. Remove the sage; peel and chop the onion. Rinse and pat dry the thyme; mince the leaves. Combine the beans, onion, and thyme in a bowl. Toss with the vinegar and olive oil and season with salt and pepper.

3 Drizzle the prunes with the white wine and set them aside for about 30 minutes turning them over occasionally.

4 Preheat the oven to 400° F (if convection oven 350° F). Drain the prunes, reserving the wine; slice them partially open and stuff them with the almonds. Press them shut. Cut the bacon in half and wrap each prune in a piece; spear with toothpicks to prevent the bacon from falling off the prunes.

5 Place the prunes in a baking dish and bake them on the middle oven rack for 10 minutes; after 5 minutes turn the prunes over and drizzle over them some of the wine. Garnish the bean salad with the warm prunes and with the sage flowers.

The right ingredients are vital parts of this classic specialty with its familiar but interesting flavors—the herbs and the bacon will lend to the dish a typical taste.

Zucchini Fritti con Noci

Fried Zucchini with Walnuts (Alto Adige)

INGREDIENTS for 4:

1 lb zucchini

Salt and freshly ground pepper

3 Tbsp walnuts

2 shallots

2 garlic cloves

1 Tbsp butter

2 Tbsp flour

$3/4$ cup dry white wine

$3/4$ cup heavy cream

$1/4$ cup olive oil

Pinch saffron

3.5 oz bacon, sliced thin (substitute with pancetta)

PREPARATION TIME: 45 minutes
PER PORTION: about 550 calories

1 Trim the zucchini; cut them lengthwise into very thin slices. Sprinkle with salt and set them aside for about 10 minutes.

Preheat the oven to 120° F and heat the serving plates.

2 Coarsely chop the walnuts. Peel and mince the shallots and garlic. Melt the butter in a skillet and briefly sauté the shallots and garlic. Stir in 1 tablespoon of the flour, the wine, and heavy cream; cook, stirring constantly, until the mixture thickens.

3 Pat dry the zucchini slices and dust them with the remaining tbsp of flour. Heat the olive oil in a skillet and fry the zucchini until golden brown. Drain on paper towels; season with salt and keep them warm in the oven.

4 Add the saffron to the cream sauce and stir in the salt and pepper. Pour it in portions on the warmed plates. Top the cream with zucchini; sprinkle the walnuts over the zucchini; garnish each portion with the bacon. Serve everything with either white or rye bread.

Recommended Wine:
Fruity, cherry-flavored red wine such as the Santa Maddalena Classico.

Variation:
Preheat the broiler. Pat dry the zucchini slices; brush with 2 tablespoons of olive oil, and broil them for 2–3 minutes or until they are golden brown. Place them on heat resistant plates, cover with slices of mozzarella (about 2 oz per portion), and broil them for about 5 minutes or until the cheese begins to melt.

Pork—smoked, dried, and cured
Every part of the animal is used

Besides the famous air-dried hams from Parma and San Daniele, pork shoulder, belly, and even neck are preserved to make a variety of cured meats and bacon.

Speck Bacon.
A specialty of Alto Adige, speck is actually not bacon but a type of ham. It is made from a lean cut of the pork's flank hind leg. The meat is freed from the bone and then rubbed with a spice mixture, brined, and exposed to a cold smoke that reaches a temperature no higher than 68° F. After this operation the ham is aged for about 22 weeks. Only about half are ultimately allowed to be labeled "Südtirol-Alto Adige." Of the controlled denomination "Speck," no one in the field of hams will dare to contest this original regional name, which comes from a century-old tradition. Speck is definitively milder in flavor than any other cold-smoked ham, but it is spicier in flavor than other Italian air-dried hams. Pancetta dell'Alto Adige, made from the belly, is cured and flavored with juniper, pepper, and salt before it is cold-smoked with beechwood. It is firm to the bite and may have a strong flavor of juniper, and is a favorite for snacks and meals served with local bread.

Coppa and Pancetta.
Because neither is made with the pork's hind legs—coppa is made from the front shoulder and the neck, pancetta is made from the belly—neither is a ham. Coppa, a specialty from the Po Basin, is made of cooked meat pieces that are rolled up and tied, brined or cured like a ham, and air-dried. It is strong in flavor and definite in taste and is very well suited for use in stew dishes. Coppa dolce is the name of an air-dried pork neck specialty that is usually prepared in the mountainous areas between Trieste and the Adriatic Sea. It is mild and very well suited to an antipasto platter.

Lardo.
Called fatback in the United States, lardo is the fat from under the pork's skin that has more or less pink lines of meat. Pure lardo is made from snow white fat with very thin striations of meat; it comes from the cutlet part that include strips of meat which are used as breakfast bacon. Lardo di Colonnata comes originally from the town of Colonnata near Carrara and is especially famous throughout Italy. Bacon fat from pigs raised in the region is rubbed with a mixture of salt, spices, and mountain herbs, then is cured in special marble containers (common marble would be corroded by the brine), and is stacked and preserved from six months to a year. This process yields a bacon that is buttery-soft and flavorful, and can be served as an appetizer or used to cook with polenta or with *pestarda*, a diced and minced mixture chopped with a sharp knife, or as a basis for hearty soups or as a *soffritto* with onions and/or herbs for other stewed dishes. Even the salt used to pickle the bacon is used to flavor. No less renowned are the bacon specialties from another town in Aosta, the lardo d'Arnad, and the lardo di Camaiore from the region of Lucca.

a The bacon from Colonnata, lardo di Colonnata, is at its best sliced very thin. It can be served simply with diced tomatoes and chopped parsley and slices of Tuscan white bread. In fact, this has been a common lunch eaten by the marble workers of the marble quarries of Colonnata near Carrara for generations.

b   Pigs are raised for specialty cured meat products throughout northern Italy.   c   South Tyrolean speck, or pancetta dell'Alto Adige, is smoked over cold beechwood to lend the characteristic flavor. It is commonly served with a flat hard rye bread during the South Tyrolean break also called *merenda*.
d   For lardo di Colonnata, brine containers need to be made from a special marble that are resistant to the corrosion caused by the brine liquid. Rubbed with coarse salt, spices, and herbs, the bacon pieces are stacked and left to age at least half a year until they are ready to be consumed.   e   In contrast to the air-dried prosciutto hams, ham in Alto Adige is sliced thick.   f   Fine bacons should appear ruby red with wide layers of fat.

Gnocchi Ripieni con Ragù di Finferli

Stuffed Gnocchi with Chanterelle Ragù (Trentino)

INGREDIENTS for 4:

For the gnocchi:

1½ lb baking potatoes (about 5 medium)

Salt and freshly ground pepper

1 small red beet

1 tsp butter

1–2 cups flour + flour for kneading

1 egg

½ lb fresh spinach

1 egg yolk

¼ cup grated Grana Trentino cheese (substitute with parmesan cheese)

Freshly grated nutmeg

For the ragù:

½ lb fresh chanterelle mushrooms

2 garlic cloves

2–3 parsley sprigs

4 Tbsp olive oil

2 Tbsp butter

Salt and freshly ground pepper

2 Tbsp lemon juice

PREPARATION TIME: 1½ hours
PER PORTION: about 545 calories

Recommended Wine:
Aromatic dry white wine with moderate acidity, such as a Pinot Grigio from Trentino.

Gnocchi are the fluffy potato dumplings often served in lieu of the pasta in northern Italy; in the same way other Italians stuff ravioli or tortellini, so Alpine cooks hide flavorful surprises in their gnocchi. For this dish, only use baking potatoes like Idahos or russet Burbanks. Older potatoes are the most suited, otherwise the gnocchi may turn out sticky and chunky. Take care not to overknead gnocchi. The less flour used, the finer and fluffier the dumplings turn out. The coloring with the red beet is typical of Trentino. Instead of red beets you can use also pureed tomatoes, but the flavor will not be the same.

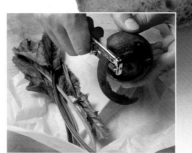

1 For the gnocchi, scrub the potatoes (do not peel) and cook them in salted water for about 25–30 minutes or until they are soft. Peel and dice the beet. Melt the butter in a skillet. Cook the beet, covered, over low heat for about 25 minutes or until it is soft.

2 Drain the potatoes and, while they are still warm, peel them and rice them through a potato ricer onto a floured work surface; dust the potatoes with flour. Puree the beets in a food processor, and if necessary heat them again until they have lost all liquid. Add the beets, egg, and salt to the potatoes.

3 With floured hands, gently knead the gnocchi ingredients and work them to soft dough; use only enough flour to prevent the dough from being sticky.

4 Meanwhile, rinse and trim the spinach; blanch it in a large pot of salted water until it wilts. Drain the spinach and rinse in cold water; squeeze it to remove as much liquid as possible. Chop the spinach and mix it with the egg yolk and grated cheese; season with salt, pepper, and nutmeg.

5 Roll out the potato dough; cut out circles 2–3 inches in diameter. Place about 1 teaspoon of spinach filling on half of the circles; dampen the borders of the circles with water and top each with an empty circle; press all circles together. Set the dumplings aside until you are ready to cook them.

6 For the ragù, clean and trim the chanterelles. Peel and mince the garlic. Rinse and pat dry the parsley; mince the leaves. Heat 2 tablespoons of oil in a saucepan. Sauté the mushrooms; add the garlic and parsley and sauté briefly. Season with salt and pepper and stir in the remaining oil and lemon juice. Keep warm.

7 Bring a large pot of salted water to a boil. Cook the gnocchi in batches for about 4 minutes or until they float to the surface, stirring them gently. With a slotted spoon, remove them from the water and place them on preheated serving plates. Top the gnocchi with the mushroom ragù and serve while still warm.

Zuppa d'Oca
Goose Soup (Friuli)

INGREDIENTS for 4:

1 goose leg (about 1 lb)

2½ lb goose parts (neck and back)

Salt and freshly ground pepper

10–11 oz. chestnuts

2 onions

1 garlic clove

1 Tbsp olive oil

2–3 red or Yukon gold potatoes

PREPARATION TIME: 2¾ hours
PER PORTION: about 610 calories

1 Remove the goose meat from the leg and remove all sinews and skin. Separately refrigerate the meat and the skin. Put the bones and the goose parts in a large saucepan and add 8 cups water. Season with salt and bring to a boil. Reduce the heat and simmer, covered, for about 2 hours; peri-odically skim the surface with a fine-meshed skimmer.

2 Preheat the oven to 425° F (if convection oven 400° F). With a sharp paring knife, cut an X in the bottom of each chestnut; place them on a baking sheet and spray them with water. Roast them on the middle oven rack for about 20–25 minutes or until the skins curl open. While the chestnuts are still warm, peel them and remove the thin brown membrane.

3 Pass the goose skin through meat grinder or mince it. Dice the goose meat. Peel and chop the onions and garlic.

4 Heat the oil in another large saucepan and fry the goose skin until crispy. Remove the skin when crispy and crumbly and transfer it to a small skillet; set aside. In the same fat, sauté the onion and garlic; add the goose meat and sauté until brown. Pour 6 cups of the goose broth through a fine-meshed sieve and add to the goose meat.

5 Peel and dice the potatoes. Chop half of the chestnuts. Add both to the goose soup; season with salt and pepper and simmer, covered, over low heat for about 30 minutes.

6 Dice the remaining chestnuts and stir them into the soup. Taste and adjust the seasonings and let the soup simmer for 10 more min-utes. Reheat the goose skin pieces and use to garnish the soup. Serve while still hot.

Instead of fresh chestnuts you may use dried chestnuts. However, these will need to be soaked overnight and cooked for about 1½ hours or until soft.

Recommended Wine:
Light fruity red wine such as a Merlot from Colli Orientali del Friuli.

Minestra Aglio ed Erbette

Garlic Soup with Herbs (Alto Adige)

INGREDIENTS for 4:

6 garlic cloves

4–5 Tbsp almonds

1 small bunch parsley

1 very small rue sprig (see Tip)

1 bay leaf

1 thyme sprig

4 cups condensed chicken broth

Salt and freshly ground pepper

Freshly grated nutmeg

2 egg yolks

1/4 cup heavy cream

2 slices stale white bread

1 Tbsp butter

PREPARATION TIME: 35 minutes
PER PORTION: about 250 calories

1 Peel and chop the garlic. Puree the almonds and garlic in a food processor.

2 Rinse and pat dry the herbs. Remove the parsley and rue leaves from the stems. Tie the parsley and rue stems with the bay leaf and thyme. Heat the broth and the puree in a large saucepan. Tie the herb bundle to the pot handle and let it dangle into the liquid. Bring to a rolling boil and cook for 15 minutes.

3 Pour the broth through a fine-meshed sieve or colander and return it to the saucepan. Mince the parsley and rue and stir them into the soup. Season everything with salt, pepper, and nutmeg.

4 Whisk together the egg yolks, cream, and some of the broth; pour the mixture into the soup, stirring to prevent the eggs from curdling.

5 Remove the crusts from the bread and tear into bite-sized pieces. Melt the butter in a skillet and toast the bread pieces, stirring, until they are golden brown. Ladle the soup in bowls and top with croutons.

Tip: The bitter rue has been a favorite digestivo since the Roman times. However, in time the herb became less popular, though it has always been used in grappa con ruta. If you can't find rue, you may flavor this soup with a shot of this special grappa.

Tagliatelle con Speck

Tagliatelle with Bacon (Alto Adige)

INGREDIENTS for 4:

1 lb zucchini

1 onion

3 oz. pancetta (substitute with any of your favorite air-dried bacon or ham)

1 Tbsp butter

2 Tbsp grappa

2 cups pureed tomatoes (substitute with 1 14–15-oz can crushed tomatoes)

Salt and freshly ground pepper

1 lb tagliatelle (or any wide egg noodles)

5–6 Tbsp freshly grated aged hard mountain cheese

PREPARATION TIME: 30 minutes
PER PORTION: about 605 calories

1 Trim and dice the zucchini. Peel and thinly slice the onion. Slice the bacon into thin strips.

2 Melt the butter in a large skillet or Dutch oven. Sauté the bacon. Add the onion and zucchini and cook over medium heat for about 2–3 minutes. Stir in the grappa and cook until it evaporates; stir in the tomatoes. Season with salt and pepper, stir and keep warm.

3 For the pasta, bring a large pot of salted water to a rolling boil. Cook the tagliatelle according to package directions or until al dente (firm to the bite). Drain the pasta; add to the sauce and toss.

4 Distribute the pasta on plates and serve hot, topped with grated cheese.

Recommended Wine:
Fruity, aromatic white wine such as a Müller-Thurgau from Alto Adige.

Maltagliati alle Ortice

Pasta with Nettles (Valle d'Aosta)

INGREDIENTS for 4:

For the pasta:

$1\frac{1}{2}$ cups semolina or bread flour + flour for kneading)

$1\frac{1}{2}$ cups buckwheat flour

2 eggs

$\frac{1}{2}$ Tbsp olive oil

Large pinch salt

For the sauce:

5 oz young tops of stinging nettles (wear gloves when gathering)

Salt and freshly ground pepper

2 shallots

1 garlic clove

2 Tbsp butter

2 Tbsp flour

$1\frac{3}{4}$ cup milk

$\frac{1}{2}$ cup heavy cream

$\frac{1}{2}$ tsp saffron

4 Tbsp grated Grana Padano cheese (substitute with parmesan cheese)

PREPARATION TIME: 50 minutes
PER PORTION: about 585 calories

1 For the pasta, sift together both flours in a large mixing bowl. Add the eggs, oil, and salt and knead until the dough is smooth and springy; add a little water if necessary.

2 Using a pasta machine, roll the dough into thin sheets (if you don't have a machine use a rolling pin). Cut the sheets into wide strips, and then into irregular triangles. Set the triangles on a well floured dish cloth and let the pasta dry for about 30 minutes.

3 Meanwhile, for the sauce, rinse the nettles (wearing rubber gloves) and blanch them for 1 minute in a large pot of salted water. Drain the nettles in a colander; rinse them with cold water and set them aside to drain.

Porcini Gratinati con Crema di Polenta

Porcini Mushrooms with Creamy Polenta (Piedmont)

INGREDIENTS for 4:

2 cups chicken broth

1 cup milk

¾ cup cornmeal (substitute with coarse harina de maís)

Salt and freshly ground pepper

1 lb small fresh porcini mushrooms

4 shallots

1 garlic clove

2–3 parsley sprigs

6 Tbsp butter

2 Tbsp olive oil

Freshly grated nutmeg

0.35 oz white truffle (you may substitute with truffle oil)

1 Tbsp finely chopped hazelnuts

6 Tbsp grated Grana Padano (substitute with parmesan cheese)

PREPARATION TIME: 1 hour
BAKING TIME: 15 minutes
PER PORTION: about 410 calories

1 Combine the broth and milk in a large saucepan. In a stream and while stirring constantly, add the cornmeal. Season with salt and cook, stirring constantly, for about 30 minutes. Keep the heat below a boil to prevent the polenta from splattering.

2 Clean and slice the mushrooms. Peel and chop the shallots and garlic. Rinse and pat dry the parsley; mince the leaves. Heat 3 tablespoons of butter and the oil in a skillet. Sauté the shallots, garlic, and parsley until translucent. Add the mushrooms and sauté over high heat for about 5 minutes; season with salt, pepper, and nutmeg. Clean the truffle and shave it very thinly over the mushrooms (or drizzle with the truffle oil). Preheat the oven to 425° F (if convection 400° F).

3 Cream the cooked polenta with a hand mixer; if necessary mix in a little hot water. Set the polenta aside and stir it periodically.

4 Distribute the mushrooms among 4 individual baking dishes or soufflé cups. Combine the chopped nuts and remaining butter in a skillet and cook until golden brown. Pour the browned butter through a fine-meshed sieve into the polenta and stir vigorously. Top the mushrooms with the polenta and dust with cheese. Bake for about 15 minutes or until the cheese has become slightly brown. Serve immediately.

Recommended Wine:
An aromatic white wine such as a *Roero Arneis* from Piedmont.

(from facing recipe:)

4 Peel and chop the shallots and garlic. Melt the butter in a saucepan. Sauté the shallots and garlic over low heat until translucent. Stir in the flour; let it bubble and remove from the heat. Add the milk and cream and simmer, stirring constantly, until the sauce has thickened; season with the saffron, salt, and pepper. Squeeze the moisture from the nettles and chop finely. Add the nettles to the sauce. Keep the sauce warm and stir it periodically.

5 Bring a large pot of salted water to a boil. Cook the noodles for about 5 minutes or until al dente; drain them and distribute them among plates. Top the noodles with the nettle sauce and serve with grated cheese.

Trota con Salsa Verde

Trout with Green Sauce (Trentino)

INGREDIENTS for 4:

$4\frac{1}{2}$ oz spinach

Salt and freshly ground pepper

4 trout (about 7 oz each; cleaned and ready-to-cook)

2 slices organic lemons

2 bunches fresh basil

$\frac{3}{4}$ cup almonds

4 Tbsp lemon juice

About $\frac{1}{3}$ cup olive oil

PREPARATION TIME: 45 minutes
PER PORTION: about 420 calories

1 For the sauce, clean, rinse well, and trim the spinach; blanch it in a large pot of salted water. Remove the spinach from the water, leaving the water at a boil; rinse it with cold water and let it drain in a colander. Squeeze the moisture from the spinach and chop.

2 Rinse the trout, inside and out. Add the fish, 2 Tbsp lemon juice, and the lemon slices to the boiling water. Reduce the heat and simmer the trout for about 10 minutes.

3 Meanwhile, remove the basil leaves from the stems and puree them in a food processor with the spinach, almonds, and the remaining lemon juice. While pureeing, add the oil in a thin stream to make a creamy sauce; season with salt and pepper.

4 Carefully remove the trout from the water and place them on heated plates. Serve them with the green sauce. Crispy diced potatoes fried in olive oil go very well with this specialty.

Quaglie al Vignaiolo

Quail, Winemaker-Style (Friuli)

INGREDIENTS for 4:

4 quail (about 5–6 oz each; cleaned and ready-to-cook)

Salt and freshly ground pepper

1 tsp dried oregano

5 oz mild or hot Italian sausage

2 Tbsp butter

2 Tbsp olive oil

2 garlic cloves

1 tsp grated lemon zest

1 cup dry white wine

$1\frac{1}{2}$ cup seedless red grapes (about $\frac{1}{2}$ lb)

PREPARATION TIME: 25 minutes
COOKING TIME: 35 minutes
PER PORTION: about 460 calories

1 Rinse the quail inside and out and pat them dry; season the outsides with salt and pepper and the cavity with oregano. Fill the birds with the sausage meat and tie the legs with kitchen string so that the cavities remain closed.

2 Heat the butter and oil in a Dutch oven. Brown the quail on both sides over medium heat for about 10–12 minutes. Peel the garlic and crush it through a garlic press into the pot. Add the lemon zest and wine. Reduce the heat to low and simmer, covered, for about 30 minutes.

3 Preheat the broiler. Rinse the grapes, add them to the quail, and let simmer in the gravy for about 5 minutes; season with salt and pepper. Place the Dutch oven under the broiler about 4 inches away from the heating elements and broil until the skin of the birds is nice and crispy. Serve hot, accompanied with boiled potatoes or slices of white bread.

Stinco di Porchetta Glassata

Honey-Glazed Pork Leg (Lombardy)

INGREDIENTS for 4:

4 legs of suckling pig (about 9 oz each—substitute with larger raw ham hocks)

4 garlic cloves

1 tsp dried oregano

Salt

1 Tbsp olive oil

1⅓ cups dry white wine

2 Tbsp light wild honey

2 Tbsp lemon juice

2 Tbsp brandy or cognac

PREPARATION TIME: 20 minutes
COOKING TIME: 2 hours
PER PORTION: about 440 calories

1 Pat the pork legs dry with paper towels. Peel the garlic and cut it into slivers. Crumble the oregano over the garlic.

2 Preheat the oven to 425° F (if convection oven 410° F). With a sharp paring knife, make short slices into various parts of the legs and insert a garlic sliver into each of the cuts; season the pork legs with salt.

3 Put the olive oil in a Dutch oven and add the pork legs. Roast on the middle oven rack for about 15 minutes. Reduce the heat to 350° F (if convection oven 325° F), pour in some wine, and roast 1 hour longer, basting the pork with either more wine or with the pan juices; toward the end the juices will evaporate.

4 Whisk the honey, lemon juice, and brandy in a bowl. Roast the meat for 30 more minutes, brushing the meat with this glaze every 10 minutes and turning the legs over occasionally.

5 Remove the pork legs from the oven as soon as they have a shiny and brown crispy coating. Let stand 10–15 minutes, covered with foil. Serve; mashed potatoes will make a tasty and hearty accompaniment.

Variation:
Instead of roasting a pork leg you might want to use a leg of lamb; in this case, however, braise the lamb on the stovetop for about 2 hours so that it will be tender and delicate. Then finish roasting and glazing the lamb in the oven at 350° F for 20 more minutes.

Recommended Wine:
Light, cherry-flavored red wine such as a Groppello from around Lake Garda.

113

Lombatina di Vitello al Finocchio
Loin of Veal with Fennel (Friuli)

INGREDIENTS for 4:

4 veal loin chops (each about 5 oz)

1 small fennel bulb, with the
    greens

1 Tbsp lemon juice

1 shallot

1 piece of carrot (about 2 inch
    long)

1 piece of leek (about 2 inches;
    white part only)

3½ oz calf's liver

3 Tbsp butter

Salt and freshly ground pepper

Flour, for dusting

1 Tbsp Sambuca or other anise-
    flavored liqueur

⅓ cup condensed veal broth

2 Tbsp heavy cream

PREPARATION TIME: 45 minutes
PER PORTION: about 255 calories

The best side dish for this
specialty is a creamy polenta
such as the recipe on page
118.

Recommended Wine:
A delicate, aromatic red wine
such as a Pinot Nero [Pinot
Noir] from Friuli.

In Italy, meat, especially veal, is still somewhat a luxury ingredient. Smaller pieces are common, and even they are stuffed in order to "stretch" or emphasize the richness of the dish. The combination of the mild veal meat with the more flavorful liver lends this recipe an almost sumptuous flavor; both ingredients complement each other. A similar dish can be found in the cuisines of Umbria and Emilia-Romagna, using ham rolls filled with chicken liver.

Early versions of this used delicate shoots of wild fennel, which have a stronger flavor and aroma, instead of fennel bulbs. Should you by chance have access to this delicate wild ingredient, trim it, cut it into small pieces, blanch it, and sauté it before using.

1   Pat the veal dry with paper towels. With a meat mallet, lightly pound and flatten the veal. With a sharp knife, cut open the chops to create a side pocket for the stuffing. Cover the chops and set them aside.

2   Trim the fennel, reserving the green tops. Cut the fennel bulb lengthwise in thin wedges. Mince 1 wedge; drizzle the remaining wedges with the lemon juice and refrigerate.

3   Peel the shallot and carrot; slice open the leek and rinse it under running water; mince the vegetables. Pat dry the veal liver and if necessary remove all membranes and veins; dice the liver.

4 Melt 1 Tbsp of the butter in a large saucepan or Dutch oven. Sauté the vegetables over medium heat. Add the liver and sauté about 5 minutes or until the pieces are firm; season with salt and pepper. Chop the fennel greens and add half of them to the liver mixture. Puree the liver mixture in a food processor to make a paste.

5 Fill the veal pockets with the pureed stuffing; close the pockets and seal with toothpicks or skewers. Season the meat with salt and pepper; dust the pockets with flour. Melt the remaining 2 Tbsp of butter in a skillet. Brown the veal over medium heat for about 5–7 minutes on each side. Pour the anise liqueur over the meat and let the liquid evaporate.

6 Remove the meat from the pan and keep it warm. Sauté the fennel wedges in the pan drippings for about 2 minutes; don't overcook them since they should remain somewhat crispy. Remove the fennel and deglaze the pan with the broth and the cream.

7 Season the sauce with salt and pepper. Arrange the veal on serving plates; garnish with the fennel wedges. Pour the cream sauce over the meat and sprinkle with the chopped fennel greens; serve while still hot.

115

Orzotto allo Zafferano
Barley with Saffron (Valle d'Aosta)

INGREDIENTS for 4:

¾ cup of pearled barley

2 shallots

1 garlic clove

5 cups of vegetable broth

2 Tbsp butter

½ tsp saffron

Salt and freshly ground pepper

4 Tbsp grated Grana Padano (substitute with parmesan cheese)

PREPARATION TIME: 20 minutes
COOKING TIME: 40 minutes
PER PORTION: about 280 calories

1 Put the barley in a colander and rinse it under hot water until the water runs clear; drain the barley. Peel and mince the shallots and garlic. Bring the broth to a boil.

2 Melt the butter in a sauce pan. Sauté the shallots and garlic until they are translucent. Add the barley and saffron and stir until the barley is coated with fat. Add about ¾ cup of broth, or enough to cover all the ingredients; cook over medium or low heat, stirring, for 40 minutes or until the barley is tender, adding more broth as it is absorbed.

3 When the orzotto is creamy and soft, like risotto, season it with salt and pepper and stir in the cheese, and stir making sure that all ingredients are folded in well. Distribute the orzotto on plates and serve while still hot. On the side, you may want to serve more cheese.

Asparagi con Midollo
Asparagus with Marrow (Piedmont)

INGREDIENTS for 4:

About 3 lb asparagus

1 marrow bone (such as beef or veal shank)

1 shallot

¾ cup condensed veal or vegetable broth

4 Tbsp dry white wine (such as Roero Arneis)

Salt and freshly ground pepper

10 Tbsp cold butter

PREPARATION TIME: 40 minutes
PER PORTION: about 360 calories

1 Trim the asparagus; if necessary peel the stems. Rinse the bone and place it in ice cold water.

2 Peel and mince the shallot. Cook the shallot in a saucepan over high heat with the broth and wine for about 15 minutes or until the liquid has reduced by half.

3 Bring a skillet of salted water to a boil. Reduce the heat and simmer the asparagus for about 10–15 minutes or until still firm to the bite.

4 Pour the shallot sauce through a fine-meshed sieve and return the liquid to the saucepan. Cut the butter into small pieces and whisk into the hot liquid until the sauce is smooth and creamy. Season with salt and pepper.

5 Remove the marrow from the bone by pushing it out; cut the marrow into slices. Add the slices to the sauce and heat to serving temperature. Drain the asparagus and arrange them on a serving platter; pour the sauce with the slices of bone marrow over them.

Recommended Wine:

An aromatic white wine such as a *Roero Arneis* from Piedmont.

Cavolini di Bruxelles con Castagne

Brussels Sprouts with Chestnuts (Alto Adige)

INGREDIENTS for 4:

1 lb chestnuts

1 lb Brussels sprouts

Salt and freshly ground pepper

1 large onion

3 garlic cloves

7 oz soft cheese (such as Taleggio
   or Bel Paese)

2 Tbsp butter

1/4 cup heavy cream

Freshly grated nutmeg

PREPARATION TIME: 1 hour
PER PORTION: about 480 calories

1 Preheat the oven to 350° F (if convection oven 325° F). With a sharp paring knife, cut an X in the bottom of each chestnut. Place them on a baking sheet and spray them with water. Cover them loosely with foil. Place the baking sheet on the middle oven rack and roast for 30 minutes or until the skins curl open.

2 Meanwhile, trim the Brussels sprouts. Bring a large pot of salted water to a boil. Add the Brussel sprouts, reduce the heat, and simmer for 10–15 minutes. Don't overcook them; they should still be firm to the bite.

3 When the chestnuts are cool enough to handle, peel them, removing the inside brown membrane. Peel and mince the onion and garlic. Cut off any rind and dice the cheese. Drain the Brussels sprouts and set them aside.

4 Melt the butter in a large sauce pan. Sauté the onion and garlic until translucent. Add the chestnuts and Brussels sprouts and let everything cook briefly. Stir in the cream and cheese and allow the cheese to melt; season with salt, pepper, and nutmeg. Serve hot.

In Alto Adige, roasted chestnuts are a favorite snack food especially during the Törggelen season when visitors check on the winemakers to taste the new wine. Chestnuts and new wine are in season at the same time. Chestnuts are also peeled and caramelized as a side dish for venison, or combined with vegetables as here with Brussels sprouts.

117

Polenta

Cornmeal Mush (Alpine Regions)

INGREDIENTS for 4:

For firm polenta:

$^3/_4$ cup coarse corn meal or polenta flour (see Tip)

Salt and freshly ground pepper

Olive oil

For soft polenta:

$^3/_4$ cup fine cornmeal or polenta flour (see Tip)

Salt

$^3/_4$ cup heavy cream

Freshly grated nutmeg

PREPARATION TIME: 45 minutes
PER PORTION (FIRM POLENTA):
about 240 calories
PER PORTION (SOFT POLENTA):
about 365 calories

Tip:

If you can find "polenta flour" at your market, by all means use it—but if you can't, perfectly acceptable (and nearly identical) substitutes are cornmeal and masa harina. Pay attention to the coarseness of the polenta flour—coarse grinds are especially favored throughout the Alpine regions, in Piedmont, and in Lombardy and those result in a firmer and coarser polenta. There is a finer cornmeal that is more suitable for a creamy and softer polenta.

Besides the classic yellow polenta flour, a white cornmeal variety is available. Made from peeled corn kernels, *polenta bianca* cooks faster and is used for sweet specialties. Finally there is also a quick-cooking polenta that is made from precooked cornmeal that can be on the table in 5 minutes.

Each region and almost every town in Italy has its own preferences on how to prepare polenta. In the northern mountainous areas polenta is so firm that it can be turned over on a wooden board and sliced with a string; leftovers are often fried in a skillet, roasted over a griddle in the fireplace, or baked with layers of cheese and tomato sauce. Further south, in the Po Basin and in Tuscany, polenta is runnier, served directly out of the pot or spread on an oiled board and when cold, cut in squares that are either fried or topped with a layer of ingredients and then baked. A softer, creamier version is prepared with milk or heavy cream.

1 **For a firm polenta:** Bring 4 cups of salted water to a boil in a large, heavy saucepan (preferably made of copper). While the water is just simmering, add the corn meal in a thin stream, stirring constantly with a wooden spoon to prevent lumps from forming.

2 Keep stirring while you add the cornmeal in a stream; reduce the heat if the polenta begins to bubble and keep stirring.

3 If the polenta begins to spatter, remove the pot from heat, continuing to stir, while you wait for the polenta to "calm down." Stir the cornmeal in the same direction; this will help to prevent spatters and will keep it from cooking too fast.

4 As the polenta becomes firm, continue to stir, adding some hot water if it becomes too firm. The polenta is done when it pulls away from the sides of the pot while you are stirring and when a thin crust appears on the bottom of the pot.

5 Divide the polenta among serving plates; drizzle each portion with some olive oil and, if necessary, season it with pepper. If you like, scrape the crust from the pot and serve it with the polenta; the crust can also be served as a snack with wine.

6 For a creamy polenta: Prepare the mush as for a firm one but add the heavy cream when the polenta is almost done and continue stirring vigorously; season the polenta with nutmeg. Polenta is delicious with veal, rabbit, or chicken.

7 Firm polenta can also be turned over on a wooden board, shaped into a rectangle or loaf, and cut into slices. In this case, serve it warm; fry cold slices in butter or top it with cheese and bake it until it is crispy.

Latte di Neve

Iced Milk (Alto Adige)

INGREDIENTS for 4–6:

5 slices stale white bread (without crusts)

$\frac{1}{2}$ vanilla bean

$\frac{3}{4}$ cup milk

$\frac{1}{3}$ cup dried figs

2 Tbsp raisins

$\frac{1}{4}$ cup grappa

2 Tbsp pine nuts

1 apple

2 tsp dried grated lemon zest

3 Tbsp sugar

1–2 Tbsp bread crumbs, if necessary

$\frac{3}{4}$ cup heavy cream

1 Tbsp ground cinnamon

Mixed berries and fresh mint leaves, for garnish

PREPARATION TIME: 1 hour
REFRIGERATING TIME: 2–3 hours
PER PORTION (WITH 6 SERVINGS): about 275 calories

For a faster, easier variation, try spooning out small dumpling-sized portions of the bread mixture and covering these with heavy cream.

Recommended Wine:
A slightly chilled dessert wine, such as a Vin Santo from Trentino for example or, for a rare and expensive treat, a *Moscato Rosa* (Rosenmuskateller) from Alto Adige.

This is an old family recipe from the Senales Valley around Vernago, where glaciers have turned the place into a summer vacation resort. Here stale bread, a typical ingredient of the frugal mountain areas, is transformed into a delicious dessert. The other ingredients are equally humble: milk, dried fruits, nuts, and apples—ingredients that are staples in this area.

1 Crumble or tear the bread into small pieces into a mixing bowl. Slice open the vanilla bean and scrape the seeds into the milk in a saucepan. Add the vanilla bean and heat the milk almost to a boil.

2 Remove the vanilla bean from the milk and pour the milk over the bread; set aside to soak for about 30 minutes. Remove the stems from the dried figs and chop the figs. Soak the figs and raisins in the grappa.

3 Toast the pine nuts in a small dry skillet until they are golden, stirring constantly so they don't burn. Peel, core, and finely chop the apple.

4 Combine the milk-soaked bread, the grappa-soaked fruit, the pine nuts, apple, lemon zest, and 2 tablespoons of sugar; mix well. If the mixture is too liquid, add breadcrumbs.

5 Place the bread mixture on a serving platter and, with a spatula or a cake knife dipped in cold water, shape it into an oblong loaf; while you shape it, keep on dipping the knife or spatula in cold water. Cover the dessert with plastic wrap and refrigerate for about 2–3 hours.

6 Before serving, whip the heavy cream and the remaining sugar until stiff peaks form. Frost the dessert with the whipped cream and dust the top with the cinnamon. Slice the loaf and serve, garnished with the berries and mint.

Toma con Cugnà

Toma with Nutty Fruit Chutney (Piedmont)

INGREDIENTS for 4:

2 cups white grape juice

1 firm pear

1 peach

2 fresh figs

2 Tbsp each hazelnuts, almonds, and walnuts

1 lb fresh toma cheese (see Tip)

Lemon balm leaves to garnish

PREPARATION TIME: 35 minutes
COOLING TIME: 1 hour
PER PORTION: about 405 calories

1 Bring the grape juice to a rolling boil in a medium saucepan and cook until it has reduced by half for about 10 minutes.

2 Peel, core, and dice the pear; peel, pit, and dice the peach. Rinse, trim, and dice the figs.

3 Toast the hazelnuts, almonds, and walnuts in a dry skillet; remove the nuts from the skillet and chop them coarsely. Add the fruit and nuts to the grape juice and let the mixture simmer for about 5–10 minutes or until the sauce has thickened. Set aside to cool for about 1 hour.

4 Either slice or spoon the cheese into dessert bowls; top the cheese with the fruit chutney and garnish with the lemon balm.

Tip: Toma is made from either cow's milk or a mixture of sheep and goat's milk; it has a semisoft texture. It is a regional favorite either plain or with dessert specialties. It is rarely available in the United States; substitute with Brie or Camembert if you can't find it. *Cugnà*, also called *cognà*, is also available in a savory mustard variation that is usually served with meats.

Gratin di Zabaione

Wine Cream Gratin (Piedmont)

INGREDIENTS for 4:

9 oz mixed berries (preferably wild berries such as small strawberries, raspberries, blackberries, cranberries, blueberries, and red or black currants)

1 organic lemon

4 Tbsp sugar

4 egg yolks

¼ cup sweet dessert wine (such as Vin Santo)

Fresh mint leaves, for garnish

PREPARATION TIME: 20 minutes
BAKING TIME: 10 minutes
PER PORTION: about 160 calories

1 Rinse all the berries; drain the berries and set aside the currants. If necessary, remove any stems parts of the berries.

2 Scrub the lemon under hot water. Using a zester or grater remove 1 teaspoon of the zest. Juice the lemon and drizzle about 3 Tbsp over the berries, including the currants. Sprinkle 1 Tbsp of sugar over the currants and let them set.

3 Preheat the oven to 425° F (if convection oven 400° F). Combine the egg yolks, remaining sugar, and lemon zest in the top of a double boiler. Over simmering water, beat on high speed until pale and fluffy. Gradually drizzle in the wine and whisk constantly to make a light zabaione cream.

4 When ready, pour the zabaione into four heat resistant flan cups or dessert bowls and top each with berries. Bake on the middle oven rack for about 10

Gelatina di Pesca con Salsa al Moscato

Peach Gelatin with Moscato Sauce (Piedmont)

minutes or until the zabaione forms a honey colored crust. Garnish with the sugared currants and mint; serve immediately.

Variation:
For a cold variation of zabaione, place the warm cream over an ice-filled bowl and whisk until it has cooled. Beat 1 cup of heavy cream with a little sugar until stiff peaks form and fold it into the zabaione. Refrigerate until ready to serve.

INGREDIENTS for 4:

1 lb sweet yellow peaches

About 5 Tbsp sugar

1 Tbsp Amaretto (almond liqueur)

3 Tbsp lemon juice

2 envelopes gelatin

½ vanilla bean

1 cup *Moscato d'Asti* (sweet sparkling wine; substitute with Prosecco or Asti Spumante)

2 tsp cornstarch or arrowroot

Lemon balm leaves and small wild strawberries, to garnish

PREPARATION TIME: 30 minutes
REFRIGERATING TIME: 6 hours
PER PORTION: about 185 calories

1   Bring a large pot of water to a boil. Cut a shallow X in the bottom of each peach. Briefly blanch the peaches; peel, pit, and dice them. Puree the peaches in a

food processor with 2–3 tablespoons of sugar, the Amaretto, and 1 tablespoon of lemon juice.

2   Soak the gelatin in ⅓ cup of cold water for 1 minute and heat up the mixture. Add the hot gelatin and 1 tablespoon of lemon juice to the peach puree. Stir and pour into pudding cups or small glasses. Refrigerate for about 6 hours.

3   Slice open the vanilla bean and scrape the inside seeds into a saucepan. Drop in the bean and add the Moscato and the remaining sugar; heat over low heat. Stir the cornstarch into 1–2 tablespoons of cold water and add to the wine. Continue stirring until the sauce has thickened; add the remaining lemon juice, stirring occasionally. Set aside to cool.

4   Before serving, remove the vanilla bean from the sauce; pour some Moscato sauce over each gelatin and garnish with lemon balm and strawberries.

Tuscany, Umbria, and Marche

In the Center: Gently Rolling Hills, Olive Groves, and a Diverse and Hearty Cuisine

The Region and Its Products

With many commonalities and many differences, Central Italy has a lot to offer

Olives, legumes, grains, grapes, vegetables, and herbs thrive especially well here, where the Mediterranean climate plays a vital role. The sea along the coast provides fish to locals, and forests and meadows are home to many game animals. These regional cuisines are deeply rooted in farming, yet they never cease to surprise with their simple but refined dishes.

Tuscany. Visitors and locals alike are fond of Pecorino Toscano, which they say is absolutely delicious; they speak of Chianti and mention the thick, juicy bistecca alla fiorentina, a sizable T-bone steak from the Chianina beef that in Tuscany is grilled medium-rare and seasoned only with salt, pepper, and a good drizzling of fresh olive oil. Besides the renowned white cattle of the Val di Chiana, numerous sheep and a special breed of pigs—*cinta senese*—provide the excellent meat for the regional main dishes. Fish is mainly featured in the coastal areas' menus, though baccalà is popular everywhere. Tuscan olive oil is especially good; olive trees thrive under the best of conditions. The oil is more aromatic than in other Italian regions. Chestnut flour is used to make flat cakes and sometimes pasta. Traditional unsalted white bread, wild and aromatic herbs, vegetables, and salads enhance this region's way of cooking.

Umbria. Olives thrive here, too, but the flavor of Umbrian oil is milder. Black truffles lend fame to the small town of Norcia. This town is also renowned for its raw and dried sausages, especially if the meat comes from free ranging pigs fed on acorns as in the old days. Lentils from Castelluccio, freshwater fish from the Lake Trasimeno and the many surrounding rivers, and vegetables and legumes combine to add variety to the regional culinary market. Many dishes are updated with new ingredients; truffles might flavor a carp, or sausages may be used as filling for a roasted pigeon, or lentils could be served with trout.

Marche. Imagine a landscape of gently rolling hills with fields of wheat throughout—a little bit more rustic than Tuscany but no less beautiful, here and there interspersed with olive groves and vineyards. During the fall season, the small town of Acqualagna, located in the northwest part of the region, spoils its guests with truffles, black or white like the famous truffles from Piedmont. An especially large olive, used as a table olive or stuffed and fried, is indigenous to the southern part of Marche. Creative chefs prepare this olive in many innovative ways; as a spread that can be eaten with pecorino cheese or in sauces that garnish an antipasti or that are served with secondi.

The landscape of Marche is marked by fields of grains. On these gently rolling hills, emmer and spelt, which are among the oldest cultivated cereals, grow especially well. For this reason many pasta factories have moved here. Hard wheat such as semolina is also grown. Many factories, especially small ones, experiment with these varieties and may mix them in their products. Some even label the pasta with a harvest date, since the quality of a cereal can vary from one year to the other and may ultimately affect the time of cooking. This is why it is less important to follow the cooking time printed on the package than to taste the pasta while it is cooking.

The ideal small town is represented by Todi; this is also why it is Umbria's favorite. The town is not only famous for its peaceful surroundings but for its *brutti ma buoni*, soft macaroons made from hazelnuts, and for other sweets that are "ugly but good."

Since the Middle Ages, hams and sausages of Norcia have been considered a special treat by gourmets throughout the world. These products are so renowned today that a butcher shop or meat market that sells them is not only known as a *macelleria* but also as a *norcineria*—and this is not only throughout Umbria.

Besides cereals, olives are among the most important crops in Marche. Some varieties are used to make olive oil, and others are used at the table or in the kitchen.

The open market in Ascoli Piceno takes place within the San Francesco Passage. Farmers of the region gather here, offering their products—in the summer whole bunches of zucchini flowers.

The Mercato Centrale in downtown Florence provides the locals with everything they need. Spread throughout two floors are locally produced and harvested foods like fish, meat, sausage, ham, cheese, pasta, vegetables, and fruits. Traditional prepared foods are available at the deli stand Nerbone.

The Cuisine

Rustic but refined, whether it is antipasti and primi, or herbed and aromatic secondi

Tuscany's love is for the crisp crostini and the juicy meat; Marche's for the wonderful assortment of pasta and fresh fish; Umbria's for earthy legumes and freshwater fish.

More than just crostini.
In Tuscany, an antipasto misto is more than just crostini. You'll also find sausage, ham, and cheese—an appetizer that more than satisfies hunger. Crostini today are a delicious change of culinary pace. These are not only spread with liver pâté but with many other creative toppings. Along the coast of Marche, fish is also available raw, similar to carpaccio or beef tartare.

Welcome legumes.
Legumes, whether they are added to soups or prepared with pasta, are a favorite food in the central part of Italy, especially in winter. Pasta is served preferably topped or tossed with herbed meat sauces that simmer for hours, developing a rich depth of flavor and aroma.

Meat above all.
With the availability of so many animals—whether cattle, sheep, or pigs, or even game—it should not come as a surprise that the secondi of this area often feature meat. The recipes of today are updated: boar is braised in grape juice; pork roast is prepared with lots of vegetables; lamb has delicate artichokes and lots of herbs. Fish is also popular here; along the coast, saltwater fish is broiled or baked or simmered in chowders. In Umbria, freshwater fish is also a favorite in mixed chowders; salads, seasonal vegetables, and rosemary potatoes are served with these.

Not only sweets.
This region's meal often ends with something that is not too sweet but is usually locally produced: grapes, fresh figs, pine nuts, or chestnuts are common. Cheese, especially the flavorful pecorinos produced in the region, is often included.

Many families in the surrounding country still today maintain their own small vineyards or olive groves. They are very proud of the wine and olive oil their crops yield, even if the production is extremely small (in one cart, they can take home the fruits of their labor).

Figs are especially delicious when they are picked fresh from the tree. They are picked the day before the market if they are from around the area and are usually available only locally. Fresh figs in Tuscany, Umbria, and Marche are not only served with ham or sausage but also with pecorino Toscano. Sometimes they are eaten fresh, sometimes they are prepared as a jam (cooked in Vin Santo with a bit of rosemary), and sometimes they are dried and served with chocolate.

Traditional Tuscan bread is prepared with dough that is not salted. In the old days, this precious ingredient was left out because of its cost; today unsalted bread is appreciated because its mild flavor goes best with the robustly seasoned, hearty specialties of the region, such as sausage from boar or a fennel sausage called *finocchiona*, an aged pecorino, or a flavorful spread used to top fire-roasted crostini.

The soft *ricciarelli* are among the most famous sweets of Siena; they have been baked there since the fifteenth century. These very soft and flavorful Tuscan cookies are made from almonds, egg whites, and sugar.

At Meletti's in Ascoli Piceno—an Art-Deco styled coffeehouse located downtown in the Piazza del Popolo—not only are espresso and cappuccino served, but also the famous anise-flavored spirit mistrà and the no less renowned liqueur anisetta.

Fresh fruits and vegetables are available daily in Acqualagna in Marche. The town is not only renowned for its black truffles, but also for the white ones that are less pretty—they thrive in a much harder soil—but just as tasty as those from Piedmont.

Pheasants live all over in Central Italy. They are usually roasted whole, seasoned with herbs and a layer of bacon.

A famous specialty from Ascoli Piceno: the large olives are stuffed and fried, then served hot as an antipasto with wine or as a main dish with other ingredients.

The Wines

From traditionally homemade fermented beverages to internationally renowned wines

The popularity of Tuscan wines, especially Chianti Classico and Super Toscano, has somehow overshadowed the wines of the other neighboring regions. This is too bad since many superb wines come from throughout those regions, and may well be much less pricey.

Tuscany's wine-making is very much dependent on Sangiovese grapes. Until a few years ago, traditional Chiantis were made by combining Sangiovese grapes with three other varieties, one of which was white. With the mandates of the consortium, several innovative winemakers created their own wines, which became known as Super Toscanos. Some of these wines were made just from Sangiovese grapes, others from mixtures that included international grape varieties; they were marketed as *vino da tavola*. These wines have gained almost a cult status, and by law Italian table wines are not allowed to be labeled with the year or date, so they are labeled as IGT (Indicazione Geografica Tipica). Besides Chianti Classico, there are six more growing areas (see page 142). Brunello di Montalcino is made from a Sangiovese

clone, Sangiovese Grosso, also called Sangioveto; the Vino Nobile di Montepulciano and the young Rosso di Montalcino are made from the Prugnolo Gentile (also a Sangiovese clone). Sangiovese wines have a high tannin content, high acidity, and a very deep red color. They have a mild scent of berries and violets. Brunello and Vino Nobile are usually milder than Chianti; Carmignano, made from Sangiovese mixed with Cabernet, is noble and fine. The most famous white wine from Tuscany is the Vernaccia di San Gimignano, made from Trebbiano grapes; when this wine is at its best it has a scent of apples and almonds and sparkles like gold in a glass. A specialty is the Vin Santo that is usually made from Malvasia and Trebbiano grapes; made from dry grapes, this wine is left to age in small wood barrels for at least two years.

The most famous wine from Umbria: Orvieto, made from Trebbiano and Grechetto grapes. While considered by many in the past a mass-production wine, today Orvieto from the Classico area can taste elegant and crisp. Grechetto grapes are also used to make other exclusive wine varieties. Reds in this area depend on the late season harvested Sagrantino; Montefalco Rosso is made from the heavy Sagrantino mixed with Sangiovese and cut with other red varieties.

The hearty, ruby-red Rosso Conero is made in Marche from Montepulciano grapes; the somewhat rustier Rosso Piceno (Superiore) is made from Montepulciano and Sangiovese. Verdicchio grapes are used to make two different wines: Verdicchio dei Castellide Jesi and the Verdicchio dei Matelica from high altitude vineyards. A crisp, lemon-scented variation is the Bianchello del Metauro.

Left: The regions of central Italy are red wine areas. In Tuscany, Sangiovese and its clones are used; Sagrantino and Sangiovese are in Umbria; Montepulciano and Sangiovese in Marche.
Above: Famous samples of the regions (from left to right) – Chianti Colli Senesi, Vernaccia di San Gimignano, Sagrantino di Montefalco, Bianchello del Metauro, Brunello di Montalcino.

Regional Recipes

Pasta, legumes, fish, and meat updated with lots of vegetables

Pappardelle—are among the widest Italian egg noodles. In Tuscany, Umbria, and Marche, they are especially popular topped with hearty sauces: with boar ragù, duck, lamb, rabbit, or also with wild flavorful mushrooms. The Tuscan bread salad called panzanella is only one example among many of how central Italians transform stale bread into a culinary specialty.

Panzanella con Verdure

Bread Salad with Vegetables (Tuscany)

INGREDIENTS for 4:

5 slices stale white bread

1/2 lb asparagus

5 oz green beans

8 zucchini blossoms

Salt and freshly ground pepper

2 medium tomatoes

4 garlic cloves

1 mild white or red onion

3 Tbsp red wine vinegar

1/2 cup olive oil

1 bunch basil

PREPARATION TIME: 30 minutes
MARINATING TIME: 1 hour
PER PORTION: about 340 calories

1 Dice the bread and toast it in a dry skillet over medium heat, stirring constantly. Trim the asparagus and cut into 3-inch long pieces. Rinse and trim the green beans; if necessary cut the long ones in half. Carefully open the zucchini blossoms and remove the stamens.

2 Bring a large pot of salted water to a boil. Blanch the asparagus for 4 minutes; rinse them under cold water. Blanch the beans for 8 minutes; rinse them under cold water. Heat 2 Tbsp of oil in a small skillet. Add the zucchini blossoms and sauté, stirring, for 2–3 minutes. Season with salt and pepper.

3 Core and peel the tomatoes; cut them into 8 wedges. Peel the onion and garlic. Thinly slice the onion and mince the garlic. Whisk together the salt, pepper, vinegar, and oil. Combine the bread and vegetables; toss with the dressing and set aside for about 1 hour. Cut the basil leaves into thin strips and add them to the salad. If necessary, season with more salt and pepper, and serve.

Flan di Ricotta

Savory Ricotta Flan with Olive Sauce (Marche)

INGREDIENTS for 4:

For the sauce:

1 large meaty tomato (preferably not entirely ripe)

3/4 cup pitted green olives (see Tip)

1 organic lemon

1/4 cup sugar

1/2 bunch basil

For the flan:

Butter, for the molds

2 eggs

1 1/2 cups ricotta cheese

3 Tbsp grated pecorino cheese

Salt and freshly ground pepper

Arugula, to garnish

PREPARATION TIME: 20 minutes
BAKING TIME: 30 minutes
PER PORTION: about 305 calories

1 Core and dice the tomato. Mince the olives. Scrub the lemon under hot water; with a zester or grater, remove the zest from half of the lemon. Extract 1 tablespoon of juice.

2 Simmer the tomato, olives, lemon zest, and sugar in a saucepan over medium heat for 15 minutes or until the sauce thickens.

3 Remove the basil leaves from the stems; cut into thin strips. Add to the sauce with the lemon juice; season with salt and set aside to cool.

4 Preheat the oven to 300° F (if convection oven 275° F). Grease 4 flan molds (about 3/4 cup in capacity) with the butter.

5 Separate the eggs. Mix the egg yolks, ricotta, and pecorino; season with salt and pepper. Beat the egg whites until stiff peaks

Branzino Crudo ai Peperoni

Bass Tartar with Peppers (Marche)

form and fold them into the ricotta mixture. Spoon into the flan molds.

6 Pour 1 inch of water into a baking dish; place the flans in it. Bake on the lower oven rack for about 30 minutes or until the flans are set. Remove from the oven and with a sharp knife carefully loosen the flans from the molds and invert them onto serving plates. Serve with the olive sauce and garnish with arugula.

Tip: Oliva tenera is the name of the most famous olive in the region of Marche. It is fried, stuffed, served as an appetizer, or used in the various local specialties. This olive is especially large and flavorful. If you find it in Italian delis, take advantage and use it. This olive is also very tasty if served with cheese, especially pecorino cheese.

INGREDIENTS for 4:

For the peppers:

1 yellow bell pepper

2 red bell peppers

1 Tbsp lemon juice (from the lemon used to prepare the fish tartar)

1 Tbsp olive oil

Salt and freshly ground pepper

1 bunch arugula

For the fish tartar:

1/2 celery rib

1/2 lb very fresh bass fillet (see Tip)

1 organic lemon

2–3 Tbsp olive oil

Salt and freshly ground pepper

PREPARATION TIME: 45 minutes
PER PORTION: about 175 calories

1 For the peppers, preheat the oven to 475° F (if convection oven

425° F); line a rimmed baking sheet with parchment paper. Seed, and cut the peppers in halves. Set the peppers, cut-down on the baking sheet. Roast the peppers on the middle oven rack for about 15 minutes or until their skins are dark. Cover the peppers with a damp dish cloth; set aside to cool.

2 For the fish, trim and chop the celery. If necessary, use tweezers to remove any bones from the fillets. Cut the fish into slices, then dice or mince. Scrub the lemon under hot water; with a zester or grater remove the zest from half of the lemon. Juice the lemon.

3 Combine the fish, celery, lemon zest, olive oil, and 1½ tablespoons of lemon juice; season with salt and pepper; cover, and refrigerate. Meanwhile, peel

and slice the peppers. Toss the peppers with salt, pepper, lemon juice, and olive oil. Rinse, trim, and chop the arugula; stir into the pepper.

4 Place the fish tartar on serving plates; garnish with the peppers and drizzle everything with olive oil.

Tip: Ask a reputable fish monger if the fish you buy is fresh enough to eat raw. Otherwise, substitute this fish with raw tuna or bream.

These peppers also make wonderful antipasti; in this case prepare a double portion.

Crostini al Tonno

Crostini with Tuna (Tuscany)

INGREDIENTS for 4:

1 small red onion

$\frac{1}{2}$ yellow bell pepper

1 celery rib

$\frac{1}{4}$ bunch fresh parsley

$\frac{1}{2}$ dried peperoncino (chili pepper)

6 oz tuna steak

4 Tbsp olive oil

5 Tbsp Vin Santo (or dry white wine)

1 organic lemon slice

1 anchovy (preserved in oil)

Salt

2 tsp lemon juice

12 slices white bread

PREPARATION TIME: 30 minutes
PER PORTION: about 375 calories

1 Peel the onion. Seed the pepper and trim the celery. Chop the vegetables. Rinse, pat dry, and chop the parsley leaves and any thin stems. Crush the peperoncino in a mortar. Cut the tuna into $\frac{1}{4}$-inch dice.

2 Heat 2 tablespoons of oil in a saucepan. Sauté the vegetables with the parsley and peperoncino. Add the tuna and sauté briefly. Stir in the Vin Santo; cover and simmer over low heat for about 10 minutes.

3 Puree the tuna, vegetables, lemon slice, anchovy, lemon juice, and the remaining olive oil in a food processor; season with salt and pepper.

4 Toast the bread until golden brown. Top the crostini with the tuna spread and serve immediately.

Crostini ai fagioli

Crostini with Bean Spread (Tuscany/Umbria)

INGREDIENTS for 4:

1 bunch basil

2 garlic cloves

$\frac{1}{2}$ cup cooked white beans (canned and drained or homemade)

$\frac{1}{2}$ tsp grated lemon zest

3 Tbsp olive oil

Salt and freshly ground pepper

2 oz lardo di Colonnata (substitute with thin sliced pancetta or bacon)

Chili powder, to taste

12 slices white bread

PREPARATION TIME: 15 minutes
PER PORTION: about 335 calories

1 Remove the basil leaves from the stems and mince them. Crush the garlic through a garlic press into a food processor.

2 Puree the beans in a food processor with the basil, garlic, lemon zest, olive oil, and 1 tablespoon of cold water; season with salt and pepper.

3 Slice the bacon in thin strips. Fry in a saucepan over medium-high heat until it becomes crispy; season with chili powder to taste.

4 Toast the bread. Top the crostini with the bean spread and bacon bits; serve immediately.

134

Bruschette al Pecorino

Bruschetta with Pecorino Cheese (Tuscany)

INGREDIENTS for 4:

2 oz aged pecorino cheese (about $\frac{1}{4}$ cup diced)

$\frac{1}{2}$ or 1 green peperoncino (chili pepper)

4 parsley sprigs

4 Tbsp olive oil

2–3 firm plum tomatoes

4 Tbsp sun-dried tomatoes (preserved in oil)

Salt and freshly ground pepper

8 slices Italian white bread

2 large garlic cloves

PREPARATION TIME: 15 minutes
MARINATING TIME: 30 minutes
PER PORTION: about 215 calories

1 Remove the rind from the cheese and dice the cheese. Rinse and trim the peperoncino and mince it with the seeds. Rinse and pat dry the parsley; mince the leaves. Mix the peperoncino and parsley with 1 tablespoon of oil and the cheese; set aside for about 30 minutes.

2 Meanwhile, core, seed, and dice the plum tomatoes. Drain the sun-dried tomatoes and cut them into thin strips. Toss both with the remaining 3 tablespoons of olive oil and season with salt and pepper.

3 Toast the bread. Peel the garlic and cut in half; rub the bread with the cut sides. Top the bruschetta with the tomatoes and the pecorino cheese. Serve while still warm.

Bruschetta agli Sgombri

Toasted Bread with Mackerel Spread (Tuscany)

INGREDIENTS for 4:

1 small eggplant (about 9 oz)

4 Tbsp olive oil

Salt and freshly ground pepper

$\frac{1}{4}$ red bell pepper

1 oz arugula

1 garlic clove

2 tsp lemon juice

8 slices white bread

1–2 oz smoked mackerel

PREPARATION TIME: 25 minutes
PER PORTION: about 240 calories

1 With a swivel peeler, peel the eggplant; chop it in small dice. Heat 2 tablespoons of olive oil in a skillet or saucepan. Sauté the eggplant; season with salt and pepper and simmer for about 8 minutes until soft and golden brown. Set aside to cool.

2 Meanwhile, mince the pepper. Rinse, trim, and pat dry the arugula. Peel the garlic. Mince the arugula and garlic. Add to the eggplant. Drizzle the remaining olive oil over the vegetables and season with salt, pepper and lemon juice.

3 Toast the bread. Top the bruschetta with the eggplant mixture. Slice the mackerel and place it over the eggplant spread. Serve immediately.

Legumes—Rich in Protein and Flavor
Lentils, chickpeas, etc. appear often on the menu—and this is good

In central Italy, legumes often compete with vegetables, in the case of antipasti as well as primi and contorni. And in this cuisine many beans reign supreme, from large cannellini and borlotti to tiny lentils.

Fagioli (Beans). Common white beans are called fagioli bianchi; the large whites are called cannellini. Other favorites are the red speckled borlotti beans that come in various sizes and varieties (such as the lamon beans from the Veneto region) and that are considered among the best. A specialty from the area of Arezzo are the fagioli zolfino which are sulfur yellow and have a skin so tender they don't need soaking before cooking. This less common and very tasty variety is served as simply as possible in Tuscany; it is only cooked and drizzled with the finest of olive oils. All other varieties are soaked overnight and cooked. The cooking time depends not only on the variety but on how old the beans are. Recently dried beans cook faster than beans that have been stored dry for a long time.

Lenticchie (Lentils). They are the tiniest of the legumes. They are flavorful and require less work than fagioli; they don't need soaking time and cook fairly quickly. In Tuscany, Umbria, and Marche lentils are often used in soups and stews, and are added to salsicce (spiced raw sausages) or served as a side dish. A favorite combination: lentils and chestnuts.

Fave (Fava Beans). Fave are similar to lima beans; they are available either whole (these have to be soaked overnight and peeled of their skins) or peeled and halved, which do not require soaking. Usually they are available in Italian markets.

Ceci (Chickpeas). This flavorful legume is cultivated almost everywhere in central Italy. It is used in salads, marinated as an antipasto, use in soups, as a side dish, or served with meat or fish as a main dish—ceci are absolutely a favorite in Tuscany, Umbria, and Marche. Chickpeas are also prepared with a type of short noodles; along the coast of Tuscany they are milled into flour that is used for a tasty flatbread called *cecina*. Whole chickpeas are usually available everywhere; the flour, however, is available in Italian or Asian stores (chickpea flour is also very prevalent in Indian cuisine).

Cicerchie (Chicklings). These look like flat, split chickpeas. Related to chickpeas, cicerchie have a long history but have fallen out of favor. Today the flavorful and aromatic beans are experiencing a comeback, but they might be hard to find in this country unless you find them through the Internet. They can be prepared like chickpeas, in salads or as side dishes and in soups.

a *Fagioli Borlotti Insalata* (Borlotti Bean Salad): Soak 1 cup dried borlotti beans overnight in cold water to cover. The next day, drain the beans and cook with a pinch of baking soda in abundant fresh water until they are soft. Drain and mix the beans with 1 trimmed, sliced fennel bulb; 1 seeded, sliced red bell pepper; 1 peeled, minced red onion; 1 tablespoon capers; 1 bunch rinsed, chopped arugula; 2 tablespoons red wine vinegar; 5 tablespoons olive oil; and salt and pepper.

b   Italy boasts a vast selection of legumes. Occasionally, different varieties are combined, perhaps in soups. The cooking advantage: small and softer varieties such as red lentils or split peas cook faster and break apart, make a soup almost velvety. Bean mixtures are available almost in every Italian food store.   c   Borlotti are not only available on the market dried but also fresh; they need only to be shelled and cooked in salted boiling water for about 20 minutes. They can be served as a side dish or in salads.   d   Lenticchie di Castelluccio from the Umbrian high plain of Castelluccio are considered among the best, and are therefore Italy's favorites.

Zuppa di Lenticchie

Lentil Soup (Umbria)

INGREDIENTS for 4:

2 garlic cloves / 1 onion / 1 carrot

1 celery rib

1 plum tomato

½ bunch parsley

1 sprig each oregano, thyme, and rosemary

¼ cup olive oil

1 cup brown lentils

5 cups beef or vegetable broth

2 tsp tomato paste

½ pound Italian sausage (salsicce)

2 Tbsp dry red wine

1 pinch chili powder

Salt and freshly ground pepper

PREPARATION TIME: 20 minutes
COOKING TIME: 40 minutes
PER PORTION: about 520 calories

1 Peel and chop the garlic, onion, and carrot. Trim and chop the celery. Bring a pot of water to a boil. Blanch the tomato; peel, core, and dice. Rinse and pat dry the herbs; remove the leaves from the stems. Set aside some parsley leaves and mince the rest of the herbs.

2 Heat the oil in a large saucepan. Sauté the garlic, onion, carrot, celery, and the minced herbs until softened. Stir in the lentils, broth, tomato paste, and the diced tomato. Simmer, covered, over low heat for about 40 minutes or until the lentils are soft but still firm to the bite. If necessary, add more water or broth.

3 Remove the sausage from the casings. Brown the sausage in a saucepan, breaking it apart as it cooks. Stir in the wine and chili powder. Mince the reserved parsley. Season the soup with salt and pepper and stir in the sausage; serve the soup topped with the parsley.

Pappa al Pomodoro

Tomato Soup (Tuscany)

INGREDIENTS for 4:

7 slices stale white bread

5 medium tomatoes

2 red onions

4 garlic cloves

1 rosemary sprig

4 Tbsp olive oil

2 cups vegetable or chicken broth

½ dried peperoncino (chili pepper)

½ bunch parsley

Salt and freshly ground pepper

PREPARATION TIME: 30 minutes
PER PORTION: about 325 calories

1 Break or tear the bread into pieces and soak it in water to cover. Bring a large pot of water to a boil. Blanch the tomatoes, then rinse under cold water. Peel, core, and dice the tomatoes.

2 Peel the onions and garlic. Thinly slice the onions and mince 2 garlic cloves. Rinse and pat dry the rosemary. Mince the leaves.

3 Heat 2 tablespoons of olive oil in a saucepan. Sauté the onions and garlic over low heat for about 3–5 minutes. Drain the bread and squeeze out the moisture; stir in the bread, tomatoes, and broth. Cook for about 15 minutes or until the tomatoes have broken down and thickened, stirring occasionally.

4 Meanwhile, slice the remaining garlic in thin strips and crush the peperoncino. Rinse, pat dry, and mince the parsley.

Crema di Ceci con Gamberi

Chickpea Soup with Prawns (Marche)

5 Heat the remaining oil in a small skillet over low heat. Add the remaining garlic, peperoncino, and parsley (don't brown it too much). Season the soup with salt and pepper and ladle into serving bowls. Top with the garlic oil and serve immediately.

Tuscan bread is traditionally unsalted, a leftover from the times when salt was expensive and a luxury ingredient. Frugal cooks couldn't afford to throw away stale bread, and many regional dishes make delectable use of this lowly ingredient. This tasty soup is just one example.

INGREDIENTS for 4:

2/3–3/4 cup dried chickpeas
2 garlic cloves
1 onion
2 thyme sprigs
1 bay leaf
1 Tbsp baking soda
1 carrot
1 celery rib
2 tsp tomato paste
Salt and freshly ground pepper
12 peeled deveined prawns
2 parsley sprigs
4 Tbsp olive oil

PREPARATION TIME: 30 minutes
SOAKING TIME: Overnight
COOKING TIME: 2 hours
PER PORTION: about 305 calories

1 Soak the chickpeas in water to cover for at least 8 hours (preferably overnight). Drain and put into a large saucepan.

2 Peel the garlic and onion and cut them into halves. Rinse and pat dry the thyme. Add the garlic, onion, thyme, the bay leaf, and 5 cups of fresh water to the chickpeas. Add the baking soda and bring to a boil. Simmer, partially covered, over low heat for about 1 hour.

3 Peel the carrot and trim the celery; chop them both. Add to the chickpeas and cook for 1 more hour or until the chickpeas are soft.

4 Remove the bay leaf and thyme from the soup; puree the soup in a food processor and season with salt, pepper, and tomato paste.

5 Meanwhile, rinse and pat dry the prawns; cut the larger ones into halves. Rinse, pat dry, and mince the parsley.

6 Heat 2 tablespoons of olive oil in a skillet over medium heat. Sauté the prawns for 2–3 minutes or until they have become pink; season with salt and pepper and stir in the parsley. Fill soup bowls with the soup and top with the prawns. Drizzle with the remaining olive oil and serve immediately.

Canned chickpeas are also used in Italy. In this case, cook the chickpeas with the vegetables, broth, and puree; ladle the soup into the soup bowls when all ingredients are done. Top the soup with the prawns.

139

Pasta con Pere e Pecorino

Pasta with Pears and Pecorino Cheese (Tuscany)

INGREDIENTS for 4:

1 lb tagliatelle, fettuccine, or pappardelle

Salt

4 rosemary sprigs

$\frac{1}{2}$ tsp organic lemon zest

2 firm ripe pears (about 12 oz)

2 dried peperoncini (chili peppers)

2 garlic cloves

$\frac{1}{4}$ cup pine nuts

$\frac{1}{4}$ cup olive oil + olive oil for serving

4 oz aged pecorino

PREPARATION TIME: 20 minutes
PER PORTION: about 680 calories

1   Bring a large pot of salted water to a rolling boil. Cook the pasta until al dente (firm to the bite).

2   Meanwhile, rinse and pat dry the rosemary. Mince the rosemary leaves with the lemon zest. Core, peel, and dice the pears. Crush the peperoncini. Peel and mince the garlic.

3   Toast the pine nuts in a dry skillet over medium heat until they are golden. Remove from the skillet. Heat the olive oil in the skillet over medium heat and sauté the rosemary, garlic, and peperoncini for 1–2 minutes; add the diced pear and continue sautéing for 1–2 minutes; season with salt.

4   Remove the rind from the cheese and shave with a vegetable peeler. Drain the pasta and toss with the pear mixture. Divide the pasta among plates; sprinkle each serving with pine nuts and cheese, drizzle with olive oil and serve.

This specialty was originally a "poor folks dish" that used leftovers. It has become a classic throughout the Tuscan area of the Val di Chiana. In the old days, this was prepared with whatever leftover from any number of ingredients. Modern times have refined the specialty by adding regional ingredients such as rosemary, olive oil, and pine nuts. Alternatives to the firm pears included tomatoes, croutons or leftover bread, or mixed herbs mixed with pecorino cheese; today fresh figs are used; with the cheese, they lend a wonderful and unique flavor.

This pear sauce goes also very well with *pici*, handmade Tuscan noodles. To make, knead to a soft and springy dough 1¾ cups of semolina or bread flour, 1 tsp of salt, and ¾ cup of water. Cover the dough with a clean dish cloth and let it rest for about 30 minutes. On a floured surface, tear small pieces of dough and shape them into ⅙-inch thick strings. Set the noodles aside to dry a little, and cook them until firm to the bite.

Pappardelle al Sugo di Cinghiale con Pesto di Porcini

Pasta with Boar Ragù and Porcini Mushroom Pesto (Marche)

INGREDIENTS for 4:

For the sauce:

1 lb boneless boar (from the shank)

2 garlic cloves

1 carrot

1 celery rib

2 rosemary sprigs

2 Tbsp olive oil

About 1 cup strong red wine (such as a Sagrantino)

Salt and freshly ground pepper

2 tsp honey

2 tsp lemon juice

For the pesto:

1½ Tbsp dried porcini mushrooms (about 0.7 oz)

1 dried peperoncino (chili pepper)

5 Tbsp olive oil

2½ Tbsp pine nuts

2½ Tbsp freshly grated pecorino cheese

Salt and freshly ground pepper

1 lb pappardelle or any wide egg noodles

PREPARATION TIME: 30 minutes
COOKING TIME: 1½ hours
PER PORTION: about 845 calories

1   For the sauce, trim the fat and sinew from the meat; cut into small cubes. Peel the garlic and carrot; trim the celery. Chop the vegetables. Rinse and pat dry the rosemary; mince the leaves.

2   Heat the oil in a large saucepan. Brown the meat well. Add the garlic, carrot, celery, and rosemary and sauté. Stir in the wine and season with salt and pepper. Cover the sauce and simmer over low heat for about 1½ hours; if necessary add some water.

3   Meanwhile, soak the porcini in ¾ cup lukewarm water for about 30 minutes. Drain the mushrooms, reserving the liquid. Mince the porcini. Strain the liquid through a fine-meshed sieve or a paper coffee filter. Crush the peperoncino. Heat 2 tablespoons of olive oil in a skillet. Sauté the mushrooms until firm, then stir in the mushroom liquid and peperoncino. Simmer, covered, for about 15 minutes.

4   Set the mushrooms aside to cool, then purée them, the pine nuts, and the remaining olive oil in a food processor. Stir in the pecorino cheese and season with salt and nutmeg.

5   Bring a large pot of salted water to a rolling boil. Cook the noodles until al dente (firm to the bite). Stir the honey and lemon juice into the meat sauce; if nec-essary season with salt and pepper.

6   Drain the noodles and fold them into the meat sauce. Serve the pasta on preheated plates with the mushroom pesto served on the side; pass grated pecorino or parmesan at the table.

For this sauce some prefer gnocchi, or potato dumplings. To make them, mix and knead to a soft dough about 7 tablespoons of floury cooked riced or mashed potatoes, 1⅓ cups of semolina or bread flour, 1 teaspoon salt, and 2 eggs. Wrap the dough in a clean dish cloth and set it aside to rest for about 30 minutes. With a pasta machine, roll out thin sheets of noodles; cut into various shapes; set them aside to dry and cook them in boiling salted water for about 3–4 minutes.

141

Searching for Chianti

Sangiovese grapes, "fiascos," and grand red wine

Long ago, when Italian food meant pizza and spaghetti and meatballs served in restaurants with red-checked tablecloths, the wine that was served came in round, straw-covered bottles that, when empty, were used as candle holders. The name for these bottles is "fiasco" (Italian for flask), but the term could have referred to the mediocre wine they contained.

Red and White. Chiantis weren't always inferior. During the nineteenth century, Baron Ricasoli found the right mixture of grapes for Chianti Classico, which included Sangiovese, Canaiolo, Trebbiano, and Malvasia. The latter two were dried after harvest and pressed and added to the first two only after these had fermented. In this way, a second fermentation took place which gave the Chianti a full body and a higher alcohol content.

Black Rooster. The *gallo nero*, or black rooster, is the identifier for Chianti Classico DOCG (Denominazione di Origine Controllata e Garantita), and indicates a higher quality wine. The Classico area is the heart of the Chianti region in Tuscany and stretches from Florence to Siena. Based on this subdivision six additional sub-areas were added: Chianti Rufina in the northeast of Tuscany from which the best non Classico wines come; Chianti Aretini, Chianti Colline Pisane, Chianti Colli Senesi, Chianti Montalbano, and Chianti Colli Fiorentini. Wines from outside these zones but still within Chainti's borders can only be labeled Chianti. Riserva is the term for wines that have been aged at least three years.

Only red now. The old production rules issued by the Consorzio del Gallo Nero allowed the partial use of white grapes and the aging of the wine in old barrels; the quality of the wine declined, and by the 1960s the rooster wasn't crowing proudly. The prices and the quality went down; the fermentation was difficult; the wine's fruitiness was lost faster than its bitter tones. Until winemakers such as Antinori and Felsina brought again the Chianti Classico wine up to fine standards. Inspired by Bordeaux wines, these winemakers added French grape varieties such as Cabernet Sauvignon or Merlot to the Sangiovese; aged the wine in small wooden barrels (French *barriques*) and created a Super Chianti that again attracted attention and was filled in bottles as a *vino da tavola* (table wine) since it did not comply with Chianti Classico conditions—and that allowed the wine to be aged on its side in bottles. Meanwhile, the Chianti consortium has amended its rules. Only red grapes are permitted, 80 percent must be the Sangiovese variety; the remaining 20 percent can be Sangiovese, other local varieties, or international varieties such as Cabernet Sauvignon or Merlot. Almost 1,000 Chianti winemakers are following those footsteps that have led to success. Their Chianti wines have ceased to taste watery or acidic or stunted, but are rich in color, with a berry and cinnamon aroma. They are smooth on the palate, without acidity and without the taste of fermentation that in the past was in the forefront. However, what still remains is the typical risky Chianti climate factor. As with all wines and all regions, not every year is the same; at times even with greatest efforts made by winemakers, the wine in the barrels turns out less superb than a previous year.

a In the old days, Chianti Classico vineyards were interspersed with olive groves; today they have almost exclusively vines that are easier to maintain and manage. The diverse soil conditions—limestone, sand, and volcanic rock—are contributing factors behind the diverse flavor facets of the Chianti wines.

b For winemakers focused on quality, harvesting the grapes by hand, during which unwanted grapes can be removed right away, is still preferred over the mechanical harvest.   c The Sangiovese grape, very important to the production of Chianti, has a characteristic ripe cherry flavor.   d The wines produced by the Felsina Estate are regularly awarded for their highest quality standards. Besides the definite and elegant Chianti Classico, the estate produces a Riserva Rancia and a Fontalloro (a pure Sangiovese wine that is aged in *barriques*).   e It is hard to believe, but in the Chianti area, winters may be cold and snowy. Frost that damages the grapes also can appear in late spring. The grape ripening process can also be slowed down by cold and humid weather; then the wines have rough fermentation flavors.

Cozze in Sugo di Finocchio
Mussels in Fennel Gravy (Marche)

INGREDIENTS for 4:

6–7 lb mussels

4 garlic cloves

2 red onions

1 large tomato

2 tsp fennel seeds

2 Tbsp olive oil

³/₄ cup dry white wine

3 Tbsp Sambuca (or other anise liqueur)

Salt and freshly ground pepper

1 Tbsp lemon juice

Pinch cayenne pepper

PREPARATION TIME: 40 minutes
PER PORTION: about 230 calories

1 Rinse the mussels under running water; discard any mussels that are slightly open or broken, or that feel heavy for their size.

2 Peel and thinly slice the garlic and onions. Bring a pot of water to a boil. Blanch the tomato; peel, core, and dice. Lightly crush the fennel seeds in a mortar.

3 Heat the olive oil in a large saucepan or skillet. Sauté the onions, garlic, and fennel seeds. Add the tomato and mix well; stir in wine, Sambuca, and ¹/₂ cup water; season with salt, pepper, lemon juice, and cayenne pepper.

4 Add the mussels and cook, covered, over high heat for about 5–7 minutes; periodically shake the pan to allow the shellfish to cook evenly. Discard any mussels that still have not opened. Serve the mussels in their broth, with crusty bread alongside.

Tonno Tagliato con Asparagi
Sliced Tuna with Asparagus (Marche)

INGREDIENTS for 4:

For the tuna:

2 garlic cloves

2 sprigs each rosemary, thyme, and oregano

1 Tbsp lemon juice

6 Tbsp olive oil

8 thin tuna steaks (4–5 oz each)

Salt and freshly ground pepper

For the asparagus:

1 lb asparagus

Salt and freshly ground pepper

1 organic lemon

1 bunch arugula

4 Tbsp pitted olives

Freshly grated nutmeg

PREPARATION TIME: 30 minutes
MARINATING TIME: 2 hours
PER PORTION: about 620 calories

1 For the fish, peel and thinly slice the garlic. Rinse and pat dry the herbs; mince the leaves. Whisk together 4 tablespoons of olive oil, the garlic, herbs, and lemon juice. Put the tuna in a glass baking dish; drizzle the mixture over the tuna. Marinate the tuna in the refrigerator for about 2 hours.

2 Trim the asparagus and cut into 2-inch-long pieces. Bring a large skillet of salted-water to a boil and blanch the asparagus; rinse under cold water and drain. Scrub the lemon with hot water. With a zester or grater, remove the zest from half of the lemon; extract the juice from half. Rinse, pat dry, and chop the arugula. Slice the olives thinly.

Filetti di Trota in Crosta
Trout Fillets with Bread Topping (Umbria)

3   Heat the olive oil in a large skillet and sauté the asparagus over high heat. Add the lemon juice, lemon zest, and olives. Season with salt, pepper, and nutmeg; let simmer for about 5 minutes over low heat.

4   In one or two small skillets, heat the remaining 2 tablespoons olive oil. Scrape off the marinade solids from the tuna; brown the tuna on both sides over high heat for about ½ minute; season with salt and pepper.

5   Stir the arugula into the asparagus; season with salt and pepper. Arrange the vegetables on preheated serving plates and top with tuna steak.

INGREDIENTS for 4:

8 trout fillets (skinless)

4 sage leaves

2 juniper berries

1 organic lemon

4 garlic cloves

3 Tbsp plain breadcrumbs

6 Tbsp olive oil + enough olive oil to grease a baking dish

Salt and freshly ground pepper

1 large tomato

4 anchovies (preserved in oil)

½ bunch parsley

1 dried peperoncino (chili pepper)

PREPARATION TIME: 25 minutes
BAKING TIME: 12 minutes
PER PORTION: about 335 calories

1   Preheat the oven to 350° F (if convection oven 325° F). Brush a baking dish with oil and put trout in it. Clean and mince the sage and juniper berries. Scrub the lemon under hot water. Using a zester or grater, remove the zest from half the lemon.

2   Peel the garlic and crush 2 cloves through a garlic press into a small bowl. Combine with the breadcrumbs, the sage and juniper mixture, the lemon zest, and 4 tablespoons of olive oil. Season the paste with salt and pepper. Season trout with salt and pepper and spread some of the paste over each fillet. Bake on the middle oven rack for about 12 minutes or until the crust is golden brown.

3   Meanwhile, core, seed, and mince the tomato. With a fork, mash the anchovies; mince the remaining garlic. Rinse and pat dry the parsley; mince the leaves. Crush the peperoncino in a mortar. Combine all these ingredients with the remaining olive oil and season everything with salt and pepper. Serve the cold tomato sauce alongside the trout.

Many varieties of freshwater fish are served at home and in the ristoranti and trattorie around Lake Trasimeno. Instead of trout, you may also use char, pike, or even large carp (which need to be trimmed to fillets); most whitefish are very tasty with this crispy breadcrumb topping.

145

Arista al Vin Santo

Pork Roast with Vin Santo (Tuscany)

INGREDIENTS for 4:

3 sprigs each rosemary and thyme

2 oregano sprigs

2 fresh bay leaves

1 organic lemon

Salt and freshly ground pepper

4 Tbsp olive oil

1 boneless pork shoulder roast (about 2 lb)

4 fennel bulbs (preferably with lots of green tops)

7 oz cherry tomatoes

1 cup Vin Santo or other sweet dessert wine

$\frac{1}{2}$ Tbsp honey

2 tsp fennel seeds

PREPARATION TIME: 20 minutes
ROASTING TIME: 2 Hours
PER PORTION: about 470 calories

1   Rinse and pat dry the herbs; mince the leaves with the bay leaves. Scrub the lemon under hot water; using a zester or grater, remove the zest from half the lemon. Mix all these ingredients with 2 tablespoons of olive oil; season with salt and pepper.

2   Preheat the oven to 325° F (if convection oven 300° F) and pat dry the roast. Rub the roast with the oil-herb mixture; heat the remaining olive oil in a roasting pan or Dutch oven and brown the pork roast on all sides over high heat. Transfer the roast to the oven and roast for about 1$\frac{1}{4}$ hours, turning the roast over once.

3   Trim and core the fennel bulbs and cut them lengthwise into quarters. Rinse the tomatoes.

4   Whisk together the honey, Vin Santo, and freshly ground pepper to taste. Add the sliced fennel and tomatoes to the roast; pour about half of the Vin Santo sauce over, then scatter the fennel seeds on top. Continue to roast for 45 more minutes, adding more Vin Santo mixture periodically.

5   Remove the roast from the oven and let the meat rest for 10–15 minutes. Slice the meat and serve it with the fennel and the tomatoes and the gravy. This dish goes well with rosemary potatoes or bread and mixed salad.

Tuscany is home of a special type of pig—the cinta senese. The name of the animal derives from its unique skin color that includes a pink back stripe (*cinta*) on its overall dark skinned body. The pig has been found in the area of Siena since the Middle Ages; it is suited for a life outdoors and has been bred accordingly. Besides the Tuscan specialty *arista* (which was originally prepared without vegetables), the meat of this animal is used to make hams or fresh sausages that are hung to dry. A favorite among gourmets, the animal is also under the protection of a consortium and of the Slow Food movement.

Pasticciata alla Cagliostro
Marinated Stewed Beef (Marche)

INGREDIENTS for 4:

2 lb bottom round beef roast

3 strips bacon

1/4 tsp ground cinnamon

Salt and freshly ground pepper

4 garlic cloves

4 whole cloves

1 cup dry red wine

1 onion

1 carrot

1 celery rib

3 medium tomatoes

2 oregano sprigs

4 Tbsp olive oil

1 tsp tomato paste

PREPARATION TIME: 40 minutes
MARINATING TIME: Overnight
COOKING TIME: 1 1/2–2 hours
PER PORTION: about 585 calories

1 With a small, thin-bladed sharp knife, make several small cuts throughout the entire roast. Cut half the bacon into matchstick sized pieces and toss with the cinnamon, salt, and pepper. Peel half of the garlic and cut into slivers. Into each cut in the roast, push a bacon piece, a clove, or a slice of garlic. Set the spiked roast in a large bowl or baking dish. Pour the wine over the roast, cover, and refrigerate overnight; occasionally turn the roast over while it is marinating.

2 Peel and chop the onion and carrot. Trim and mince the celery. Bring a large pot of water to a boil. Blanch the tomatoes and rinse under cold water. Core, peel, and dice them. Rinse and pat dry the oregano; mince the leaves.

3 Heat 2 tablespoons of olive oil in a Dutch oven. Remove the roast from the marinade, pat it dry, and brown it all over on high heat. Remove the roast from the Dutch oven and season it with salt and pepper. Sauté the onion, carrot, celery, and oregano in the Dutch oven. Stir in the wine and tomato paste; season with salt and pepper. Return the roast to the Dutch oven and simmer over low heat, covered, for about 1 1/2–2 hours or until the roast is tender.

4 Remove the roast; let it stand for 10 minutes, then slice it thinly. Finely chop the remaining bacon and peel and mince the remaining garlic. Pour off the gravy and strain it through a fine-meshed sieve; press the vegetables well to extract the juices.

5 Heat the remaining oil in the Dutch oven. Sauté the bacon and garlic; moisten these with the gravy; if necessary let the gravy simmer and cook down to thicken. Return the sliced roast to the gravy and heat to serving temperature.

In the region of Marche as well as in Umbria and Tuscany, meats that are stewed or braised in red wine are a favorite. In Florence, cooks prepare *peposo*, a simple dish with beef, red wine, garlic, and lots of pepper; the specialty was already a popular food when masons worked on Florence's cathedral. For a peposo, a 2-pound beef roast is sliced not too thick; cloves from a whole head of garlic are peeled but kept whole and layered between the meat slices; freshly ground pepper is used to season each slice (at least 1 tablespoon of pepper for the entire stew), and 2 cups of Chianti are poured over the stack of slices. The meat is braised in a covered Dutch oven at 250° F (if convection oven 210° F) for about 8 hours.

147

Agnello al Formaggio

Lamb with Cheese (Marche)

INGREDIENTS for 4:

2 lb boneless lamb shoulder or leg

1 bunch mint

4.2 oz aged sharp pecorino cheese

Salt and freshly ground pepper

¼ cup olive oil

1 cup dry white wine

4 garlic cloves

1 head Romaine lettuce

PREPARATION TIME: 20 minutes
ROASTING TIME: 1¼ hours
PER PORTION: about 810 calories

1 Trim the lamb, removing the sinews and fatty parts. Slice open the meat to make a butterfly piece. Rinse and pat dry the mint; mince the leaves. Set some mint aside for garnish. Cut the rind off of the cheese and dice the cheese.

2 Season the meat with salt and pepper; top it with mint and diced cheese. Fold the meat closed and tie it together with kitchen string.

3 Preheat the oven to 350° F (if convection 325° F). Heat the oil in a roasting pan and brown the lamb over high heat until it is golden brown. Transfer the roast to the middle oven rack and roast for about 15 minutes. Pour the wine over the meat and roast for 30 more minutes.

4 Peel and slice the garlic. Rinse and trim the lettuce; spin or pat dry and slice. Add the vegetables to the roast. Continue roasting for 30 minutes. Remove the meat from the pan; let rest for 10–15 minutes, then slice and set on a serving platter. Stir the reserved mint into the lettuce; season with salt and pepper and use to garnish the lamb roast. Serve hot.

Agnello ai Carciofi

Lamb with Artichokes (Tuscany)

INGREDIENTS for 4:

2 lb boneless leg of lamb

10 large sage leaves

3 rosemary sprigs

10 thyme sprigs

4 large garlic cloves

1 organic lemon

6 Tbsp olive oil

½ cup dry white wine

Salt and freshly ground pepper

Freshly grated nutmeg

6 small artichokes

¼ bunch parsley

4 Tbsp pine nuts

PREPARATION TIME: 30 minutes
COOKING TIME: 1¼ hours
PER PORTION: about 755 calories

1 Trim the lamb, removing the sinews and fatty parts. Cut the meat into 1-inch cubes. Rinse and pat dry the herbs; mince the leaves. Peel and chop the garlic. Scrub the lemon under hot water; with a zester or grater, remove the zest.

2 Heat 3 tablespoons of olive oil in a large saucepan or Dutch oven. Brown the meat over high heat in batches. In the pan drippings, briefly sauté the herbs and garlic. Pour in the wine and deglaze the pot. Return the meat to the pot and add the lemon zest (keep a little for garnish); season with salt, pepper, and nutmeg. Simmer, covered, for about 1 hour.

3 After 30 minutes, rinse and trim the artichokes, removing as many leaves as necessary until the tender leaves and the heart come forth. Cut the pointy tops of the leaves and slice the artichokes lengthwise in eighths.

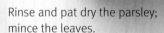

Arrosto di Cinghiale con Castagne e Mosto

Roasted Boar with Chestnuts and Grape Juice (Umbria)

Rinse and pat dry the parsley; mince the leaves.

4 Heat the remaining olive oil in a skillet. Sauté the artichokes over medium heat for about 8 minutes or until they are golden brown, stirring occasionally. Add the parsley and season with salt and pepper. Add the artichokes to the lamb; cook for 15 more minutes.

5 Toast the pine nuts in a dry skillet until they are golden brown. Add the reserved lemon zest to the meat; season with salt and pepper and serve, sprinkled with pine nuts. This goes well with rosemary potatoes or bread.

INGREDIENTS for 4:

2 lb boneless boar leg

2 onions

2 carrots

2 celery ribs

5 bay leaves

3 cups dry red wine

4 Tbsp white wine vinegar

Salt and freshly ground pepper

$\frac{1}{2}$ lb chestnuts

4 garlic cloves

4 rosemary sprigs

$\frac{1}{4}$ cup olive oil

1 cup unsweetened grape juice

4 Tbsp mosto cotto or honey

PREPARATION TIME: 1 hour
MARINATING TIME: 2 days
COOKING TIME: 1$\frac{1}{2}$ hours
PER PORTION: about 715 calories

1 Trim the boar meat, removing any sinews and fatty parts. Place the meat in a container suitable for marinating. Peel and slice the onions and carrots. Trim and chop the celery. Combine the onions, carrots, celery, bay leaves, wine, and vinegar and pour over the meat. Cover and refrigerate for 2 days, turning the meat over occasionally.

2 Bring a large pot of water to a boil. With a sharp paring knife cut a cross into the chestnut peels. Boil the chestnuts for about 10 minutes. Drain the chestnuts and rinse them under cold water; peel them and remove the brown membranes. Peel the garlic and cut into quarters. Rinse and pat dry the rosemary; remove the leaves from the stems.

3 Preheat the oven to 300° F (if convection oven 275° F). Remove the meat from the marinade; pat it dry and season with salt and pepper. Strain the marinade through a fine-meshed sieve and reserve. Heat the oil in a roasting pan or Dutch oven and brown the meat all over on high heat.

4 Add the chestnuts, garlic, and rosemary to the pan; pour the grape juice and $\frac{1}{2}$ cup of the marinade over the meat. Roast the meat on the lower oven rack for about 1$\frac{1}{2}$ hours, basting often with the pan juices; if necessary use more marinade.

5 Remove the roast from the pan and cover it with foil. Mix the pan juices with the honey and season it with salt and pepper. Slice the meat thinly and serve with the chestnuts and gravy. Roasted potatoes go well with this dish.

Pecorino – Sharp Sheep Cheese
The best and most famous pecorinos come from Central Italy and Sardinia

Innumerable sheep live in Tuscany, Umbria, Marche, and Sardinia. No wonder then that inhabitants are able to deal so well with these animals and make such fine cheese. Sardinia's inhabitants have made cheese since prehistoric times and later made it popular throughout the Italian peninsula.

From the milk to the cheese. *Pecorino* means "little sheep," and the cheese with this name is made from sheep's milk. After heating the milk, the cheesemaker adds rennet, which causes milk to coagulate and curdle. The solid mass then is cut. For cheese that will be consumed fresh, the curds are left no larger than nuggets; for cheese that is destined to be aged, the curds are of the size of corn kernels. The cheese curds are then placed in sieves that allow them to drain; later the cheese is pressed, and finally seasoned with salt. During this stage the cheese is either dipped in a salt bath or rubbed with dry salt.

The cheese aging time is vital. The cheese's flavor and texture are determined by how long it is left to ripen and how the cheese is processed. A young pecorino is left to ripen between 20 and 60 days, has a light and thin rind and a soft texture, and its taste is relatively mild and slightly acidic. An aged pecorino has a thicker, straw-yellow or brown rind and acquires in time (after a few months up to a year) a stronger, more pungent flavor and a firmer texture. Pecorino is sold according to its age: the young cheese is called dolce, the medium aged cheese is the semi-stagionato, and the very aged cheese is stagionato.

Fine differences. Pecorinos are also marketed by their region of origin; the four main varieties are pecorino Romano, from Rome; pecorino Sardo, from Sardinia; pecorino Siciliano, from Sicily; and pecorino Toscano, from Tuscany. Tuscan pecorinos include the mild and young pecorino bacellone that after a 24-hour-long salt bath is left to ripen only two to five days. The medium-aged and very aged toscanos include the pecorino della Garfagnana, from the coastal region (made from Massese sheep milk), pecorino di montagna from southern and central Tuscany, pecorino di Pienza from the southern Siena region, pecorino Senese (that is often available young), and pecorino Toscano, from throughout the region. Pecorino di Norcia from the Nerina Valley is often brushed with oil during the aging process and is renowned in Umbria. In the region of Marche, pecorino dei Monti Sibillini, which comes from the Sibylline mountains, is often still made with raw milk and aged in cellars up to two years. Pecorino di montagna is made throughout the mountains of the region of Marche.

Fine cheeses are also made in the region of Abruzzi: pecorino abruzzese, made from raw sheep's milk; pecorino del Parco, from the regional national park; pecorino del Sannio (whose milk is only heated to 85° F and takes longer to curdle), made from the milk of Camisana sheep; pecorino di Capracotta (which was also made by the ancient Sannites); and pecorino di Farindola (which is the only one made with pork rennet).

From the region of Basilicata come the traditional pecorino di Filiano and the pecorino Moliterno; from Emilia-Romagna comes the pecorino dolce dei colli bolognesi that ages for no longer than four months. Calabria pecorinos include pecorino del Monte Poro, made with baby goat rennet and famous for its pungent and herb flavored aroma. From Campania come the pecorino bagnolese, often used as a grating cheese, and pecorino laticauda, made with milk from Laticauda sheep. Pecorino Siciliano is only authentic if it is aged for at least four months. Pecorino veneto, made with milk from Massese sheep, is hard to find.

a   A Tuscan springtime gourmet specialty: remove *fave* from their pods and arrange them on a plate. Add young shaved or chopped pecorino (*bacellone* or *marzolino*) and season with salt and olive oil; serve with fresh baked white bread.

b Sheep that graze freely among the olive groves and mountain ranges are a common sight throughout the central Italian regions. Almost all animals are raised for their milk, which is used to make pecorino.   C Umbria's specialty: loaves of ricotta rolled in wheat bran (made from milk left over from the production of pecorino).   d To allow the cheese to solidify, the curds are ladled in molds and left to drain after the coagulation and the cutting process.
e The formaggio di fossa a pecorino is aged in a special sealed earth cavity (*fossa*) and has an unusual, indescribably pungent flavor. It is a specialty of Marche (and Emilia-Romagna). This cheese goes especially well with a side dish of honey.

Pollo in Padella

Braised Chicken (Marche/Umbria)

INGREDIENTS for 4:

1 chicken (about 3 lbs)

Salt and freshly ground pepper

5 celery ribs

2 red onions

1 red bell pepper

6 oz cherry tomatoes

2 Tbsp olive oil

5 fresh bay leaves

½ cup dry white wine or chicken broth

½ organic orange

3 Tbsp nonpareil capers

PREPARATION TIME: 30 minutes
COOKING TIME: 45 minutes
PER PORTION: about 535 calories

1 Rinse and pat dry the chicken. With a heavy, sharp knife or poultry shears, cut the chicken into 8 portions. Season the chicken with salt and pepper.

2 Trim and cut the celery into 2-inch long pieces. Reserve the celery leaves. Peel and cut the onions into eighths. Trim, seed, and thinly slice the pepper. Rinse the tomatoes.

3 Heat the oil in a Dutch oven. Brown the chicken on all sides over high heat. Remove the chicken from the Dutch oven. Sauté the celery, onions, pepper, and bay leaves in the pan drippings; deglaze the pan with wine or broth. Add the tomatoes and the chicken pieces; cover and simmer over low heat for about 45 minutes.

4 Scrub the orange under hot water. With a zester or grater, remove the zest from half of the orange. Add the orange zest, capers, and celery leaves to the chicken; season with more salt and pepper if necessary and serve.

Petto d'Anitra all'Arancia

Duck Breast with Orange Sauce (Tuscany)

INGREDIENTS for 4:

4 boneless duck breasts (7 oz each)

4 oranges (1 organic)

3 rosemary sprigs

4 garlic cloves

Salt and freshly ground pepper

½ cup Vin Santo or dry white or red wine

1 Tbsp lemon juice

¼ cup pitted black olives

Pinch ground cinnamon

1 tsp sugar

PREPARATION TIME: 30 minutes
PER PORTION: about 545 calories

1 With a sharp knife, score the skin of the duck breasts to make a grid. Scrub the organic orange under hot water. With a zester or grater, remove the zest. Peel 2 of the remaining oranges, making sure that the white part is removed. Cut these oranges into sections over a mixing bowl to catch any juice. Over the same mixing bowl, juice the organic orange and the remaining orange. Rinse and pat dry the rosemary; mince the leaves. Peel and slice the garlic.

2 Set a large skillet over medium-high heat. When it is hot, add the duck, skin-side down. Roast over medium heat for about 8 minutes. Turn the duck over and roast for about 3–4 more minutes. Season with salt and pepper and cover in foil.

3 Pour all but 1–2 tablespoons of fat out of the skillet. Sauté the rosemary and garlic until fragrant. Deglaze skillet with the Vin Santo, the reserved orange juice, and lemon juice. Add the olives and allow the sauce to simmer down a

Coniglio all'Etrusca
Rabbit with Olives and Pine Nuts (Tuscany)

little bit. Season the sauce with the salt, pepper, cinnamon, and sugar; add the orange sections and heat to serving temperature.

4 Uncover the duck breasts, slice them thinly and add them to the sauce. Serve the duck while still warm.

This recipe is a fast version of papero all'arancia, or ducking with oranges. The classic recipe was apparently brought to France by Catherine de Medici from her Florentine homeland.

INGREDIENTS for 4:

1 rabbit, with its liver (about 3–4 lb; cut into 12 pieces)

Salt and freshly ground pepper

4 oz lardo di Colonnata (substitute with pork belly or fatback)

1 onion

2 garlic cloves

1 carrot

1 celery rib

2 sage sprigs

3 rosemary sprigs

2 Tbsp olive oil

1 cup dry white wine

1/2 cup chicken broth

1 bay leaf

1 cinnamon stick

1/2 cup pitted black olives

1 Tbsp lemon juice

2 Tbsp pine nuts

PREPARATION TIME: 25 minutes
COOKING TIME: 50 minutes
PER PORTION: about 655 calories

1 With paper towels, pat dry the rabbit pieces; if necessary remove any bone splinters. Season the rabbit with salt and pepper. Chop the bacon; peel and mince the onion, garlic, and carrot. Trim and mince the celery with its green leaves. Rinse and pat dry the herbs; mince the leaves.

2 Heat the oil in a Dutch oven. Fry the bacon. Add the rabbit and brown well. When the pieces are brown, remove them from the pot. Add the vegetables and herbs; sauté for about 2–3 minutes. Deglaze with the wine and broth; add the bay leaf and cinnamon. Return the rabbit to the pot; cover and simmer over low heat for about 30 minutes. Cut the rabbit liver into small pieces; add it to the rabbit and simmer for 10 more minutes.

3 Remove the rabbit from the Dutch oven. Strain the sauce through a fine-meshed sieve and return it to the Dutch oven. Add the olives; season with salt, pepper, and lemon juice, and return the rabbit to the pot. Simmer, covered, for additional 10 more minutes.

4 Meanwhile, toast the pine nuts in a dry skillet until they are golden brown. Serve the rabbit, sprinkled with the pine nuts.

Recommended Wine: Serve a chilled white wine such as a Vernaccia di San Gimignano.

153

Pomodori e Cipolle
Tomato and Onion Salad (Tuscany)

INGREDIENTS for 4:

¼ cup red wine vinegar

½ Tbsp sugar

2 red onions

3 medium firm, ripe tomatoes

½ bunch basil

2 Tbsp nonpareil capers (prefer-ably preserved in salt; see Tip)

¼ cup olive oil

Salt and freshly ground pepper

PREPARATION TIME: 20 minutes
PER PORTION: about 140 calories

1   Heat the vinegar and sugar in a small saucepan. Cook over high heat for about 4 minutes or until the mixture has thickened and reduced; set aside to cool.

2   Peel and slice the onions. Core the tomatoes and cut into wedges. Rinse and pat dry the basil; cut the leaves into thin strips.

3   Rinse the capers. Mix the vinegar reduction with the olive oil; season with salt and pepper.

4   Toss the tomatoes, basil, and onions with the vinegar-oil dressing; serve, sprinkled with the capers.

Tip: Tiny capers are sold as non-pareil; they may be packed in salt or brine. If you can't find them, try using the larger type of capers.

Insalata al Pecorino
Salad with Pecorino Cheese (Tuscany)

INGREDIENTS for 4:

2 eggs

7 oz mixed salad greens (prefer-ably several varieties such as Romaine, arugula, radicchio, and chicory or Belgian endive)

3.5 oz aged pecorino cheese

2 Tbsp raisins

¼ cup pine nuts

8 anchovies (preserved in oil)

2 Tbsp white wine vinegar

Salt and freshly ground pepper

5 Tbsp olive oil

PREPARATION TIME: 20 minutes
PER PORTION: about 355 calories

1   Cook the eggs in simmering water for about 10 minutes and rinse them with ice cold water. Rinse, trim, and pat dry the salad greens; tear them into bite-sized pieces.

2   Cut the rind off the cheese and shave it with a vegetable peeler. Soak the raisins in hot water. Toast the pine nuts in a dry skillet until they are golden brown. Mince the anchovies.

3   Whisk the vinegar and olive oil to a creamy consistency; season with salt and pepper (taste before salting, as anchovies and pecorino are already salty). Peel the eggs and cut in wedges. Drain the raisins.

Insalata di Erbette con Fiori di Sambuco
Mixed Green Salad with Elderberry Blossoms (Umbria)

4   Toss the salad greens, cheese, raisins, anchovies, and pine nuts with the dressing; if necessary season with salt and pepper. Garnish the salad with the eggs and serve.

This is another specialty that originated during the time of Catherine de Medici (as did the duck in orange sauce on page 152); for this reason this salad is sometimes called insalata Caterina de'Medici.

The salad goes very well with grilled meats, such as bistecca alla fiorentina; however, it is also a fine antipasto. If you wish, you may leave out the eggs.

INGREDIENTS for 4:

4 oz mixed wild greens (such as young borage leaves, young dandelion leaves, young nettle leaves, summer or winter purslane, and fennel greens)

2 oz arugula

12 young elderberry blossoms

4 asparagus spears

2 garlic cloves

1/4 cup lemon juice

Salt and freshly ground pepper

1 tsp honey or pinch sugar

6 Tbsp olive oil

PREPARATION TIME: 15 minutes
PER PORTION: about 205 calories

1   Rinse well, pat dry, and trim the greens; if necessary tear the larger leaves into bite-sized pieces. Rinse the elderberry blossoms well but gently; if necessary remove the woody stems. Trim the asparagus. Slice the asparagus thin and lengthwise.

2   For the dressing, peel and mince the garlic. Whisk together the lemon juice, salt, pepper, and honey; add the olive oil and whisk to a creamy consistency. Toss the greens, elderberry blossoms, and asparagus with the dressing and serve immediately.

Throughout Umbria, Marche, and Tuscany, wild greens are often mixed and offered for sale at farmers' markets during spring-time; these mixed greens might

include young Swiss chard leaves and spinach, or other field greens. The flavor of the salad changes with the variety; you might find some of these herbs and vegetables at your local farmers' market.

Fagiolini al Sedano

Green Beans with Celery (Umbria)

INGREDIENTS for 4:

1 lb young green beans

1 large tomato

Salt and freshly ground pepper

3 celery ribs

3 garlic cloves

¼ cup olive oil

½ bunch basil

PREPARATION TIME: 35 minutes
PER PORTION: about 155 calories

1 Rinse and trim the green beans; cut the beans into 2-inch long pieces. Bring 4 cups of salted water to a boil. Cook the beans for about 3–4 minutes and with a slotted spoon or strainer, transfer them to a colander. Rinse them with ice water; set them aside to drain.

2 Blanch the tomato in the boiling water; rinse it under cold water. Core, peel, and dice. Trim the celery; set aside the green leaves. Thinly slice the celery; peel and mince the garlic.

3 Heat the oil in a saucepan. Sauté the beans, celery, and garlic. Add the tomato and celery leaves; season with salt and pepper. Cover and simmer over low heat for about 12 minutes or until the beans are still firm to the bite; if necessary add a little water or broth.

4 Rinse and pat dry the basil; cut the leaves into thin strips. Add the basil to the green beans. Season with salt and pepper and serve either warm or cold.

If the green beans are very young and tender, they may not need to be blanched. This dish is also tasty as an antipasto.

Scafata

Bean and Pea Salad with Fennel (Umbria)

INGREDIENTS for 4:

1 white or red onion

3½ oz sliced pancetta (or fairly lean bacon)

1 lb hulled lima beans (or 1½ lb beans in their pods; see Tip)

1 fennel bulb

2 red or Yukon gold potatoes

6 oz cherry tomatoes

¼ bunch marjoram

2 Tbsp olive oil

3½ oz hulled peas (about 1 lb in their pods)

Salt and freshly ground pepper

PREPARATION TIME: 40 minutes
PER PORTION: about 580 calories

1 Peel and mince the onion. Slice the pancetta. Peel the lima beans if they are large.

2 Trim the fennel; quarter it lengthwise and slice it. Scrub and peel the potatoes; dice them. Rinse the tomatoes and cut them in halves. Rinse and pat dry the marjoram; mince the leaves.

3 Heat the olive oil in a saucepan. Sauté the onion and pancetta. Add the fennel, potatoes, and lima beans and cook over medium heat, stirring occasionally.

4 Add the tomatoes, marjoram, and peas; moisten with about 1/2 cup of water. Season with salt and pepper and simmer over low heat for about 15–20 minutes or until the potatoes and the lima beans

Patate al Lardo di Colonnata
Roasted Potatoes with Lardo di Colonnata (Tuscany)

are tender. Taste and season if necessary; serve. This goes well with toasted white bread.

Tip: If you don't find fresh lima beans at the grocery store, you might want to use frozen lima beans, or visit your local farmers' market.

INGREDIENTS for 4:

2 lb red or Yukon gold potatoes

3 oz lardo di Colonnata (substitute with bacon or fatback)

2 garlic cloves

2 rosemary sprigs

2 tsp fennel seeds

2 Tbsp olive oil

Salt and freshly ground pepper

PREPARATION TIME: 15 minutes
COOKING TIME: 45 minutes
PER PORTION: about 280 calories

1 Preheat the oven to 350° F (if convection oven 325° F). Scrub and peel the potatoes; cut them in quarters or eighths. Slice the bacon into strips. Peel and thinly slice the garlic. Rinse and pat dry the rosemary; with kitchen shears, cut the sprigs into short pieces.

2 Toss the potatoes, garlic, rosemary, bacon, fennel seeds and olive oil in a baking dish; season with salt and pepper. Roast for about 45 minutes or until the potatoes are tender and golden brown, stirring occasionally.

These potatoes go well with roasted or grilled meats, and with grilled or broiled fish.

Lardo di Colonnata comes originally from the town of the same name located in the Apuane Alps; the lard is aged in special containers that are made of Carrara marble. It is layered with rosemary, minced garlic, and various spices (each family has its own special secret formula). You may substitute the lardo di Colonnata with your favorite bacon, preferably flavored with herbs or spices.

157

Schiacciata ai Fichi
Flatbread with Figs (Tuscany)

INGREDIENTS for 4:

For the dough:

1 oz fresh yeast

$\frac{3}{4}$ cup lukewarm milk

$\frac{2}{3}$ cup sugar

4 cups all-purpose flour

Pinch salt

$\frac{1}{4}$ cup raisins

2 Tbsp Vin Santo

7 Tbsp walnuts

1 tsp fennel seeds

7 Tbsp softened butter

1 egg, at room temperature

For the topping:

1 lb fresh figs

3 rosemary sprigs

2 Tbsp pine nuts

2 Tbsp sugar

PREPARATION TIME: 40 minutes
RESTING TIME: 1½ hours
BAKING TIME: 35 minutes
PER PORTION (FOR 10 SERV-INGS): about 470 calories

Fall is when the high season of the *schiacciata* begins. The handmade flatbread is covered with various toppings; favorites are the grapes that are ripe and ready during this season. Figs are also in season; though different in flavor and appearance, they are appealing as well. Rosemary, soaked raisins, nuts, and fennel seeds (which can be substituted with anise seeds) that are the ingredients give this *schiacciata* its special flavor.

Originally the flatbreads were a Carnival season specialty during which they were simply sprinkled with sugar.

Recommended Wine:
Serve this with a dry dessert wine such as Vin Santo.

1   Combine a little of the milk with 1 teaspoon of sugar. Crumble in the yeast and let stand a few minutes. Mix the flour with the remaining sugar and salt in a mixing bowl. Make a well in the flour and pour in the yeast sponge; cover the well with the surrounding flour, cover the mixing bowl loosely, and set it aside for about 15 minutes.

2   Meanwhile, soak the raisins in the Vin Santo. Chop the walnuts. Toast the fennel seeds in a dry skillet, then crush them in a mortar.

3   Pour the remaining milk, the butter, egg, and fennel seeds in the flour mixture. Knead all ingredients to smooth and springy dough; add the raisins and walnuts, work the dough again. Set the dough aside, covered, for about 1 hour or until it has doubled in volume.

4 Punch down the dough and knead again; shape it into a 1/2-inch thick round flatbread. Line a baking sheet with parchment paper and place the dough on it, leaving it to rise again for about 15 minutes. Preheat the oven to 350° F (if convection oven 325° F).

5 Rinse the figs; cut off the stems. If the skins of the figs are thick, peel them. Based on their size, cut the figs into slices, quarters, or eighths. Rinse and pat dry the rosemary; remove the leaves from the stems.

6 Making sure to distribute the ingredients, evenly top the flatbread with figs, rosemary, and pine nuts. Sprinkle the bread with sugar and bake for about 35 minutes or until the bread has increased in height and appears golden brown. Set aside to cool.

Caffé in Forchetta

Coffee Cream (Marche)

INGREDIENTS for 6:

²/₃ cup sugar

6 Tbsp anise liqueur (such as Anisetta or Sambuca)

1 cup cold brewed espresso

1 cup milk

2 eggs

4 egg yolks

1 tsp vanilla sugar

PREPARATION TIME: 30 minutes
COOKING TIME: 50–60 minutes
PER PORTION: about 225 calories

1 In a small saucepan over medium heat, melt and brown about ½ cup of the sugar, if possible, without stirring. Add the liqueur and loosen the mixture. Pour the caramel among six heat resistant ¾–1 cup flan molds or custard cups.

2 Preheat the oven to 300° F (if convection oven 275° F). Combine the milk and the coffee. Beat the eggs, egg yolks, the remaining sugar, and the vanilla sugar in a large bowl with a hand mixer. Gradually beat in the milk mixture.

3 Pour the coffee cream over the caramel and place the flan cups in a baking dish. Pour about 1 inch of hot water into the baking dish so that the flan cups are half immersed. Bake for about 50–60 minutes or until the mixture is set. Remove the cups from the water and set them aside to cool. Refrigerate until they are to be served.

4 With a sharp knife, loosen the creams from the cups and invert them onto dessert plates.

Lonzino di Fico

Fig Sausage (Marche)

INGREDIENTS for 10–12:

1 lb dried figs

¾–1 cup blanched almonds

½ cup shelled pistachio nuts

3.5 oz semisweet baking chocolate

1½ Tbsp candied orange

¾ Tbsp candied lemon

1 organic lemon

PREPARATION TIME: 35 minutes
REFRIGERATION TIME: 1 day
PER PORTION (WITH 12 SERV-INGS): about 225 calories

1 Remove the stems from the fig. Chop the figs in a food processor. Transfer to a mixing bowl. Chop the almonds and pistachio nuts; add to the figs.

2 Break the chocolate into pieces and melt in the top of a double boiler. Meanwhile, chop the candied fruits. Scrub the lemon under hot water; with a zester or grater, remove the zest from half of the lemon.

3 Add the chocolate, candied fruit, and lemon zest to the mixing bowl; combine all the ingredients. Shape the mixture into 3 or 4 "sausages" about 2 inches in diameter; wrap the sausages in plastic wrap and refrigerate for at least 1 day. Serve the sausages sliced.

This flavorful, sweet "sausage" has a long tradition in the region of Marche; it was even awarded the title of regional specialty by Slow Food.

Crema di Cioccolato

Chocolate Mousse (Marche/Umbria)

INGREDIENTS for 4:

7 oz unsweetened baking chocolate (at least 70 percent cacao)

4 fresh eggs

3 Tbsp sugar

²⁄₃ cup heavy cream

2 tsp freshly ground black pepper

PREPARATION TIME: 20 minutes
REFRIGERATION TME: 4 hours
PER PORTION: about 500 calories

1 Break the chocolate into pieces and melt in the top of a double boiler. Set aside to cool until lukewarm. Separate the eggs. With a hand mixer, cream and beat the egg yolks with the sugar in a large bowl.

2 Gradually pour the melted chocolate into the egg yolks. In another bowl, beat the egg whites until stiff peaks form, adding the heavy cream and then the pepper. Fold the whites into the chocolate mixture, then spoon this into a mold. Refrigerate for at least 4 hours or until firm. To serve, use two spoons to scoop ovals of mousse and place on dessert plates.

Fresh fruits such as figs, peaches, or apricots marinated in lemon juice and sugar go well with this chocolate mousse.

Castagne alla Ricotta

Chestnuts with Ricotta Cream (Tuscany)

INGREDIENTS for 4:

1 lb chestnuts

1 organic orange

1 Tbsp lemon juice

1 cinnamon stick

7 Tbsp sugar

2 oz semisweet baking chocolate

1½ cups ricotta cheese

PREPARATION TIME: 45 minutes
PER PORTION: about 475 calories

1 With a sharp paring knife, cut crosses on the smooth and curved side of the chestnuts. Cook the chestnuts in boiling water for about 10 minutes; rinse them under cold water and peel them, removing the brown membranes as well.

2 Meanwhile, scrub the orange under hot water; with a swivel peeler, peel the orange, cutting long rings of peel and avoiding as much of the white part of the rind as possible. Cut the orange in half and juice it. Simmer the orange peel, orange juice, lemon juice, cinnamon, sugar, and ³⁄₄ cup of water in a small saucepan about 5 minutes. Add the chestnuts and cook for 10 more minutes or until they are soft. Remove the chestnuts from the syrup, and strain the syrup through a fine-meshed sieve.

3 Break the chocolate into pieces and melt in the top of a double boiler. Beat the ricotta and syrup with a hand mixer. Serve the ricotta in dessert bowls, topped with the chestnuts and melted chocolate.

Lazio, Campania, and Sardinia

The full life: large, bustling cities, magic coastal resorts, nature

The Region and Its Products

Busy life along the Mediterranean Coast, contemplative peace inland

From Campania's and Lazio's fertile backcountry to the rich fishing grounds along the coastal regions to the mountains and meadows of Sardinia, where sheep and herbs are abundant, these regions boast the ingredients for traditional Italian cuisine.

Centuries ago, ancient Romans spent the hot summer months along the attractive coastal areas of Campania, where they had built their beautiful villas. The rich waters of the Mediterranean Sea and the fertile backcountry, especially around Caserta, provided them with culinary treasures that enhanced their paradise. The region is still called today *terra di lavoro*, the land of farming; it is where myriad vegetables grow abundantly, especially around Vesuvius and Cilento (famous for its tomatoes and for its artichokes), where wheat is cultivated and where water buffalo graze. This rich land is the cradle of a cuisine called *cucina povera*, or food of the poor. Meat is scarce—animals require a great deal of land, and those that are raised are usually kept for their milk. This cuisine is instead based on pasta, pizza, and especially on vegetables, which are the main ingredients for a rich variety of antipasti and primi. Along the shores of the coastal areas and throughout the islands of Ischia, Capri, and Procida, seafood and fish are the local specialties. Inland rabbit, pork, and more recently buffalo are the basis of many main dishes, called secondi.

Interspersed throughout the areas that surround the Eternal City are small gastronomical treasures. Whether hidden behind the Sabine Mountains, where one of Italy's best olive oil is pressed, or in Bolsena Lake, which provides freshwater fish or where the harvests from rich and fertile farmlands provide first quality fruits and vegetables. The pigs and the *abbacchio*, or suckling lambs, are also famous here. Dishes from these regions are part of an ancient but overall simple cuisine based on the land, the sea, and pristinely fresh ingredients. Flavors are robust, reflecting a love of good food that extends to the ristoranti, which are everywhere. Since ancient times, Romans were forbidden to cook over open fires in their homes—it was simply too dangerous in the very large and densely populated city. Wanting to eat well meant going out to eat—a pastime Italians everywhere relish.

The Mediterranean's second largest island is nearer to Corsica than to Italy's mainland; Spaniards and French, who were from French Savoy, left their traditions on Sardinia, which today is inhabited by four million sheep and fewer than two million people. Along the shores, the landscape is defined by steep rocks, wide white beaches, and turquoise clear water. Throughout the backcountry, mountains, valleys, and meadows are filled with wild herbs, olive trees, and suberous oaks. The local cuisine is based on the lean and meager ingredients available. There is wheat for pasta and bread, wine, olive oil, cheeses from sheep's milk, and fruits and vegetables. Local treasures lend to the simple yet tasty way of cooking with a special touch; these include saffron, herbs and *bottarga* (dried fish eggs).

Roccia dell'orso—Bear Rock—is a granite formation on the island of Sardinia built by nature in the form of an imposing 394-feet-high bear. At its peak of Capo d'Orso, not far from Palau, the rock formation seems to watch the entire island.

Along the mainland's coast and around Sardinia fishermen hoping for a good catch still go out to sea today—if successful, they prepare the fish as *frittura* (fried fish) or as a soupy chowder.

Large and aromatic lemon trees, typical of the breathtakingly beautiful Amalfi coast, are planted along terraced gardens for the delight of those who take a stroll around them. Lemons have been grown here since the eleventh century; the oblong citrus fruits called *limone sfusato amalfitano* have almost no pits and a juicy, almost sweet, flesh. *Limoncello*, as well as sweets and numerous savory dishes, are marked by their flavor.

The small villages along the mountainous Amalfi coast can only grow upward. No land was wasted, as terraces carved into the hills have become the foundation for many lovely homes. Positano—one of the most beautiful places along the costa amalfitana, has almost all rooms with a sea view.

Even in the large city of Naples, people prefer to buy their groceries in small shops around the corner. Not everything is available there, but gossip and recent news keep marketers informed of what is happening.

The stress of the metropolis hasn't yet infiltrated the small towns and villages of Lazio. It is still possible to watch the world go by through the mirror of a little glass of wine.

The Cuisine
Cucina Povera—the cuisine of the poor—rich in flavor

Tomatoes, eggplants, peppers, garlic; an array of cheeses; lamb, pork, and fresh-caught fish—these basic ingredients were used for centuries by the inhabitants of the region who turned them into culinary masterpieces that have become famous throughout the world.

Golden apples—pomodori.
The first tomatoes brought to Naples from the New World were golden yellow fruits; it was for this reason that the round yellow fruit became known as the golden apple. Tomatoes were first thought to be poisonous. When it was discovered that they weren't, these tasty fruits became a major ingredient in the cuisine of Naples and throughout the region of Campania. It is no wonder that there are at least two especially flavored varieties: the San Marzano, a fine egg-shaped plum tomato that is ideal for sauces, and the small pomodorino del piennolo del Vesuvio, a hardy, tough-skinned cherry tomato that grows on volcanic soil and is especially suitable for preserving and canning. Preserved or fresh, raw or cooked, simmered into sauces, or sliced as antipasti, tomatoes are essential to this cuisine. Other vegetables, cheeses, sausage, meat, and fish complement the tomato classics from Naples and the Campania.

The finest lamb.
On Sardinia, innumerable sheep graze free-range. Their milk is not only used to make delicious pecorino sardo cheese but their meat is prepared in fine lamb dishes. The same goes for Rome and the surrounding areas, where lamb is a favorite, especially the tender and young suckling lamb called *abbacchio*. While in the old days the meat was prepared simply, often either roasted over charcoal or stewed, now it is flavored with herbs, moistened with wine, seasoned with either peperoncino or honey or both, or braised with aromatic regional vegetables.

An authentic pizza napoletana is made according to strict guidelines; it has a thin crust that is made without any fat, and it is baked in brick ovens that are fired by wood. Pizza has been sold on the streets of Naples since the eighteenth century; shortly after then the first pizzerias were opened.

Alici—Anchovies are tasty fresh and preserved. A special dish are the alici di menaica from the Cilento area; in the small village of Marina di Pisciotta there are still fishermen that between April and July leave the place with their boats and nets to fish for them (this was what was called *menaica*). In the wide meshed nets are caught only the larger fish that are beheaded and cleaned directly on the boat. On the mainland the fish are either sold fresh or preserved with salt in clay pots for about three months.

Besides the famous mozzarella di bufala, the regions of Campania and Lazio and the island of Sardinia also produce many other types of flavorful cheeses: a wonderful pecorino comes from Sardinia; *caciocavallo* from Campania; and pecorino Romano and the fresh cheese called ricotta (fresh and creamy, or aged and salted, which is called ricotta salata) from Lazio.

Typical of Sardinia. The specialties of the island are offered in every small beach bar and trattoria: flavorful salami, air-dried prosciutto, and pancetta with a pecorino made from the milk of local sheep. Favorite accompaniments with these specialties: a glass of wine and crusty bread.

Friarielli are a variation of cime di rapa, or broccoli rabe, that are only available in Campania, in Naples, and in the surrounding areas and only during cold months of the year. Their taste is more pungent and bitter than other varieties of broccoli. *Friarielli* are often prepared with olive oil, garlic, and *peperoncino*, and are served as a side dish.

The daily offering of the fishermen varies as well as the way the fish is cooked. While seafood during the old days was fried or stewed with tomatoes and peperoncino, today's cooks have become much more creative: fish enhances dishes of pasta, or is prepared with ingredients such as ham, or combined with herbs and spices that have much more intensive flavors.

Shepherds required bread that was made for storage; it needed to remain edible during long journeys. In Sardinia, the long-lasting bread is called *pane carasau*; this is a very thin and crispy flatbread that can be kept for several months. Since the bread is as thin as a sheet of paper it is also called *carta da musica* which refers to the paper on which musical scores are written.

The Wines

From common table wines to specialty wines, everything is available here

From the days of the Roman Empire, wines from around the Vesuvius area as well as wines from the Castelli Romani have been renowned. Over the centuries, some winemakers resorted to shortcuts, and wines of the area lost their reputation for quality. Thanks to modern winemaking techniques and open-minded winemakers who combine tradition with progress, new and superior vines and wines are putting these regions back on the map.

Campania's flagship wines are from the Aglianico and Greco di Tufo grapes. The Aglianico is known to be the noblest red vine among the South Italian varieties; its wines are deep red. Aglianico that carries the Taurasi DOCG label is very highly regarded. It is a ruby-red wine with a very definite aroma and body and is best when aged. The Aglianico del Vulture or the DOC wines Cilento, Sannio or Sant'Agata de'Goti can give fine wines. Greco di Tufo is a white-wine grape. This vine grows in the northern area of Avellino around the small town of Greco, and makes a fruity white wine that has a scent of peach and apples but that can also have an aroma of almonds. It goes very well with fish dishes that are prepared throughout the coastal region. Fiano di Avellino wines from the same area have an aroma of hazelnuts and pears; they are also very fine wines.

Wines from Lazio are made predominantly from Malvasia and Trebbiano (white wine grapes) and Sangiovese and Montepulciano (red wine grapes). Usually these are light wines that should be consumed while they are still new since their character remains fairly mediocre and is not suited to long aging. The most popular wines of the Lazio region are the Frascati and the Est!Est! Est! ; these wines have no particularly outstanding personality and should be consumed well chilled. Sometimes a lucky wine lover might be able to find here and there a Frascati made from grapes grown on volcanic soil and that has retained its special white wine character with a fresh and herblike aroma.

Sardinia, the second largest Mediterranean island, has its own grape varieties. Grenache grapes, here called Cannonau, are made into a full-bodied dark wine that goes very well with the island's lamb specialties. The best Cannonau come from the Nuoro area. Milder and lighter are the Monica wines from the plain of Cagliari. The white Vermentino di Gallura has an intense, fruity and herblike aroma, Nuragus di Cagliari more modest, and the Vernaccia di Oristano is made from very ripe grapes, like a sherry.

Left: Suberous oaks grow especially well in the northeastern part of Sardinia. The trees can be shaved for the first time when they are about 25 years old and later require from seven to 10 more years to grow a new bark.
Above: Famous samples of the region (from left to right) – Greco di Tufo, Cannonau di Sardegna, Taurasi, Petrizza.

Regional Recipes

Traditional dishes enhanced by herbal flavors and lots of fresh lemons

Specialties of the region include dishes made of delicate artichokes and pungent *bottarga*—both delicious on their own, but especially if paired. Sun-blessed herbs turn stuffed squid into a gourmet specialty; juicy, almost sweet lemons lend aroma and flavor not only to risotto and vegetables but also to fish and meat.

Polpo d'Insalata con Mele e Sedano

Octopus Salad with Apples and Celery (Campania)

INGREDIENTS for 4:

1 octopus (about 2 lbs)
2 small organic lemons
2 bay leaves
1 dried peperoncino (chili pepper)
Salt and freshly ground pepper
3–4 celery ribs
1 large firm tart apple
5 Tbsp olive oil

PREPARATION TIME: 35 minutes
COOKING TIME: 1½ hours
PER PORTION: about 315 calories

1   Rinse the octopus under cold water and place it in a large pot. Scrub 1 lemon under hot water; slice it and add it with the bay leaves to the octopus. Crush the peperoncino and add this too to the octopus. Add water to cover, season with salt and bring to a boil. Reduce the heat and simmer the octopus for 1½ hours, partially covered (use a wooden spoon for this). The octopus is ready when it is tender as butter and a sharp knife cuts it easily.

2   Remove the octopus and rinse it in a colander under cold water; scrub or brush it to remove as much purple skin as possible. Set the octopus aside to cool.

3   Extract the juice from the remaining lemon. Trim the celery; mince the leaves and slice the ribs. Core, peel, and slice the apple. Toss the celery ribs and apple with 1 tablespoon of lemon juice; reserve the celery leaves.

4   Cut the octopus tentacles into bite-sized pieces; finely chop the rest of the octopus, discarding the inedible parts. Whisk the remaining lemon juice with salt and pepper; add the olive oil and whisk until almost creamy.

5   Combine the octopus, celery, apple, and dressing. Season with salt and pepper and serve, sprinkled with the celery leaves.

Try insalata di gamberi, rucola, e mele. For this variation, core, peel, and dice 2 apples. Rinse and trim about 5 ounces of arugula; pat dry and tear in bite-sized pieces. Combine with about a pound of peeled and cooked shrimp. Whisk a dressing of 2 tablespoons of lemon juice, 5 tablespoons of olive oil, salt, and freshly ground pepper; toss all the ingredients with the dressing and serve with toasted white bread.

Guanciale alla Griglia

Grilled Pork Jowls (Lazio)

INGREDIENTS for 4:

For the pork jowls:

1 carrot

1 onion

2 garlic cloves

1 celery rib

2 bay leaves

1 tsp peppercorns

1/4 cup white wine vinegar

Salt

1 lb trimmed pork jowls (order these from your butcher; or substitute these with veal jowls)

1/4 cup olive oil

For the marinade:

2 dried red peperoncini (chili peppers)

4 garlic cloves

1/2 bunch of parsley

2 Tbsp white wine vinegar

Salt

1/4 cup olive oil

4 lemon wedges

PREPARATION TIME: 15 minutes

COOKING TIME: 55 minutes

MARINATING TIME: 4 hours

PER PORTION: about 1165 calories

1   Peel and chop the carrot, onion, garlic, and celery. Put these ingredients in a pot and add the bay leaves, peppercorns, vinegar, and 6 cups of water. Season with salt and bring to a boil. Add the pork jowls to the boiling liquid and simmer for about 45 minutes. Turn off the heat and allow everything to cool.

2   Remove the pork jowls from the liquid and slice them. Pat the slices dry and brush them with oil. Preheat the grill or broiler.

3   Meanwhile, for the marinade trim the peperoncini and crush them with the seeds. Peel the garlic and cut into thin strips. Rinse and pat dry the parsley; mince the leaves.

4   Whisk together the vinegar, oil, and salt to make an almost creamy marinade. Add the peperoncini, parsley, and garlic.

5   Place the pork jowls on the grill or under the broiler, about 4 inches from the heat. Grill or broil for about 10 minutes or until they are nice and brown, turning them once. Let cool briefly.

6   Transfer the jowls to a shallow bowl and pour the marinade over them. Cover and refrigerate for about 4 hours. Serve, garnished with lemon wedges.

In ancient Rome, lesser cuts of meat and organs called quinto quarto, or fifth quarter, were given to the workers of the slaughterhouse or to the poor. (Carcasses were usually quartered; these cuts comprised the "fifth.") Housewives who received these parts managed to make culinary delicacies out of them.

Recommended Wine:

A hearty white wine, such as a Vermentino di Gallura, or a red Aglianico from the region of Campania.

Spinaci al Pecorino

Garlic Spinach with Pecorino Cheese (Sardinia)

INGREDIENTS for 4:
About 1 lb spinach
Salt and freshly ground pepper
4 garlic cloves
½ bunch basil
2 Tbsp olive oil
About 5 oz medium-aged pecorino
  cheese

PREPARATION TIME: 35 minutes
PER PORTION: about 160 calories

1 Rinse and trim the spinach, removing the stems. Make sure to clean the spinach very well. Bring to a rolling boil a large pot of salted water and cook the spinach for 1–2 minutes, until wilted. Rinse it in a colander under cold water and set it aside to drain and cool. Squeeze out as much liquid as possible.

2 Preheat the oven to 425° F (if convection oven 400° F). Peel and thinly slice the garlic. Rinse and pat dry the basil; shred the leaves.

3 Toss the spinach with the garlic, basil, oil, salt, and pepper. Divide the spinach into four portions and place each portion in individual baking dishes. Remove the rind from the cheese; use a vegetable peeler to make shavings. Top each portion of spinach with cheese.

4 Bake the spinach on the middle oven rack for about 4 minutes or until the cheese has melted (don't allow the cheese to become brown). Serve.

Carciofi alla Bottarga

Artichokes with Bottarga (Smoked Fish Eggs) (Sardinia)

INGREDIENTS for 4:
4 small young artichokes
2 garlic cloves
½ bunch parsley
2 thyme sprigs
1 dried peperoncino (chili pepper)
4 Tbsp olive oil
Salt
1–3 Tbsp *bottarga*
4 lemon wedges

PREPARATION TIME: 35 minutes
PER PORTION: about 120 calories

1 Rinse and trim the artichokes; remove the outer leaves, peel the stems and with scissors cut off the tops of the remaining central leaves. Cut the artichokes in half.

2 Peel and slice the garlic. Rinse and pat dry the herbs; mince the leaves. Lightly crush the peperoncino.

3 Heat 3 tablespoons of oil in a skillet. Sauté the artichokes over high heat. Add the herbs, garlic, and peperoncino. Moisten with ⅓ cup of water and simmer, covered, for about 10 minutes. Allow the artichokes to cool off in their juice.

4 Drain the artichokes and place them on a serving platter. Shave the *bottarga* and add, then drizzle with the remaining olive oil. Serve, garnished with lemon wedges.

Mozzarella con Salsa di Pomodori

Mozzarella with Tomato Dressing (Campania)

INGREDIENTS for 4:

4 medium tomatoes

5 anchovies (preserved in oil)

1 bunch basil

8 Tbsp olive oil

Salt and freshly ground pepper

12 zucchini blossoms

1 lb buffalo mozzarella

PREPARATION TIME: 25 minutes
PER PORTION: about 475 calories

1 Core and dice the tomatoes. Mince the anchovies. Rinse and pat dry the basil; shred the leaves. Combine the tomatoes, anchovies, basil, and 6 tablespoons of olive oil; season with salt and pepper.

2 Carefully rinse the zucchini blossoms and with a small paring knife remove the stamens. Cut the mozzarella into thin slices and arrange on four salad plates.

3 Heat the remaining 2 tablespoons of olive oil in a saucepan. Sauté the zucchini blossoms over medium heat for 3–4 minutes, turning them over occasionally. Season with salt and pepper. Garnish the mozzarella slices with the blossoms and top with the tomato dressing; serve immediately.

It has recently become fashionable to use balsamic vinegar with salads of mozzarella, tomatoes, and basil; however, the majority of Italians seem not to care for this. Italians believe that tomatoes should have the necessary acidity and flavor to make vinegar unnecessary, and that the delicate flavor of mozzarella should not be overpowered by vinegar. Of course there are still tomato fans who love drizzling vinegar over tomatoes. If you typically serve tomatoes with vinegar try something new—but be sure that you have fresh and ripe tomatoes with lots of flavor.

Mozzarella di Bufala—A White Delicacy

Mozzarella can be made from cow's milk, but when made with buffalo milk it is prized by gourmets

A delicate, somewhat acidic flavor and a soft, almost juicy consistency characterize the authentic mozzarella di bufala. The mozzarella made from cow's milk is definitely firmer, slightly drier, and blander in flavor.

Mozzarella is not just mozzarella.
Many cheeses sold as mozzarella are cheeses made from cow's milk, buffalo milk, or from a mixture of both. In Italy, mozzarella is also called fiori di latte or flower of the milk; the authentic mozzarella is recognizable from the DOC or the DOP label on the container. Imported mozzarella is rare—this fresh cheese does not travel well and is at its best when younger than two days old. For nearly two millennia, buffalo have been raised in Campania, near the areas of Caserta and Salerno, which is the place of origin of this cheese. Mozzarella from Salerno is still produced as it was in the old days. During a visit to those areas seeing the large and imposing brown buffalos with their long horns is still a common event.

Cheese production with a special touch.
The difference between the various mozzarellas is still dictated by the type of milk used to produce them. The milk of the buffalo has a higher content in fat—it can be as high as 9 percent—and is creamier. It has no carotenoids and is snow white. For the production of mozzarella, milk is heated (usually from two milkings) and is made to curdle with a coagulant. The curdled mass is then stirred and kneaded in boiling water until it has the consistency of a dough. Pieces are further kneaded by hand or by machine in lukewarm water until they become elastic. This is called *pasta filata* because it is cooked and the cheese is kneaded (the same techniques are used to make *caciocavallo* and *provolone*). At this point the cheese can be shaped, usually in the shape of a ball. The mozzarella is ready and delicious after a short stage in a lightly salted marinade. It is available to be sold either shaped as a ball (which in the marinade usually weighs about ½ pound), as tiny balls (*bocconcini*), as a braid (*treccia*), or as a tied rope.

A well chosen pairing.
Of course mozzarella tastes best when it is fresh. Ideally, it should be served at cool room temperature; if cooked, it should not be exposed to direct heat. Mozzarella in carrozza, made of cheese sandwiches that are coated with egg before frying, are tasty. Avoid using authentic mozzarella di bufala on pizza; it is far too succulent and delicately flavored; use cow's milk mozzarella instead. Another tip: the slightly acidic taste of the authentic mozzarella goes best with tomatoes that are also acidic in nature; this pairing goes especially well if no other acidic ingredient is added. Avoid using vinegar of any type on insalata caprese (mozzarella with tomatoes); instead, use a truly aromatic carefully chosen olive oil.

a

a   Original and authentic mozzarella makers use only milk of buffalo raised the traditional way. The animals range free with access to water; if natural sources of water are not available, the animals are hosed down daily. Water buffalo are incapable of expelling sweat through their skin and would be dehydrated without wetness.

b/c The most important stage of mozzarella making has lent its name to the cheese. As the curds are kneaded, cheese makers break off ball-shaped pieces; the operation of breaking off pieces from the cheese dough in Italian is called *mozzare*. d At the ball-shaping stage, the cheese has not yet acquired its best flavor; it will be at its best after being left to marinate in a salt brine. A couple of hours in the brine will be sufficient. e Mozzarella nella mortella is a specialty of the Salerno area: the mozzarella is placed on a bed of myrtle leaves. It both looks beautiful and tastes delicious.

Fusilli alla Pancetta

Fusilli with Bacon Rolls (Lazio)

INGREDIENTS for 4:

4 garlic cloves

1/2 small bunch parsley

8 sage leaves

2 dried peperoncini (chili peppers)

4 Tbsp freshly grated pecorino or parmesan cheese

5 oz thinly sliced pancetta (substitute with bacon)

3 –4 medium tomatoes

1 lb fusilli pasta

Salt

4 Tbsp olive oil

PREPARATION TIME: 25 minutes
PER PORTION: about 705 calories

1 Peel the garlic. Rinse and pat dry the parsley and sage; mince the leaves with the garlic and peperoncini. Combine with the cheese.

2 Cut the pancetta into strips, then cut each into halves; line with the herbed cheese mixture and roll them up. Bring a large pot of salted water to a boil; blanch the tomatoes. Core, peel and dice them. Cook the fusilli in the boiling water according to package directions or until al dente.

3 Meanwhile, heat 2 tablespoons of oil in a saucepan or skillet. Sauté the bacon rolls until crispy on all sides. Set aside, reserving the fat.

4 Heat the remaining oil in another saucepan. Sauté the tomatoes; season with salt. Drain the fusilli and add to the tomatoes, mixing well. Distribute among serving plates; garnish with the bacon rolls and drizzle with the bacon fat.

Pasta Caprese

Pasta with Mozzarella and Tomatoes (Campania)

INGREDIENTS for 4:

2 medium tomatoes

2 garlic cloves

1–2 dried peperoncini (chili peppers)

8 oz mozzarella (preferably buffalo mozzarella)

1/4 cup olive oil

1 lb penne or maccheroni pasta

Salt

1 bunch basil

1 small can tuna (preserved in oil)

1 Tbsp small capers

PREPARATION TIME: 25 minutes
MARINATING TIME: 1 hour
PER PORTION: about 665 calories

1 Core and dice the tomatoes. Peel and mince the garlic. Crush the peperoncini. Cut the mozzarella in 1/2-inch cubes.

2 Combine the tomatoes, garlic, peperoncini, mozzarella, and olive oil; cover and refrigerate 1 hour to marinate.

3 Bring a large pot of salted water to a rolling boil. Cook the penne according to package directions.

4 Meanwhile, rinse and pat dry the basil. Shred the leaves. Drain and flake the tuna. Combine both ingredients.

5 Drain the pasta and return it to the pot on the hot burner. Stir in the mozzarella mixture and the tuna mixture, tossing to combine. Season with salt and cover the pot, leaving it on the burner for about 1–2 minutes (keep the burner off). Serve in heated plates.

Gnocchetti al Pesce Spada
Gnocchetti Pasta with Swordfish (Lazio/Sardinia)

INGREDIENTS for 4:

1 lb swordfish

1 cup fish broth

2 Tbsp lemon juice

1 rosemary sprig

2 thyme sprigs

4 anchovies (preserved in oil)

2 garlic cloves

3 medium tomatoes

1 lb *gnocchetti sardi* pasta (see Tip)

Salt

8 Tbsp olive oil

1 bunch basil

½ bunch oregano

3 Tbsp plain breadcrumbs (preferably grated from old stale white bread)

1 dried peperoncino (Italian chili pepper)

PREPARATION TIME: 25 minutes
PER PORTION: about 765 calories

1 Rinse the swordfish with cold water. Bring the fish broth and lemon juice to a rolling boil. Add the swordfish, reduce the heat and simmer for about 5 minutes. Remove the fish and cut it into bite-sized pieces.

2 Rinse and pat dry the rosemary and thyme; mince the leaves. Mince the anchovies and peel and mince the garlic.

3 Bring a large pot of salted water to a boil; blanch the tomatoes and rinse under cold water. Core, peel and chop them. Cook the pasta in the boiling water according to package directions or until al dente.

4 Heat 2 tablespoons of olive oil in a saucepan. Sauté the minced herbs and garlic. Add the tomatoes and anchovies and simmer for 10 minutes.

5 Meanwhile, rinse and pat dry the basil and the oregano. Puree the leaves with 4 tablespoons of olive oil in a food processor. Heat the remaining oil in a small skillet and toast the breadcrumbs and peperoncino.

6 Add the swordfish to the tomato sauce. Drain the pasta and add it, tossing well. Distribute among serving plates; drizzle each portion with herbed oil and serve with the toasted bread crumbs on the side.

Gnocchetti sardi, sometimes called *malloredus,* are small, narrow shell-shaped noodles made from hard wheat. They are usually available in Italian gourmet stores or supermarkets. Use another type of small pasta in case they are hard to find; try rigatoni or caserecce since this pasta is rilled and retains particularly well any type of sauce.

Instead of swordfish, try this recipe with canned tuna or sardines.

177

Risotto al Limone

Lemon Risotto (Campania)

INGREDIENTS for 4:

1 organic lemon

3 Tbsp butter

1 lb risotto rice

5 cups hot vegetable or veal broth

1 small bunch parsley

2 Tbsp pine nuts

3 Tbsp freshly grated caciocavallo or parmesan cheese

Salt and freshly ground pepper

PREPARATION TIME: 35 minutes
PER PORTION: about 590 calories

1 Scrub the lemon under hot water. With a zester or grater, remove the zest. Juice the lemon.

2 Melt the butter with the lemon juice in a saucepan. Add the rice and stir until the rice is coated with fat.

3 Pour in ½–1 cup broth and stir. Cook the rice over medium heat, stirring constantly while waiting until the broth has been absorbed before adding more. The rice will be firm to the bite or al dente, when done.

4 Rinse and pat dry the parsley; mince the leaves and combine with the lemon zest. Toast the pine nuts in a small skillet with a little butter until they are golden brown. Set the pine nuts aside.

5 Cut the remaining butter into small pieces and fold it into the risotto with the parsley, lemon zest, and the cheese. Season the risotto with salt and pepper and serve, sprinkled with toasted pine nuts.

Torta Rustica

Savory Pie with Ricotta and Zucchini Blossom (Lazio)

INGREDIENTS for 4:
For the crust:

2¼ cups all-purpose flour

8 Tbsp olive oil

Salt

For the filling:

6 zucchini blossoms

1 bunch mixed greens (such as arugula, borage, parsley, and oregano)

Salt and freshly ground pepper

1½ cups ricotta cheese (see Tip)

2 eggs

⅓ cup freshly grated *caciotta* cheese (sheep milk cheese; you may substitute with middle-aged pecorino or *caciocavallo*)

Freshly grated nutmeg

PREPARATION TIME: 45 minutes
RESTING TIME: 30 minutes
BAKING TIME: 15 minutes
PER PORTION: about 680 calories

1 Combine the flour, 5 tablespoons of oil, ½ teaspoon of salt, and about ⅓ cup of water in a mixing bowl and knead to make a soft smooth dough. Wrap the dough in a clean dish towel and set aside to rest for about 30 minutes.

2 Carefully open the zucchini blossoms and remove the stamens. Rinse and pat dry the greens and the herbs; if necessary trim all the stems. Bring a pot of salted water to a rolling boil. Blanch the zucchini blossoms for ½ minute and drain. Blanch the herbs until they are just limp. Drain and mince everything.

3 Cream the ricotta and eggs in a bowl with a mixer. Add the grated cheese and season with salt, pepper, and nutmeg.

4 Preheat the oven to 475° F (if convection oven 425° F). Brush a pizza pan or a pie plate (9–12

Pizza Scarola e Salsiccia
Pizza with Escarole and Sausage (Campania)

inches in diameter) with oil. Knead the dough once more and divide the dough in two pieces. Place each between two pieces of plastic wrap and roll out each one to a flat round pie crust.

5   Place one dough wheel in the pan and fill it with the herbed ricotta mixture; place the zucchini blossoms over the layer of ricotta. Prick the second wheel of dough with a fork and place it on top. Push the top crust against the bottom crust and press it beyond the rim of the pan, pinching both crust edges together. Brush the pie with the remaining oil and bake it on the middle oven rack for about 15 minutes. Serve the torta rustica either warm, luke-warm, or cold, cut into wedges.

Tip: Throughout the Roman countryside, the authentic ricotta Romana is made from sheep milk; it is soft, spreadable, and slightly curdled.

INGREDIENTS for 4:

For the dough:

4 cups bread flour

salt

2½ tsp active dry yeast (1 envelope)

2 Tbsp olive oil

For the topping:

1 head escarole or Romaine lettuce

4 garlic cloves

2 Tbsp olive oil

Salt and freshly ground pepper

1 Tbsp walnuts

2 Tbsp pitted black olives

8 oz Italian sausage

5 oz *caciocavallo* cheese

PREPARATION TIME: 40 minutes
RESTING TIME: 1 hour
BAKING TIME: 14 minutes per baking sheet
PER PORTION: about 815 calories

1   For the dough, mix the flour and salt in a large bowl. Sprinkle the yeast over ¾–1 cup of luke-warm water. Let stand until foamy then add it and the oil to the salted flour. Knead on a floured work surface to make a smooth dough (it should be soft but not sticky). Return the dough to a mixing bowl; cover with a clean dish towel and set it aside to rest at room temperature for about 1 hour.

2   For the topping, rinse, pat dry, and trim the escarole; cut into ½-inch slices. Peel and mince the garlic. Heat the oil in a skillet or saucepan. Sauté the garlic, then add the escarole and sauté over high heat for about 3–4 minutes. When the greens are wilted, trans-fer them to a mixing bowl and season with salt and pepper. Chop the walnuts and add, with the olives, to the greens.

3   Remove the sausage from its casing and brown in a skillet. Remove the rind from the *cacio-cavallo* and dice.

4   Preheat the oven to 450° F (if convection oven 425° F). Divide the dough into fourths. Brush four individual pizza pans or two large baking sheets with oil; or line the pans with parchment paper. Shape each piece of dough into a flat round. Place the dough on the pans.

5   Top each pizza with sausage and the greens. Distribute the cheese among the pizzas. Bake the pizzas, two at a time, on the middle oven rack for about 14 minutes. Cut into halves and serve hot. If you wish you can bake the other two while you eat the first.

Zuppa Sarda

Bread and Cheese Chowder, Sardinian-Style (Sardinia)

INGREDIENTS for 4:

8 oz mozzarella cheese

1 bunch parsley

1 small fennel bulb (with greens)

8 slices stale white bread

Freshly ground pepper

Freshly grated nutmeg

4 cups good beef broth

¼ cup grated pecorino Romano or Sardo cheese

2 Tbsp olive oil

PREPARATION TIME: 40 minutes
PER PORTION: about 350 calories

1 Cut the mozzarella into very thin slices. Rinse, and pat dry the parsley; mince the leaves. Trim and chop the fennel with the greens. Preheat the oven to 425° F (if convection oven 400° F). Line a round heat resistant serving bowl with a layer of the bread; top this with a layer of cheese, then with chopped fennel, parsley, and grated nutmeg. Pour some broth over the layers. Continue layering until you run out of ingredients. Pour some broth over the last layer and finish with a layer of pecorino; drizzle with the olive oil.

2 Bake the soup on the middle oven rack for about 15 minutes or until the top layer is nice and golden. Briefly set aside and serve.

This is a farmers' specialty and reflects typically the Sardinian way of cooking; in Sardinia the dish is prepared with fresh pecorino or mozzarella, but the latter is more readily available here. Crumbled dried peperoncini are also tasty between the layers of cheese. Sardinian cooks make the broth usually from meat of lamb.

Cauraro

Springtime Soup (Campania)

INGREDIENTS for 4:

2 small red potatoes

2 red onions

8 oz Swiss chard

1 fennel bulb with greens

5–6 oz mixed wild greens and herbs (such as dandelion, arugula, mint, borage, parsley, and oregano)

4 Tbsp olive oil

4 cups vegetable broth

1 cup canned tomatoes

4 anchovies (preserved in oil)

Salt and freshly ground pepper

Freshly grated pecorino or cacio-cavallo cheese, to serve

PREPARATION TIME: 45 minutes
PER PORTION: about 245 calories

1 Scrub the potatoes, but do not peel. Cover with cold water in a saucepan. Cook, covered, for about 20 minutes. Drain and set aside to cool.

2 Meanwhile, peel and chop the onions. Rinse, trim, and chop the Swiss chard. Rinse and trim the fennel. Remove the woody part of the fennel's center and thinly slice the fennel lengthwise. Rinse and pat dry the fennel greens and the herbs. Remove the leaves from the stems. Set aside about ¼ of these; mince the rest. Peel the potatoes and slice them not too thin.

3 Heat 2 tablespoons of oil in a saucepan. Sauté the minced herbs over medium heat. Add the Swiss chard and the fennel and sauté. Pour in the broth. Dice the tomatoes and add them and the potatoes to the soup. Simmer over low heat for about 15 minutes or until all the vegetables are still firm to the bite.

4 Mince the anchovies with the remaining herbs. Season the soup

Zavardella

Mixed Vegetables with Grilled Bread (Lazio)

with salt and pepper. Ladle the soup into bowls. Top each portion with the anchovy mixture and drizzle with olive oil. Serve the grated cheese at the table.

A similar soup is prepared in Sardinia. For the specialty called *s'erbudzu* all sort of herbs and vegetables used are from farmers' fields, gardens, and wild meadows.

INGREDIENTS for 4–6:

- 1 ham hock
- Salt and freshly ground pepper
- 4 small celery ribs
- 1 small head catalogna (or dandelion small greens, about 8 oz; available in Italian supermarkets or farmers' markets)
- 4 young artichokes
- 4 young carrots
- 7 oz broccoli
- 7 oz spinach or Swiss chard
- 3–4 spring onions
- 1 cup shelled peas (or about 1 lb unshelled)
- 2–4 dried peperoncini (chili peppers)
- ½ cup olive oil
- 4–6 slices stale white bread

PREPARATION TIME: 30 minutes
COOKING TIME: 1 hour
PER PORTION (FOR 6 SERVINGS): about 290 calories

1 Bring the ham hock and 4 cups of water to a boil. Reduce the heat and simmer for about 1 hour. Remove the bone and season the broth with salt and pepper.

2 Rinse, trim, and peel the vegetables. Slice the celery and catalogna in 2-inch long pieces. Tear off the outer leaves of the artichokes and cut off the points. Cut the trimmed artichokes into eighths. Cut the carrots lengthwise into quarters; cut the broccoli into florets. Trim and slice or chop the spinach. Cut the spring onions, including the green tops, into 2-inch long pieces.

3 Heat again the broth; add the artichokes, carrots, celery, broccoli, and peas and cook for about 6–7 minutes. With a slotted spoon remove the vegetables from the broth. Preheat the oven to 150° F and keep the vegetables warm. Cook the onions for about 5 minutes; add the spinach and catalogna and cook for 1–2 more minutes. Remove these vegetables and add them to those in the oven.

4 Meanwhile, trim the peperoncini and crush or mince them. Heat the oil in a small skillet and add the peperoncini. Toast the bread. Line serving plates with the toasted bread; season the vegetables with salt and pepper and distribute them over the bread; moisten with a little broth. Drizzle with the peperoncini oil.

When Roman cooks prepare this one-pot specialty, they always use eight different types of vegetables. The ones they choose vary upon the time of year and what is available: They go to market every day and choose what looks attractive and fresh.

181

Sarde in Tortiera

Sardine and Potato Casserole (Lazio)

INGREDIENTS for 4:

1½ lb red potatoes

8 plum tomatoes

1½–2 lb fresh sardines

1 organic lemon

4 garlic cloves

1 bunch parsley

Salt and freshly ground pepper

8 Tbsp olive oil

2 eggs

3 Tbsp freshly grated pecorino
    Romano cheese

PREPARATION TIME: 45 minutes
BAKING TIME: 30 minutes
PER PORTION: about 560 calories

1 Scrub the potatoes, but do not peel. Cover with cold water and cook for about 20 minutes. Remove with a slotted spoon and set aside to cool. Blanch the tomatoes in the boiling water. Rinse under cold water. Core, peel, and slice the tomatoes. Slice open and butterfly the sardines;

with the end of a spoon remove the central bone. Rinse and pat dry the deboned sardines.

2 Scrub the lemon under hot water. With a zester or grater, remove the peel from half the lemon. Peel and mince the garlic. Rinse and pat dry the parsley; mince the leaves. Mix the parsley, garlic, and lemon zest. Peel and slice the potatoes.

3 Preheat the oven to 350° F (if convection oven 325° F). Brush a baking dish with oil and layer the potatoes, tomatoes, and sardines in it, sprinkling the potatoes with the parsley mixture and seasoning each layer with salt and pepper. Drizzle the potatoes with a little olive oil but use only salt for the tomatoes and sardines.

4 Whisk the eggs and cheese with the remaining olive oil. Pour over the final layer. Bake for about 30 minutes until golden brown.

Cassola di Pesce

Fish in Marinara Sauce (Sardinia)

INGREDIENTS for 4:

1 onion

4 garlic cloves

2 dried peperoncini (chili peppers)

1½ lb tomatoes

6 Tbsp olive oil

½ cup dry white wine

Salt

1½–2 lb mixed fish fillets (such as
    red mullet, sea bass, sardines,
    and bream)

½ bunch parsley

4 thick slices of bread

PREPARATION TIME: 40 minutes
PER PORTION: about 465 calories

1 Peel and mince the onion and garlic. Crush or mince the peperoncini. Bring a large pot of water to a boil. Blanch the tomatoes; rinse under cold water. Core, peel, and dice them.

2 Heat 2 tablespoons of oil in a saucepan. Sauté the onion, garlic,

and peperoncini. Add the tomatoes and wine; season with salt and simmer, covered, over low heat for about 15 minutes.

3 Remove any fish bones with tweezers. Cut the fish into bite-sized pieces and season with salt and pepper. Stir the tomato sauce; add the fish. Simmer for 15 more minutes.

4 Meanwhile, rinse and pat dry the parsley; mince the leaves. Toast the slices of bread. Place the toasted bread in a deep dish; top with the fish and sauce. Sprinkle with parsley and drizzle with the remaining olive oil. Serve immediately.

Tomatoes and fish are paired often, especially in the sunny southern regions of Italy where the best tomatoes—those that have a fine acidic aroma and also

Saltimbocca di Triglie con Spinaci
Red Mullet Saltimbocca with Spinach (Lazio)

a sweet flavor—are grown. Cooks in Campania prepare a very similar dish. There, fish is cooked in a somewhat runnier sauce (more water or fish broth is added) and it is called *pesce in acqua pazza*—"fish in crazy water."

INGREDIENTS for 4:

For the vegetables:

1 lb spinach

1 bunch each parsley and arugula

Salt

2 dried peperoncini (chili peppers)

2 Tbsp olive oil

Lemon juice

For the saltimbocca:

15–20 sage leaves

4 garlic cloves

1 organic lemon

4 large red mullet fillets (about 1½ lb)

Salt and freshly ground pepper

4–8 slices bacon

¼ cup olive oil

¼ cup dry white wine

PREPARATION TIME: 40 minutes
PER PORTION: about 505 calories

1 For the vegetables, rinse, pat dry, trim, and chop the spinach. Rinse and pat dry the herbs.

Remove the leaves from the stems; set aside a few leaves. Bring a large pot of salted water to a boil. Cook the spinach and greens for 1 minute. Rinse in cold water and drain.

2 For the saltimbocca, cut the sage leaves into strips. Peel and mince the garlic. Scrub the lemon under hot water and with a zester or grater, remove the zest from half the lemon. Juice the whole lemon.

3 Mix the sage, garlic, and lemon zest. Season the fish with salt and pepper; top the meaty side of the fillets with some of the sage mixture. If necessary, cut the bacon in half (each piece of bacon should be about the size of each fish piece). Top each fillet with a piece of bacon and use toothpicks to secure bacon and fish.

4 Heat the ¼ cup of oil in a large skillet. Sauté the fillets for about 3 minutes, placing them skin-side down. Turn the saltimbocca over and cook for 3 more minutes.

5 For the vegetables, crush the peperoncini. Heat the 2 tablespoons of oil in another skillet. Sauté the peperoncini. Add the spinach and cook until everything is hot. Season with salt, lemon juice (reserve 2 tablespoons), and the remaining sage mixture.

6 Place the fish on serving plates. Deglaze the pan juices with wine and the reserved lemon juice. Pour over the fish; add the spinach and serve.

183

Calamari Ripieni
Stuffed Squid (Campania)

INGREDIENTS for 4:

For the squid:

1½ lb cleaned squid (see Tip)

4 slices stale white bread

4 oz mixed greens and herbs (such as borage, arugula, fennel greens, oregano, and mint)

2 garlic cloves

1 dried peperoncino (chili pepper)

2 Tbsp olive oil

4 anchovies (preserved in oil)

1 organic lemon

1 egg white

2 Tbsp freshly grated parmesan or pecorino cheese

Salt and freshly ground pepper

For the sauce:

1 each red, yellow, and green bell pepper

2 medium tomatoes

3–4 spring onions

½ bunch parsley

¼ cup olive oil

½ cup dry white wine

Salt and freshly ground pepper

1 Pinch sugar

PREPARATION TIME: 1 hour
COOKING TIME: 30–45 minutes
PER PORTION: about 410 calories

Tip: The key to success with this recipe is to choose calamari, or squid, that's the right size. Ideally, they should be between 2½ and 3½ inches in length. This size will not only look appealing when served but will be easy to fill and will have better flavor.

There are thousands of squid recipes throughout the Mediterranean region; these saltwater creatures are among the least expensive types of seafood. It is for this reason that home cooks came up with all sorts of ways to prepare them.

Larger squid are often stuffed. Breadcrumb mixtures are common; squid are also prepared with mixtures of potatoes, egg yolk, and grated cheese. However, not too much cheese should be added since its flavor should not overpower or compete with the taste of this seafood.

1   Clean, rinse, and drain the squid. Soak the bread in a bowl filled with lukewarm water and allow it to soften.

2   Meanwhile, rinse and pat dry the herbs; if necessary remove the leaves from the stems and mince the herbs. Peel and mince the garlic; crush the peperoncino.

3   Heat the oil in a large skillet. Sauté the herbs, garlic, and peperoncino. When limp, place these ingredients in a large bowl. Mince the anchovies. Scrub the lemon under hot water. With a zester or grater, remove the zest from half of the lemon.

4 Drain and squeeze the soaked bread; break it into small pieces into the bowl with the herbs. Add the anchovies, egg white, cheese, and lemon zest; season with salt and pepper and knead all the ingredients to blend. Fill the squid bodies with the bread mixture and close the ends of the bodies with a toothpick or kitchen twine.

5 For the sauce, core, seed, and chop the peppers. Bring a pot of water to a boil. Blanch the tomatoes; rinse them under cold water, and core, peel, and dice them. Trim and slice the spring onions into thin rings.

6 Rinse and pat dry the parsley. Mince the leaves. Heat the oil in a large saucepan. Sauté the squid over high heat until they are golden brown on all sides. Remove the squid from the pan; in the same oil, sauté the peppers, parsley, and onions.

7 Stir in the tomatoes and white wine; season with salt, pepper, and sugar. Add the squid and simmer, covered, for about 30–45 minutes or until they are tender.

Bottarga—Caviar of the Islands
A local specialty made from eggs of tuna or mullet is increasingly prized the world over

In Sardinia, *bottarga* from the gray mullet—*bottarga di muggine*—is called the gold of Cabras; since the Middle Ages it has been a favorite and sought-after barter item. Discovered by the Egyptians, *bottarga* became a delicacy throughout the Mediterranean thanks to Arabian traders. In fact, its name originated with the Arabic word *battarikh*, which means salted fish eggs. Today, bottarga is distributed by a variety of small businesses located on Sardinia and located along the Tuscan coast. Tuna bottarga, or *bottarga di tonno*, is considered inferior; it comes primarily from Sicily and along the coast of Calabria.

At the end of the summer. In and around September, female mullets are carrying a precious specialty, their eggs (tuna roe is harvested in May and June). Only the larger fish are caught in order to provide *bottarga*—the fish should weigh at least 6–8 pounds. As soon as the fish are caught, fishermen slice open their bellies and carefully remove the egg sac, taking care not to damage the thin membranes. The *bottarga* is then either rubbed in salt or placed a few hours in salty brine. Afterward, the *bottarga* is rinsed well, pressed slightly, and

dried—in the old days the egg sacs were dried under the sun on specially built rafters, but today this occurs in climate-controlled drying rooms. After 7 to 14 days (depending on size) the *bottarga* has lost about half of its weight and is sufficiently dry. *Bottarga* that has a nice shape and an undamaged sac is sold whole (it is sold wrapped in vacuum-packed foil). Those that are less than perfect are grated or shaved and sold preserved in glass jars. Of course preserved *bottarga* cannot be compared in flavor with whole *bottarga* that is freshly shaved or grated just before use.

A fine difference. Mullet *bottarga* is a rich golden orange in color. It is still soft after the drying stage and has an intense but yet delicate flavor. On the other hand, tuna *bottarga* has a rougher sea flavor and firmer consistency. Its color is brown and gray. Whatever fish it is from, *bottarga* is a food that is either loved at first bite or not loved at all: People who are indifferent to it are rarely found. *Bottarga* can be purchased in gourmet markets or from a fish monger. You might have to special-order it, or you might find it through the Internet. *Bottarga* is rather expensive, and mullet *bottarga* costs considerably more than tuna *bottarga*. On the positive side, you will probably need only a small amount since this ingredient is typically used very sparingly.

Suitably served. A food as special as *bottarga* does not appear too often at a table. It can be an extraordinary appetizer, thinly shaved with fresh celery, a couple of tomatoes, and simply dressed with only a little olive oil. In first courses, or primi, bottarga is typically used to garnish pasta and risotto; in main courses, or secondi, it can enhance any fish or seafood dish. When *bottarga* is shaved, the sac is treated like a sausage casing; it is removed from the area to be used and discarded.

a *Bottarga* goes well with cooked spaghetti. Mince 3 peeled garlic cloves with 1 crushed peperoncino and the leaves of $\frac{1}{4}$ bunch of fresh parsley. Sauté for 2–3 minutes over low heat in $\frac{1}{4}$ cup of olive oil. Boil a pound of spaghetti in salted water. Toss with the garlic and top with approximately 3 ounces of freshly grated or shaved bottarga.

b *Bottarga* of tuna is larger than b*ottarga* from mullet (the Sicilian *bottarga di Favignana* is perhaps the best known). *Bottarga di tonno*, shaved very thin with lemon juice and olive oil tastes delicious with toasted white bread.   c/d Mullet *bottarga* is finer and more delicate and has a bright gold or orange-red color. In Tuscany it is found especially in the Lagoon of Orbetello.   e   The best tool for shaving *bottarga* is a truffle shaver or mandoline: the thinner the slices, the better. The coarser *bottarga di tonno* is usually sliced with an electric slicing machine or with a very sharp knife.   f Catching tuna in Sicily has been a centuries-long tradition. The factories in which the tuna is processed immediately after arrival were and are still called today *tonnerie*.

Agnello al Pesto di Menta
Lamb Chops with Mint Pesto (Lazio)

INGREDIENTS for 4:
For the meat:
1 organic lemon
2 garlic cloves
$\frac{1}{4}$ cup olive oil
8 lamb chops (about 5 oz each)
Salt and freshly ground pepper
For the pesto:
1 large bunch mint
3 Tbsp blanched almonds
$\frac{1}{3}$ cup olive oil
Salt and freshly ground pepper

PREPARATION TIME: 20 minutes
PER PORTION: about 1035 calories

1 For the meat, scrub the lemon under hot water. With a zester or grater, remove the zest from half of the lemon. Extract 2 teaspoons of the juice; set aside. Peel and mince the garlic. Combine the lemon zest and garlic with the oil.

2 Wipe the lamb with a clean, damp cloth; if necessary, remove the bone splinters. To prevent the chops from curling while they cook, make small cuts in the fat. Brush the meat on all sides with the garlic oil and set them aside to marinate.

3 For the pesto, rinse and pat dry the mint; chop the leaves. Chop the almonds in a food processor. Add the mint and olive oil and puree; season with salt, pepper, and the reserved lemon juice.

4 Heat a grill pan or skillet. Cook the lamb on both sides over high heat for about 2–3 minutes. Season with salt and pepper; serve with the mint pesto.

Purpugia
Sautéed and Marinated Pork (Sardinia)

INGREDIENTS for 4:
2 sage sprigs
4 rosemary sprigs
$\frac{1}{2}$ bunch mint
4 fresh bay leaves
4 garlic cloves
2 tsp black peppercorns
2 tsp fennel seeds
2 cups dry white wine
$\frac{1}{2}$ cup white wine vinegar
$1\frac{3}{4}$ lb tenderloin
4 Tbsp olive oil
Salt

PREPARATION TIME: 25 minutes
MARINATING TIME: 1–2 days
PER PORTION: about 315 calories

1 Rinse the herbs and pat them dry; remove the leaves from the stems. Set aside $\frac{1}{2}$ tablespoon of mint and mince the remaining herbs and bay leaf. Peel and thinly slice the garlic. Crush the peppercorns and fennel seeds with a blade of a large knife or in a mortar.

2 Mix the chopped herbs, crushed spices, garlic, wine, and vinegar in a large bowl. Trim the sinewy parts from the meat; cut the meat into slices $\frac{1}{5}$-inch thick. Place the meat in the marinade and set it aside to marinate for about 1–2 days. Occasionally turn the slices of meat over and stir them into the marinade.

3 Remove the meat from the marinade and pat it dry. Heat two skillets and pour in the oil (or cook the meat in batches in the same skillet). Brown the meat over high heat for about 4 minutes on each side or until they are slightly brown. Mince the reserved mint leaves. Season the meat and serve sprinkled with the mint.

Involtini di Cotiche al Ragù

Pork Belly Rolls in Ragù Sauce (Campania)

INGREDIENTS for 4:

¾ pound beef stew meat (shank or chuck)

1 onion

1 sprig each thyme, rosemary, oregano, and borage

1 fresh bay leaf

1 piece organic lemon zest

2 Tbsp olive oil

1 can peeled tomatoes (about 14–16 oz)

1 small can tomato paste (about 4 oz)

1 cup dry red wine

½ cup beef or vegetable broth

Salt and freshly ground pepper

4 garlic cloves

1 small bunch parsley

3 Tbsp raisins

3 Tbsp pine nuts

¼ cup freshly grated pecorino cheese

1 lb thinly sliced pork belly, free of rind and gristle (see Tip)

PREPARATION TIME: 45 minutes
COOKING TIME: 2½ hours
PER PORTION: about 700 calories

1 Cut the beef into 2-inch cubes. Peel and mince the onion. Rinse and pat dry the herbs. Mince the leaves and the lemon zest.

2 Heat the oil in a large saucepan or Dutch oven. Working in batches, if necessary, brown the beef. Add the herb mixture and onion and sauté briefly. Add the tomatoes, tomato paste, red wine, and broth. Season with salt and pepper and simmer for about 1½ hours or until the meat is tender.

3 Remove the meat from the sauce and set it aside to cool. When the meat has cooled, chop it into small pieces; peel and

mince the garlic. Rinse and pat dry the parsley; mince leaves.

4 Combine the chopped meat with the garlic, parsley, raisins, pine nuts, and cheese; stir to combine and season with salt and pepper (taste before seasoning as the pecorino is already salty). Spread some of this mixture over each slice of pork belly; roll the pieces up and secure them with toothpicks.

5 Place the rolls in the tomato sauce and cook over low heat for 1 more hour; serve them with the sauce.

Tip: In the original regional version, this specialty is made with meat-filled pork rind; pork belly is lighter, but it may be difficult to find. Substitute with pancetta if you like.

189

Manzo Arrotolato con Lenticchie
Beef Roll with Lentils (Campania)

INGREDIENTS for 4–6:

For the roast:

4 garlic cloves

1 large red onion

2 sprigs each rosemary, thyme, oregano, sage, and basil

6 Tbsp olive oil

3 oz sun-dried tomatoes (preserved in oil)

1 ball fresh mozzarella cheese (about 4–5 oz)

Salt and freshly grated pepper

1 beef (about 2 lb shoulder or flank steak)

¾ cup dry red wine

2 bay leaves

For the lentils:

1 cup brown lentils

1 dried peperoncino (chili pepper)

2 garlic cloves

1 carrot

1 celery rib

2 medium tomatoes

3 Tbsp olive oil

1 cup dry red wine

2 tsp sugar

½ bunch basil

Salt

1 Tbsp red wine vinegar

PREPARATION TIME: 1 hour
COOKING TIME: 2 hours
PER PORTION (WITH 6 SERVINGS): about 630 calories

Recommended Wine:
A robust red wine such as Aglianico or Taurasi.

In the Cilento area, Campania's most fertile coastal land, there are many buffalo that provide the milk for the famous mozzarella di bufala. The buffalo bulls graze free on the large plains around the cheese factories. Their meat is flavorful; originally, this roast was made with buffalo meat. If you travel through Cilento, you should try buffalo at least once (it tastes somewhat similar to the American beefalo) and the air-dried meat called *bresaola*.

1 For the roast, peel and mince the garlic and onions. Rinse and pat dry the herbs; mince the leaves. Heat 3 tablespoons of oil in a Dutch oven or roasting pan. Sauté the onion and garlic over low heat for 10 minutes or until they are limp and translucent. Add the herbs and continue sautéing. Dice the mozzarella and sun-dried tomatoes. Allow the onion mixture to cool and mix it with the tomatoes and cheese; season with salt and pepper.

2 Preheat the oven to 350° F (if convection oven 275° F). If the piece of beef is thick, butterfly it by cutting it open like a book; take care not to cut through the entire piece. Season the meat with salt and pepper. Top with the onion mixture, roll it up, and tie it with kitchen twine.

3 Heat the remaining 3 tablespoons of oil in the pan. Brown the meat roll on all sides. Transfer it to the oven and roast for about 30 minutes. Add the red wine and bay leaves and continue to roast for about 1½ more hours; check the roast occasionally and add more wine if necessary.

4 After the meat has roasted for about 45 minutes, rinse the lentils in a colander. Crush the peperoncino. Peel and chop the garlic and carrot. Trim, and chop the celery. Bring a pot of water to a boil, Blanch the tomatoes; rinse under cold water. Core, peel, and finely chop them.

5 Heat 2 tablespoons of oil in a large saucepan. Sauté the garlic, peperoncino, carrot, and celery. Add the lentils and 2 cups of water. Bring to a boil, reduce the heat, and simmer for about 40–60 minutes; do not let the lentils get too soft. If necessary, add some water to the simmering lentils.

6 Meanwhile, sauté the tomatoes in the remaining oil in a small skillet for about 10 minutes or until they have fallen apart. Heat the wine and sugar in a small saucepan and cook down to about a half. Shred the basil leaves in small pieces. Mix the lentils, tomatoes, and the reduced wine, and season with salt and pepper. Sprinkle with basil.

7 Let the roast stand for 10 minutes at room temperature, then slice it thin and arrange on a platter. Taste the sauce and season if necessary; add it to roast. Serve the lentils separately. White bread or rosemary potatoes make a fine accompaniment to this dish.

Carciofi al Forno

Artichoke Gratin (Sardinia)

INGREDIENTS for 4:

12 small artichokes

Juice of $\frac{1}{2}$ lemon

Salt and freshly ground pepper

$\frac{1}{2}$ bunch parsley

4 garlic cloves

$\frac{1}{2}$ cup ricotta cheese

1 egg

2 Tbsp plain breadcrumbs

3 Tbsp freshly grated pecorino cheese

$\frac{1}{4}$ cup olive oil

PREPARATION TIME: 30 minutes
BAKING TIME: 20 minutes
PER PORTION: about 295 calories

1 Rinse the artichokes and remove the external leaves. Peel the stems and slice off the pointed tops of the leaves. Cut the artichokes lengthwise in half; remove the chokes.

2 Bring $\frac{1}{2}$ cup salted water and the lemon juice to a rolling boil in a saucepan. Add the artichokes and simmer for about 5 minutes. Drain and place the artichokes in a baking dish.

3 Preheat the oven to 400° F (if convection 375° F). Rinse and pat dry the parsley and peel the garlic; mince the garlic and parsley leaves. Mix these with the ricotta, egg, breadcrumbs, and cheese; season with salt and pepper.

4 Spoon the ricotta mixture over the artichokes; drizzle with the olive oil. Bake the artichokes for about 20 minutes or until the ricotta has browned and the artichokes are soft; they are tasty hot, warm, at room temperature, or cold.

Fiori di Zucca al Forno

Baked Zucchini Blossoms (Lazio)

INGREDIENTS for 4:

3 medium tomatoes

1 bunch borage (substitute with arugula and fresh lemon balm)

2 garlic cloves

1 small green peperoncino (chili pepper)

12 zucchini blossoms (substitute with pumpkin blossoms)

Salt

$\frac{1}{4}$ cup olive oil

PREPARATION TIME: 25 minutes
BAKING TIME: 20 minutes
PER PORTION: about 135 calories

1 Bring a large pot of water to a boil. Blanch the tomatoes; rinse under cold water. Core, peel and cut them into eighths.

2 Rinse and pat dry the borage and slice the leaves. Peel and slice the garlic. Trim and thinly slice the peperoncino, including the seeds.

3 Preheat the oven to 350° F (if convection oven 325° F). Carefully open the zucchini blossoms and using a small paring knife remove the stamens. Rinse the blossoms in cold water and pat dry.

4 Mix the tomatoes with the borage, garlic, and peperoncino; season with salt. Stir in the blossoms and transfer to a baking dish. Drizzle with the oil and bake on the middle oven rack for about 20 minutes or until the blossoms have fallen apart.

Parmigiana di Zucchini e Acciughe
Zucchini Casserole with Anchovies and Mozzarella (Campania)

At the Campo de' Fiori, the most beautiful market of the Italian capital, shoppers and visitors find an amazingly diverse selection of vegetables. Roman cuisine is famous for its abundance of vegetarian and vegetable dishes; many of these are of Jewish origin. Another common filling for zucchini blossoms is mozzarella and anchovies. Pumpkin blossoms are somewhat larger than those from zucchini; however, the flavors of both are very similar and they can be used interchangeably.

INGREDIENTS for 4:

2 lb zucchini (5–6 small)

1 large red bell pepper

2 red onions

$\frac{1}{2}$ bunch oregano

10 anchovies (preserved in oil)

8 Tbsp olive oil

Salt and freshly ground pepper

2 balls fresh mozzarella cheese (about 4–5 oz each)

3 Tbsp freshly grated parmesan cheese

PREPARATION TIME: 30 minutes
BAKING TIME: 30 minutes
PER PORTION: about 455 calories

1   Trim and cut the zucchini lengthwise into very thin slices.

2   Trim, seed, and slice the pepper. Peel and slice the onions. Rinse and pat dry the oregano; mince the leaves. Cut the anchovies into slivers.

3   Heat 4 tablespoons of oil in a skillet. Working in batches if necessary, sauté the zucchini over medium heat until golden brown on both sides. Season with salt and pepper and set on a paper towel–lined platter.

4   When all zucchini slices are fried, heat 2 more tablespoons of olive oil and sauté the pepper, onions, and oregano for about 5 minutes. Combine vegetables with the anchovies in a mixing bowl; season with salt and pepper. Thinly slice the mozzarella.

5   Preheat the oven to 350° F (if convection 325° F). In a baking dish, layer the zucchini, sautéed vegetables, and mozzarella.

Sprinkle with the parmesan and drizzle with the remaining olive oil.

6   Bake on the middle oven rack for about 30 minutes or until the top is golden brown. Serve hot, at room temperature, or cold.

Both Campania and Calabria compete for credit of this vegetarian dish that is most often prepared with eggplant. Campania is known for its mozzarella; Calabria for its eggplant. Whoever may be the creator, this parmigiana is delicious hot as a side dish for fish or meat, or as a room temperature or cold antipasto. Made with zucchini, the specialty is healthy and light; during summertime the dish can be a main course for two.

Insalata di Zucchini Crudi

Raw Zucchini Salad (Lazio)

INGREDIENTS for 4:

1 lb small zucchini

Salt and freshly ground pepper

2 medium pears

3–4 arugula leaves

1 organic lemon

Pinch sugar

$\frac{1}{4}$ cup olive oil

3 Tbsp pine nuts

2 oz ricotta salata (aged ricotta cheese or pecorino)

PREPARATION TIME: 30 minutes
PER PORTION: about 260 calories

1 Trim the zucchini and cut into matchsticks; season with plenty of salt and set them aside to drain.

2 Peel, core, and cube the pear. Rinse, pat dry, trim, and chop the arugula. Scrub the lemon under hot water. With a zester or a grater, remove the zest from half of the lemon; extract the juice from half.

3 Whisk together the lemon juice, salt, pepper, and sugar to make an almost creamy dressing. Drain the zucchini and toss with the pear, arugula, and dressing. Arrange the salad on serving plates.

4 Toast the pine nuts in a dry skillet and sprinkle them over the salad. Shave the cheese over the salad and serve immediately.

Ceci al Finocchio

Chickpeas with Fennel (Sardinia)

INGREDIENTS for 4:

$\frac{2}{3}$ cup dried chickpeas

1 tsp baking soda

2 small fennel bulbs (with lots of green tops)

2 garlic cloves

$\frac{1}{2}$ bunch dill

1–2 oz pancetta (substitute with bacon)

4 Tbsp olive oil

2 tsp fennel seeds

$\frac{1}{2}$ cup beef or vegetable broth

1 Tbsp tomato paste

Salt and freshly ground pepper

PREPARATION TIME: 30 minutes
SOAKING TIME: Overnight
COOKING TIME: $1\frac{1}{4}$ hours
PER PORTION: about 300 calories

1 Soak the chickpeas in plenty of water overnight.

2 Drain the chickpeas, place them in a pot, and cover them with fresh water. Add the baking soda and bring to a rolling boil. Simmer the chickpeas, covered, for about 1 hour or until relatively soft.

3 Rinse and trim the fennel; set aside the greens. Cut the fennel bulbs lengthwise into quarters. Remove the core and slice the fennel $\frac{1}{4}$-inch thick. Peel and mince the garlic. Rinse and pat dry the dill. Mince the fennel greens and dill; set aside 1 tablespoon. Slice the pancetta into strips or chop it.

4 Heat the pancetta and 2 tablespoons of oil in a large saucepan. Sauté the fennel, garlic, and fennel seeds. Add the chickpeas, broth, minced herbs, and tomato paste. Season with salt and pepper and simmer, covered, for about 15 minutes or until

Cavolfiore Gratinato
Cauliflower Gratin (Campania)

the fennel has softened but is still firm to the bite. Taste for seasoning and add the reserved herbs. Drizzle with the remaining olive oil and serve.

Finocchio selvatico is the wild fennel that thrives throughout the hot Mediterranean regions in meadows and field. Outside of Italy, it is not easily available; the flavor of wild fennel can be best recreated with a mixture of dill, fennel seeds, and fennel green as is in this recipe.

INGREDIENTS for 4:

1 large cauliflower (1–2 lb)
2 medium tomatoes
Salt and freshly ground pepper
4 anchovies (preserved in oil)
1 Tbsp capers
1/2 bunch parsley
2 garlic cloves
3 Tbsp pine nuts
5–6 oz *caciocavallo* (aged cow's milk cheese or young pecorino)
6 Tbsp olive oil
1/3 cup plain breadcrumbs

PREPARATION TIME: 45 minutes
PER PORTION: about 540 calories

1 Rinse and trim the cauliflower; divide it in small florets. Chop the core. Bring a large pot of salted water to a boil. Blanch the tomatoes; rinse under cold water, leaving the water on the

stove. Cook in it the cauliflower florets for about 5 minutes or until they are still firm to the bite. Drain and rinse under cold water.

2 Preheat the oven to 425° F (if convection oven 400° F). Mince the anchovies; drain, rinse, and chop the capers. Rinse and pat dry the parsley; mince the leaves. Peel the garlic and crush it through a garlic press. Core, peel, and dice the tomatoes. Chop the pine nuts. Remove the rind from the cheese and grate the cheese.

3 Heat 3 tablespoons of oil in a skillet. Cook the breadcrumbs and pine nuts over medium heat for about 2–3 minutes. Stir in the anchovies, capers, parsley, garlic, tomatoes, and cheese.

4 Put the cauliflower in a gratin dish and top with the breadcrumb

mixture; drizzle with the remaining olive oil. Bake on the middle oven rack for about 15 minutes or until golden brown.

Cauliflower and broccoli are favorites throughout Italy. In Lazio, cauliflower and broccoli are also prepared *alla vignarola*, or vineyard-style. For this specialty, bacon is rendered together with chopped hazelnuts or walnuts and olive oil. The vegetables are dressed with this mixture.

195

Olive Oil—Liquid Gold

It is used for roasting; it dresses the salad and is used as a flavoring

Sabina, located in the northern most area of Lazio is renowned for its excellent olive oil and is home of the oldest olive tree in Europe. It is apparently 1500 years old. Olive oil has been a part of the cuisines of Italy for centuries (although butter predominates north of Bologna).

Attention to detail from tree to bottle. In the production of olive oil several factors play a role in determining the quality of the oil: How the trees are tended; the time of harvest; how ripe the olives are (very ripe olives have high acidic content); the soil and climate; whether the olives are pressed immediately after the harvest (to prevent them from fermenting). How the olives are processed affects the oil as well. The most prized oils are pressed without heat—thus the term "cold-pressed"—and are from the first pressing of the olives.

Markers of quality. Olive oils are labeled based on their level of acidity. In Italy, olio di oliva extra vergine (extra virgin olive oil) has less than 1 percent acidity; sopraffino vergine (superfine virgin) less than 1.5 percent; fino vergine (fine) has less than 3 percent; vergine has not more than 4 percent. Oils labeled vergine must also be from the first pressing. Oil that has higher acidity content will be refined (heated and purified) and will only be sold labeled as "olive oil."

However, not only the acidity determines the quality and flavor of the olive oil. Where the olives grow is also a factor. Some olive growers are labeling their products with the region of origin, much like wines. "Bottled in Italy" means only that the oil—which could be from Spain or France—was bottled in Italy. "Produced and bottled in Italy" is somewhat better but still not precise enough. Look for the region of origin on the label and either DOP (certified and protected designation of origin) or DOC (certified designation of origin within a delimited regional area). Olive oil producers are also beginning to include the olive variety that was used to produce the oil. Because different olives have different flavor profiles, so too do their oils. This helps cooks to select oils for their character and flavor.

Differences in flavor. Olive oils in Italy are subdivided in three main categories. Light olive oils are called *fruttato leggero* and taste mild; their scent is light and somewhat reminiscent of grass and herbs; they have an aroma of nuts such as almonds or pine nuts. These oils go well with steamed fish, vegetables, and white meats that were prepared without lots of spices. The medium-fruity oils are *fruttato medio*; these oils' scent is somewhat stronger. In flavor these oils are still reminiscent of grass and herbs; however, their aroma is also reminiscent of not yet ripe tomatoes or of leaves of tomato vines. These oils are mildly bitter and somewhat tart; they go well with fish and seafood and are well suited for salads or for drizzling over pasta. The stronger oils are called *fruttato intenso*; they still smell of grass but also of tomatoes and artichokes. They are bitter, intense, and almost spicy; they go well with grilled meat and fish, vegetables, and especially with roasted or toasted bread. Olive oil loses flavor when heated. For this reason, even if dishes are cooked with olive oil, for flavoring purposes it is best using cold-pressed oil for drizzling over the food.

a In Italy, many people still make their own olive oil. Even the smallest quantities are accepted for processing by olive oil mills. One needs only to take good care of the trees (especially with pruning, to allow the fruits to get enough sun), harvest the olives at the ideal time, and carry the olives to the mill.

b An especially gentle method of harvesting olives: the olives are raked from the branch by hand with a special rake tool. Netting at the foot of the tree catches the olives as they fall. c The farmer recognizes when harvesting time is right: the olives begin to turn purple, yet are still tinged with green. d In the oil mill, olives move on a conveyor belt and are first rinsed. A few leaves and twigs are no big deal; however, there should not be too many. e According to ancient tradition, some mills still process and crush the olives between two huge stone wheels until they are reduced to a pulp; other mills have modernized their methods with stainless steel machinery. f Freshly pressed olive oil is still cloudy and can be filtered or not before being filled into bottles.

Crostata al Limone
Lemon Tart (Campania)

INGREDIENTS for 12:

For the dough:

1¾ cups all-purpose flour

¼ cup sugar

1 tsp vanilla sugar

Pinch salt

5 Tbsp butter

1 egg yolk

For the filling:

4 large organic lemons

2 eggs

1¼ cup sugar

1 container ricotta cheese (about 16 oz)

2 Tbsp confectioners' sugar

PREPARATION TIME: 1 hour
REFRIGERATION TIME: 30 minutes
BAKING TIME: 45 minutes
PER PORTION: about 330 calories

The Amalfi coast is famous for its winding roads that overlook the sea, for its beautiful scenic landscapes, and for its scented lemon groves. And the citrus fruits there are indeed remarkable: they are larger than those that grow anywhere else in southern Italy, and they are also juicy and full of flavor. Those from Minori are especially renowned; they are not only used for desserts but also processed to make the fine limoncello liqueur that should be served frozen or ice cold in small frosted glasses.

Tip: The sugar syrup in which the lemons will cook will have a wonderful flavor. Drizzle it over the crostata to make a sweet, delicious glaze that will not run over the top of the tart when sliced.

Recommended Beverage:
Ice-cold limoncello

1 For the dough, mix the flour, sugar, vanilla sugar, and salt on a work surface. Make a well in the mixture. Cut the butter in small cubes and put it and the egg yolk in the well.

2 Work all ingredients by hand, kneading to make a smooth, silken dough. Add a few drops of water if the dough is too dry. Shape the dough into a ball.

3 Roll out the dough between two sheets of plastic wrap or waxed paper slightly larger than your tart pan (you can also use an 11–12-inch springform pan. Line the pan with the dough, leaving a ¾-inch high border. Refrigerate the dough for about 30 minutes.

4 Meanwhile, for the filling, scrub 2 lemons under hot water. With a zester or grater, remove their zest; juice 1 lemon. Cream the eggs with ¾ cup of sugar; fold in the ricotta and mix everything well. Add the lemon zest and juice.

5 Preheat the oven to 350° F (if convection oven 325° F). Spoon the ricotta mixture into the dough shell. Bake on the middle oven rack for 45 minutes or until the crust is golden brown. Cool on a rack.

6 Meanwhile, scrub the remaining lemons under hot water. Slice the lemons very thin and cut each slice into quarters. Combine the remaining sugar with 10 tablespoons of water in a saucepan and bring to a boil. Add the lemon and simmer for 5 minutes; set aside to cool.

7 Before serving, drain the lemon slices and arrange them over the filling. Dust the crostata with confectioners' sugar and caramelize the topping either with a salamander or by placing the pie very briefly under the broiler.

Torta di Fragole

Strawberry Cake (Campania)

INGREDIENTS for 10–12:

For the dough:

Butter and plain breadcrumbs for the baking pan

1 organic lemon / 5 eggs / ³⁄₄ cup sugar

Pinch salt

½ cup flour

1 Tbsp arrowroot or cornstarch

1 tsp baking powder

For the filling:

1 envelope unflavored gelatin

2 lbs fresh small strawberries

3 Tbsp strawberry syrup

2 vanilla beans

1½ cups milk / ½ cup sugar

3 Tbsp arrowroot or cornstarch

4 egg yolks

1 cup heavy cream

PREPARATION TIME: 45 minutes
REFRIGERATION TIME: 2–3 hours
BAKING TIME: 35-40 minutes
PER PORTION (FOR 12 SERVINGS): about 310 calories

1 Preheat the oven to 350° F (if convection oven 325° F). Brush a springform pan (about 11 inches in diameter) with softened butter and dust with the breadcrumbs.

2 For the dough, scrub the lemon under hot water. With a zester or grater, remove the zest. Separate the eggs. Combine the egg whites, 5 tablespoons of cold water, and the salt; beat until stiff peaks form. Lower the mixer speed and add the sugar and lemon zest; add the egg yolks, one at a time, and continue beating until the yolks are thoroughly incorporated. Mix the flour, arrowroot, and baking powder in a medium bowl. Gradually add to the egg mixture, folding well after each addition.

3 Pour the dough in the pan and bake for about 35–45 minutes or until it has risen, it is golden brown and a cake tester comes out clean. Cool the cake in

the pan for 15 minutes, then turn it over on a cooling rack; let the cake cool completely.

4 For the filling, make the gelatin, according to package direction. Clean, hull, and trim the strawberries. In the food processor, puree about one third of the strawberries with the strawberry syrup. Following the gelatin directions, combine the strawberry puree and the gelatin; refrigerate for about 2–3 hours.

5 With a sharp paring knife, slice open the vanilla beans and scrape out the seeds. Combine half of the milk, the vanilla bean and seeds, and the sugar in a small saucepan. Warm the flavored milk over low heat. With a hand mixer, beat the arrowroot, egg yolks. and the remaining milk.

6 Remove the vanilla bean from the simmering milk. Gradually

beat the egg mixture into the simmering milk and heat until it has acquired a pudding-like texture and appearance. Remove from the heat and transfer to a mixing bowl; stir periodically to prevent a skin from forming.

7 Cut the remaining strawberries into small pieces. Beat the heavy cream until stiff peaks form and fold it into the vanilla-flavored cream. Fold in half of the remaining strawberries.

8 Cut the cake horizontally. Spread the bottom layer of cake with about half of the vanilla cream. Cover this with the top layer of cake. Mix the remaining vanilla cream with the strawberry gelatin and cover the entire cake with this. Cut the cake into slices and serve, garnished with the remaining strawberries.

Seadas

Sweet Pecorino Ravioli with Honey Sauce (Sardinia)

INGREDIENTS for 6:

For the dough:

1 large organic lemon

2 cups bread flour + flour for working

2 eggs

3 Tbsp lard or vegetable shortening

2 Tbsp honey

Pinch salt

1 egg white

2 cups olive oil

For the filling and the sauce:

1 quince

1 cup dry white wine

1/3 cup honey

1 Tbsp lemon juice

5 1/2 oz very fresh pecorino cheese (see Tip)

Confectioners' sugar, to dust

PREPARATION TIME: 1 hour
RESTING TIME: 30 minutes
PER PORTION: about 505 calories

1   Scrub the lemon under hot water. With a zester or grater, remove the zest. Extract 1 tablespoon of juice and reserve for the filling. Combine the lemon zest and flour; make a well in the flour and add the egg, lard, salt, and honey. Knead to make a silken dough. Form into a ball, wrap in plastic wrap, and set aside at room temperature for about 30 minutes.

2   For the sauce, peel, core, and dice the quince. Bring the wine, honey, lemon juice, and quince to a simmer over low heat. Cook for about 30 minutes or until the quince is soft. Cut off the rind and grate the cheese.

3   Knead the dough once more and cut it into halves. On a floured work surface, roll out the dough about 1/10-inch thick and cut out as many 4-inch diameter dough circles as you can. Brush the borders of each circle with egg white and put a little pecorino in the middle of each circle, leaving some space around the borders. Roll out the remaining dough and cut out the same number of circles. Top the cheese circles with the plain circles; press the two circles together, sealing well.

4   Heat the olive oil in a saucepan or deep frying pan; the oil is ready for frying when small bubbles of oil show around a wooden spoon dipped in the hot oil.

5   Fry the ravioli in the hot oil in batches until they are golden brown. Remove them with a slotted spoon and drain them on a thick layer of paper towels. Distribute the ravioli among serving plates; drizzle the ravioli with some honey and dust them with confectioners' sugar.

Tip: Sardinian cooks use a very fresh pecorino cheese that is usually 2 days old. In this country, this fresh pecorino is rarely available; to substitute for it, use a fresh, mild, plain-flavored cheese such as a goat cheese or ricotta. Sardinian cooks also season the fresh pecorino with a pinch of salt before encasing the raviolis. Taste your cheese before you add any salt to it—you may very well find that it doesn't need any.

201

Abruzzi, Molise, and Apulia

Mountains and Sea: high peaks, gentle hills, and lots of beaches

The Region and Its Products
From the highest peaks of the Italian Apennines to the heel of the boot

Natives of these regions ski and hike along and around Abruzzi's Gran Sasso with its fascinating nature landscape. Since ancient times, people have also called Marina di Leuca the most southern point of Apulia's coast, where the Adriatic meets the Ionian Sea, the end of the world. In between there are woods, rolling hills, and places of absolutely breathtaking beauty and wonderful scenery.

The Land of the Shepherds.
The backcountry of Abruzzi and Molise are mountainous and isolated; these are ideal conditions for shepherds who move throughout the area with their sheep. Sheep and goat (as well as lamb and kid) provide the meat and cheese that make the base for the very tasty cuisine of this area. These isolated areas are also where precious ingredients come forth: Saffron grows throughout the plateau of Navelli and especially flavorful lentils around San Stefano. Throughout the entire region, dishes are spiced generously with peperoncino. The locals say that they need the fiery spice especially in winter to keep enough inner warmth. The pod, which locals lovingly call diavolino, or the little devil, thus has become synonymous with this way of cooking. Should a dish be labeled all'abruzzese, it will be for sure marked by the spiciness of peperoncini.

The Coast of Fishermen.
Apulia—the "heel" of Italy's boot—is rather long and narrow and offers about 500 miles of coastline; Abruzzi and Molise add another 125 miles. It is no wonder that fishing plays a major role in the local cuisine. Bream, mullet, sardines, squid, tuna, and swordfish are caught wild, whereas mussels and oysters are cultivated by Apulians in the warm and shallow waters of the lagoons of Varano and Taranto (also called *mar piccolo*, or small sea).

The Land of Farmers.
The Tavoliere is the second largest plain in Italy after the Po Basin. Since ancient times, wheat has been the staple grain. Other major crops include legumes, olives, and many vegetables, including the especially flavorful cime di rapa (also called broccoli rabe or rapini), cicoria (a type of dandelion), artichokes, tomatoes, eggplants, and an amazing array of peppers and potatoes. The peninsula of Salento is home to numerous vineyards, and has many olive groves as well.

Campo Imperatore, around the Gran Sassa, is an imposing plateau that is approximately 17 miles long and 5 miles wide. On this land there is plenty of space for sheep, and it is a popular grazing spot in summer.

Around Alberobello in the Apulia is *trulli* land. The small white huts have pointed and gray-scaled roofs that are built with stones simply positioned one on top of the other.

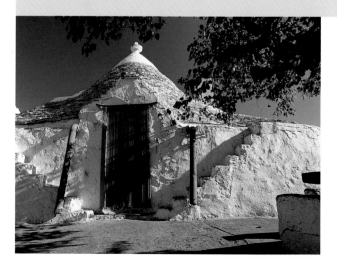

It isn't just Apulian sheepherders who tend their flocks throughout the region. Sheepherders from the surrounding regions have for generations made this area a temporary home for themselves and their animals. In this land of rugged beauty, they find innumerable plants and herbs that ultimately give the sheep's meat such wonderful flavor.

Pure spring waters such as those from Fara San Martino make doughs for bread and pasta especially delicious. Many pasta manufacturers have moved to this region (as well as Marche). Proximity to the wheat, which grows especially well here, is another factor.

Isola di San Domino is the largest island of the Tremiti island group along the Gargano in Apulia. The island is rich with pine groves and oak forests, and has a wonderfully clear sea water.

Mediterranean peace: When it is very hot, the best place to be is in the shade, perhaps doing work that allows one to stay seated. Dried herbs like oregano are preserved in jars after they are shredded, which adds aroma to sauces during the winter months.

The Cuisine

Marked by farmers and sheepherders, generously blessed with nature's bounty

Mountains, hills, and sea; in the backcountry are sheep, goats, and pigs; from the coastal area are the riches of the sea; from all over abundant vegetables, legumes, and lots of olive oil.

Main ingredient wheat. Plenty of fine-quality wheat is grown throughout these regions, and it is used to make legendary breads and wonderful pastas. Focaccie (flatbreads) might be flavored simply with herbs or olives in the dough or topped or stuffed with vegetables such as small tomatoes or zucchini slices. Focaccia dough is also used to make the twice-baked, long-lasting *taralli* and *friselle*. Taralli are small crunchy dough rings that go very well with an aperitivo (often they are made with herbs and spicy peperoncini in the dough); friselle are larger flat pieces of dough that in the old days farmers took to the field and that today are briefly soaked and topped with diced tomatoes and offered as antipasto. The most famous pasta in Apulia are orecchiette, or "little ears." Other varieties are also usually small in size. People in Abruzzi have created an especially interesting dish that is prepared with a type of guitar shaped tool that works with pulled side strings. Cooks prepare a pasta dough with or without eggs; roll out the dough like a sheet, and place the dough on the tool's sides. A rolling pin is once more passed over the sheet of dough, and the strings of the tool cut the pasta into what is called *maccheroni alla chitarra*. The dish is served either with spicy tomato sauce or with an aromatic sauce made of lamb.

Not without vegetables. Perhaps no region in Italy uses more vegetables than Apulia. Vegetables are grilled or braised or marinated or preserved in oil for antipasto; they are prepared with pasta and legumes for primo; they are stewed in ragùs or as side dishes. Legumes, especially chickpeas, borlotti, and fava beans, which are large beans that look like lima beans, are cooked and dressed with olive oil and spices and are offered on the antipasti table; they are added to thick soups and to pastas, or are pureed to be served with other vegetables. Legumes can also come with a secondo, such as a squid stew cooked with a spicy tomato sauce or a fresh sausage served grilled.

Fish or meat. Here, too, diners may be overwhelmed by the variety. Along the coastal area there is fish—it might be a spicy calamari salad or orecchiette with swordfish or stuffed and baked mussels. Inland, choices will include specialties of lamb, pork, and occasionally also baby goat. Alla Molisana, the baby goat, is prepared with herbs and peperoncini in a tomato sauce moistened with wine. Lamb is often roasted in the oven or stewed in a Dutch oven. A favorite specialty of Abruzzi is a hearty ragù made of lamb, egg, and cheese, flavored with lemon juice.

c

d

e

a   Apulia's most famous pasta, orecchiette, shaped like little ears, are still homemade. Their texture is rough to make sure that they trap and absorb the sauce.

b   Vegetables are important ingredients in the southern regions. Grilled or roasted peppers are especially tasty; try them peeled and flavored with garlic, lemon juice, and olive oil.

c   Many small farmers from the surrounding areas attend the open market L'Aquila. Only those products that are in season and that are ripe for picking are offered.

d   Apulia's bread is famous throughout Italy—because it is tasty and healthy and because in this region it is prepared with many variations. Sometimes it is prepared with potato dough, sometimes it is prepared with olives, and sometimes it is flavored with herbs. It is also always prepared with the wheat that grows in the region.

e   Confetti are the colorful sugar almond candies made in Sulmona; they are distributed during weddings or used to put together fantastic sweet creations.

The Wines

Blessed by the sun, kept cool by a sea breeze—reds are here at their best

Apulia and Abruzzi are large wine-producing regions, but the wines are not known for their quality. People of the region heartily enjoy these robust and interesting wines—still purchasable at very reasonable prices.

Between two seas. Apulia has a coast that is especially long and relatively flat. During hot summer days, the cool breeze that blows the Adriatic to the Ionian Sea creates a mild current that favors the vines. Three grapes are Apulia's best: the Negroamaro, Primitivo, and Uva di Troia. Negroamaro thrives especially throughout the lower southern peninsula of Salento and is used to make smooth, long-lasting wines and a refreshing rosé. Wines that are made from the Negroamaro include Copertino, one of the best wines of Salento and the DOC wines from around Brindisi, Leverano, and Lizzana. Negroamaro is sometimes mixed with other red varieties, for example, in Salice Salentino it is added to Malvasia Nera. Primitivo grows in the south and is closely related to California's Zinfandel; in this case the name Primitivo indicates that the grapes ripen relatively early. Wines made from this robust grape variety are purplish and very fruity. Their best flavor comes through when the wine is one to two years old. Primitivo wines are especially found around Manduria and Sava. The red Uva di Troia plays a major role in the northern area of Apulia around the famous Castel del Monte. Apulia's white wines are made with Trebbiano (called here Bombino), Malvasia Bianco, and other international grape varieties. Gravina, made with Malvasia, Greco di Tufo, and Bianco d'Alessano, is also a light, pleasant wine of this area.

Reds, Rosés, and Whites. In the Abruzzi area dominate two grape varieties: the Montepulciano and the Trebbiano d'Abruzzo, a high quality sub-variety of Trebbiano. These were the two original DOC wines. Currently the distinction is made between the Montepulciano; there is the Montepulciano d'Abruzzo and the DOCG wine made from grapes of the Colline Teramane, which grow in cooler and hilly climates and produce the best reds of the regions. Montepulciano is a deep red, well rounded wine that is rich in tannins; in a similarly delicious rosé variation the same wine is called Cerasuolo. Local Trebbiano grapes make a full-bodied, aromatic white wine that can be also aged. Wines from the Molise region are rarely exported; both DOC wines from Biferno and Molise are almost always consumed locally. Biferno wines are available as red, rosé, and white; they taste pleasantly refreshing and fruity. They are made from Montepulciano (with Aglianico and the rosé also with Trebbiano) and Trebbiano (with Malvasia).

Left: In the renowned vineyard owned by Gianni Masciarelli as in almost all vineyards, olive trees grow alongside the grape vines.
Above: Famous samples of the region (from left to right)—Salice Salentino, Montepulciano d'Abruzzo, Trebbiano d'Abruzzo, Amina.

Regional Recipes

Focus: Vegetables, pasta, legumes—alone or combined with fish and meats

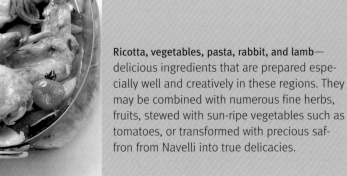

Ricotta, vegetables, pasta, rabbit, and lamb—delicious ingredients that are prepared especially well and creatively in these regions. They may be combined with numerous fine herbs, fruits, stewed with sun-ripe vegetables such as tomatoes, or transformed with precious saffron from Navelli into true delicacies.

Polpette di Ricotta

Ricotta "Meatballs" (Apulia)

INGREDIENTS for 6:

9 slices stale white bread

1 bunch parsley

1 red peperoncino (chili pepper)

2 garlic cloves

1 organic lemon

$\frac{1}{2}$ cup pitted green olives

1 cup ricotta cheese

2 eggs

1–2 oz freshly grated pecorino Romano or parmesan cheese (about 3–4 Tbsp)

Salt and freshly ground pepper

2 cups olive oil

PREPARATION TIME: 40 minutes
PER PORTION: about 360 calories

1   Crumble the bread and soak it in lukewarm water for about 10 minutes. Rinse and pat dry the parsley and mince the leaves. Rinse and trim the peperoncino and mince it with the seeds. Peel and mince the garlic. Scrub the lemon with hot water. With a zester or grater, remove the zest from half of the lemon. Chop the olives.

2   Drain the bread and squeeze out the remaining water. Tear the bread into small pieces and mix it well with the garlic, peperoncino, parsley, lemon zest, olives, ricotta, eggs, and cheese; season with salt and pepper.

3   Heat the oil in a large, deep skillet. With a melon baller, form small balls of the mixture and fry these for about 4 minutes. Remove with a slotted spoon and place them to drain on several layers of paper towels. Serve hot.

Ricotta al Forno

Baked Ricotta Roll (Abruzzi)

INGREDIENTS for 6:

For the dough:

4 cups all-purpose flour

1 tsp salt

$\frac{1}{2}$ cube fresh yeast (about 1 Tbsp)

Pinch salt

2 Tbsp olive oil

2 dried peperoncini (chili pepper)

1 sprig each rosemary, thyme, oregano, and borage

4 garlic cloves

3 Tbsp freshly grated pecorino cheese

2 cups ricotta

For the salad:

1 small head radicchio

1 bunch arugula

3–4 Romaine lettuce

$\frac{1}{2}$ bunch mint

1 fennel bulb

1 carrot

1 small onion

1 Tbsp white wine vinegar

$\frac{1}{4}$ cup olive oil

Salt and freshly ground pepper

PREPARATION TIME: 50 minutes
RESTING TIME: 1 hour
BAKING TIME: 20 minutes
PER PORTION: about 495 calories

1   For the dough, mix the flour and salt. Sprinkle the yeast and the sugar over $\frac{3}{4}$ cup of lukewarm water; let stand until foamy. Add the yeast sponge and the oil to the flour mixture. Knead to make a smooth dough. Place the dough in a bowl, cover loosely, and set aside to rest at room temperature for 1 hour.

2   Crush the peperoncini. Rinse and pat dry the herbs and mince the leaves. Peel and mince the garlic.

3   Preheat the oven to 425° F (if convection oven 400° F). Line a baking sheet with parchment. Punch down the dough and knead it once more. Roll out the dough to a flat round and place it

Tortino di Verdure

Bean and Dandelion Tartlets (Apulia)

on the baking sheet. Sprinkle with the peperoncini, herbs, garlic, and the pecorino. Top one half of the dough with the ricotta and fold the other half over the ricotta. Press and pinch shut the stuffed dough.

4 Bake the stuffed dough on the middle oven rack for about 20 minutes or until it has puffed and become golden brown.

5 Meanwhile, for the salad, rinse and trim all the greens and the mint. Shred or cut everything into bite-sized pieces. Trim the fennel and peel the carrot; thinly slice both vegetables. Peel and slice the onion. Make a dressing with the vinegar, olive oil, salt, and pepper. Dress the salad greens and vegetables with the dressing; if necessary season everything with more salt. Slice the ricotta roll and serve it with the salad.

INGREDIENTS for 8:
For the filling:
3 Tbsp dried lima beans
Pinch baking soda
7 oz chicory (frisée) or dandelion greens
1–2 small zucchini
½ bunch parsley
1 Tbsp olive oil
1 egg
⅓ cup freshly grated pecorino Romano cheese
Salt and freshly ground pepper
For the dough:
2 cups all-purpose flour
1 tsp salt
6 Tbsp olive oil
1 egg yolk

PREPARATION TIME: 20 minutes
COOKING AND BAKING TIME: 1 hour + 10 minutes
PER PORTION: about 280 calories

1 For the filling, bring the lima beans, baking soda, and 2 cups of water to a boil in a small saucepan. Simmer, partially covered, for about 45 minutes or until the beans are soft. Drain the beans and set them aside to cool.

2 For the dough, mix the flour and salt in a bowl. Mix in the olive oil and egg yolk; one at a time, stir in 4 tablespoons of water. Knead to make a smooth dough. Roll out the dough forming eight 5-inch rounds and transfer these to eight tartlet pans. Refrigerate the crusts.

3 Rinse and trim the chicory, cut into ½-inch slices. Bring a pot of water to a boil. Blanch the chicory for about 1 minute; rinse under cold water and drain.

4 Trim, thinly slice, and cut the zucchini into matchsticks. Rinse

and pat dry the parsley; mince the leaves. Heat the oil in a skillet. Sauté the zucchini for 2–3 minutes or until they are golden brown. Add the parsley.

5 Preheat the oven to 400° F (if convection oven 350° F). With a large fork, mash the lima beans in a large bowl. Mix in the egg and pecorino. Fold in the zucchini and chicory; season with salt and pepper. Fill the tartlet crusts with this mixture. Bake on the middle oven rack for 25 minutes or until the tops are nice and golden brown. Serve, if you like, with cubed tomatoes dressed with salt, pepper, olive oil, and fresh basil.

Pasta—Dough in the Best of Ways
Noodles in a thousand variations—sometimes with and sometimes without egg

Nobody really knows exactly how many pasta variations there are. The shape is perhaps the most important part: the length, size, and texture will determine the suitable sauce. Long noodles prefer creamy, smooth sauces; short and wavy noodles and shapes go well with chunky sauces. The flour used to make the pasta, and whether it includes eggs, are also important.

Pasta secca. Hard wheat, water, and salt – nothing more is required for dry pasta. However, the variations wrought with these three ingredients can be gigantic. The wheat should be hard—that is, it should have a very high protein content. Durum wheat, or semolina, and bread flour are widely available hard wheat flours. When making hard wheat noodles, spelt or farro can be suitable. Water of prime quality is a necessity. In Abruzzi, water flows from the Gran Sasso or from the Maiella—pure mountain spring water.

During production, more details come into play. In the large factories, time is often more important than quality. The dough is processed rapidly, pressed under heavy layers of cutting machines, and dried very rapidly. Producers concerned with quality take a different approach. They use bronze cutters through which the dough is processed slowly. The dough stays tender and the noodles have a rougher texture, which allows the sauce to coat them better. After cutting and pressing, the noodles are dried for about 2 days at a temperature of about 100° F (in a large factory, drying typically takes place at a temperature of 210° F for about 3–4 hours).

Pasta all'uovo. Unlike *pasta secca*, *pasta all'uovo*—pasta with eggs—can be made of soft or hard wheat flour. Other types of flour (for example chestnut flour) can also be viable since the egg keeps the dough together better. Dough prepared with fresh eggs will of course taste better than the one made with powdered eggs. Egg noodles are made similarly to *pasta secca*: The dough should be rolled under heavy bronze presses and the noodles should be allowed enough time to dry before being sold fresh in the stores.

Quality cooking. Pasta requires a *lot* of water in order to cook properly: at least four quarts of water are necessary for a pound of pasta. Salt is added when the water is boiling: for every 4 cups of water 1 teaspoon of salt (for tasting purposes, the water should taste lightly salty). Oil should never be added—it will prevent the sauce from coating the noodles. Noodles should be stirred occasionally to prevent them from sticking to the bottom of the pot and to allow them to cook evenly. Fresh pasta requires only about 3 minutes to cook; dried pasta requires from 7 to 13 minutes depending on size and shape. Don't be a slave to the cooking time indicated on the package. The age of the pasta and the quality of water will affect cooking time. Lifting a noodle out of the boiling water and tasting for doneness is still the best way to know whether the pasta is ready or not. In the center of the pasta should be visible a tiny yellow dot which indicates the pasta is al dente. This is especially important in the case of quality pasta since the noodles will continue to cook after they are drained. When the pasta is done it should be drained immediately, but it should not be rinsed (unless they are used for a pasta salad). To prevent the noodles from sticking together, toss them right away with the sauce or a bit of oil or butter; adding a little of the pasta water is a fat-free alternative.

a Pasta dough is easy to make. The quality of the flour, and in the case of fresh pasta how many eggs are added, are key factors. The basic rule: 1 egg for each cup of flour. In some regions, such as in Piedmont, pasta is made with egg yolks, which impart a lovely yellow color. Kneading the dough well in order to activate the proteins in the flour is also vital.

b–d A skilled pasta maker knows well what is important during the pasta making process: time and patience are essential, especially when making pasta by hand. The dough needs to be as thin as possible since the noodles increase in thickness during the cooking process. The rolling pin should be very dry, dusted liberally with flour; the pasta can be rolled out and cut into favorite shapes. Pasta should be loosened and separated by hand; this helps to prevent the noodles from sticking and allows them to dry out evenly until they are ready to be cooked. e Look on the pasta package: *trafilata al bronzo* indicates that the pasta was rolled and processed with highly valued bronze rollers. f Pasta all'uovo is available fresh or dried. In the latter case, good quality egg noodles are layered thinly on paper sheets included in the package.

Pasta alla Menta con Frutti di Mare
Mint Pasta with Seafood (Apulia)

INGREDIENTS for 4:

For the pasta:

1 large bunch mint

2$\frac{1}{2}$ cups semolina or bread flour

1 tsp salt

3 eggs

1 Tbsp olive oil

For the sauce:

1 lb unpeeled shrimp

4 garlic cloves

2 thyme sprigs

1 dried peperoncino (chili pepper)

4 Tbsp olive oil

$\frac{3}{4}$ cup dry white wine

7 oz cherry tomatoes

1$\frac{1}{2}$ lb clams in the shell

$\frac{1}{2}$ bunch parsley

Salt

Pinch sugar

PREPARATION TIME: 1$\frac{1}{2}$ hours
RESTING AND DRYING TIME:
1$\frac{1}{2}$–2$\frac{1}{2}$ hours
PER PORTION: about 560 calories

Pasta with seafood is a favorite throughout all coastal Italian regions. With its 500-plus miles of coast, Apulia has access to a vast array of fish to prepare—and Apulians have an equally vast number of recipes to prepare these delicious gifts of the water.

Small squid can be used in place of clams. Simply cook them for 1 minute in the shrimp water, and sauté them with the shrimp before adding them to the sauce.

Cut down on the prep time by substituting with dry, flat noodles such as tagliatelle pasta. Arugula, borage, or basil can be used in lieu of mint.

Tip: Fresh pasta can be easily prepared ahead of time and placed to dry on clean dish cloths (for example, in the morning to be ready for dinner that night). Just be sure to turn and loosen the pasta occasionally so it dries evenly and doesn't stick. If necessary, lengthen the cooking time by 1 or 2 minutes. However, don't forget to test the noodles when they are cooking!

Recommended Wine:
A robust white wine such as a Trebbiano d'Abruzzo.

1   For the noodles, rinse and pat dry the mint; mince the leaves. Combine flour, salt, and mint; add the eggs and the oil and knead to make a smooth dough. Set the dough aside to rest for about 30 minutes, wrapped in a clean dish cloth.

2   Knead the dough once more and roll it by hand or through a machine to make very thin pasta sheets. Let the pasta sheets rest for a few minutes, then cut them into $\frac{1}{3}$–$\frac{1}{2}$-inch wide strips. Let the pasta dry on clean, well-floured dish cloths.

3   For the sauce, peel the shrimp, reserving the shells. Slit the shrimp down the outside curve and remove the vein; rinse them and pat dry. Peel and mince the garlic. Rinse and pat dry the thyme; mince the leaves. Crush and crumble the peperoncino.

4 Heat 1 tablespoon of the oil in a skillet. Sauté the shrimp shells over high heat. Add the garlic, thyme, and peperoncino. Stir in the wine and simmer for about 15 minutes; press all the ingredients through a fine-meshed sieve and set the liquid aside.

5 Cut the tomatoes in half. Rinse the clams well; discard those that are open. Rinse and pat dry the parsley; mince the leaves. Bring the shrimp liquid to a simmering boil. Add the tomatoes; season them with the salt and sugar. Add the clams and cook on high heat for about 4 minutes or until they are open. Discard clams that do not open.

6 Meanwhile, for the noodles, bring a large pot of salted water to a boil. Add the pasta and cook for 3 minutes or until al dente.

7 Heat the remaining 3 table-spoons of oil in a skillet. Cook the shrimp for about 1 minute per side. Season them with salt and add them and the parsley to the tomato sauce. Drain the pasta and place in the serving bowls; top with the sauce.

215

Pasta alle Melanzane

Pasta with Eggplant Ragù (Abruzzi)

INGREDIENTS for 4:

1 small eggplant (about 1 lb)

2 dried peperoncini (chili peppers)

4 garlic cloves

1 sprig each thyme, oregano, sage, and mint

3–4 medium tomatoes

$\frac{1}{4}$ cup olive oil

Salt

1 lb *maccheroni alla chitarra* (slightly square long pasta; or spaghetti or linguine)

$\frac{1}{2}$ cup ricotta cheese

PREPARATION TIME: 30 minutes
PER PORTION: about 570 calories

1 Trim, peel, and cube the eggplant. Crush and crumble the peperoncini. Peel and mince the garlic. Rinse and pat dry the herbs; mince the leaves. Bring a large pot of salted water to a boil. Blanch the tomatoes and rinse

them under cold water, leaving the water boiling. Core, peel, and cube them.

2 Heat the oil in a large skillet. Sauté the eggplant; add the peperoncini, garlic, and herbs. Add the tomatoes, season with salt, and simmer, covered, over low heat for about 15 minutes. If necessary moisten the ragù with a few tablespoons of water.

3 Meanwhile, cook the pasta in the boiling water according to label directions or until al dente.

4 Taste the eggplant and adjust the seasonings. Distribute the ricotta evenly over the ragù and allow it to melt. Drain the noodles and distribute them in preheated serving plates; top the noodles with the eggplant ragù.

Orecchiette ai Funghi

Orecchiette with Mushrooms (Apulia)

INGREDIENTS for 4:

1 lb broccoli rabe

Salt

10 oz fresh porcini or cremini mushrooms

2 garlic cloves

2 peperoncini (chili peppers)

1 piece organic lemon zest

2 anchovies (preserved in oil)

1 lb orecchiette pasta (see Tip)

3 slices stale plain white bread

8 Tbsp olive oil

2–3 basil sprigs

PREPARATION TIME: 30 minutes
PER PORTION: about 465 calories

1 Rinse the broccoli rabe well; trim the ends and coarsely chop the greens. Bring a large pot of salted water to a boil. Blanch the broccoli rabe for about 1 minute. Drain in a fine-meshed sieve and set aside.

2 Clean and trim the mushrooms and slice them thinly. Peel and thinly slice the garlic. Rinse the peperoncini; remove the stem and mince with the seeds. Mince the lemon zest and anchovies.

3 Bring a large pot of salted water to a boil. Cook the orecchiette according to package directions or until al dente.

4 Meanwhile, cube the bread, removing the crust. Heat 4 tablespoons of oil in a skillet. Toast the bread cubes. Remove from the skillet and set aside.

5 In the same skillet, heat 3 more tablespoons of oil. Sauté the mushrooms over high heat for 3–4 minutes. Stir in the garlic, peperoncini, lemon zest, and anchovies; cook for about $\frac{1}{2}$ minute. Add the broccoli rabe and

Pasta al Sugo d'Agnello e Zafferano

Pasta with Lamb—Saffron Sauce (Abruzzi)

let simmer for a few more minutes. Season the vegetables with salt.

6 Rinse and pat dry the basil; slice the leaves. Drain the pasta and add to the vegetable mixture, stirring to coat. Let the pasta heat up a little and drizzle with the remaining olive oil. Distribute in preheated serving plates and top with the toasted croutons.

Tip: Orecchiette is the typical pasta of Apulia. These "little ears" are served usually either with cauliflower or broccoli seasoned with anchovies and peperoncini. They are also often combined with cime di rapa—usually called broccoli rabe in this country—and arugula, and sometimes with cubed potatoes, fresh sausage, and ricotta; or with tomatoes and cheese; or with seafood such as squid or mussels.

INGREDIENTS for 4:

1 envelope saffron (or a pinch)

$3/4$–1 cup beef broth or dry rosé wine (such as Cerasuolo)

1 lb boneless leg of lamb

1 onion

2 garlic cloves

1 sprig each rosemary, thyme, oregano, and sage

2 bay leaves

$1/4$ cup olive oil

Salt and freshly ground pepper

1 lb tagliatelle or *maccheroni alla chitarra* (see Tip)

10–11 oz cherry tomatoes

$1/2$ bunch basil

Freshly grated pecorino cheese

PREPARATION TIME: 30 minutes
COOKING TIME: 55 minutes
PER PORTION: about 795 calories

1 Soak the saffron in the broth or in the wine. Trim the lamb and

remove all fatty and sinewy parts. Cut the meat into $1/2$-inch cubes. Peel and slice the onion and garlic. Rinse and pat dry the herbs and mince the leaves; leave the bay leaf whole.

2 Heat the oil in a large skillet. Sauté the onion, herbs, and garlic. Add the lamb and brown for about 1–2 minutes. Add two thirds of the saffron liquid and season with salt and pepper. Cook the ragù, covered, for about 45 minutes.

3 Bring a large pot of salted water to a boil. Cook the pasta according to package directions or until al dente. Meanwhile, trim and quarter the tomatoes; rinse and pat dry the basil; slice the leaves.

4 Add the tomatoes and

remaining saffron liquid to the lamb ragù; cook for 10 more minutes. Season with salt and pepper and fold in the basil. Drain the pasta and toss with the ragù. Serve in preheated serving plates with pecorino cheese on the side.

Tip: Maccheroni alla chitarra are *the* noodle specialty of Abruzzi. Since they require some work they are also called *maccheroni domenicali*, or Sunday noodles. The noodles are made with eggs and should be relatively firm. They are shaped or cut on a special pasta machine that has strings like a guitar. The machine is positioned flat, with its strings up, and the sheets of pasta are cut over the strings with the rolling pin. The mountain of thin, almost squarish, long noodles collects underneath.

217

Zuppa di Ceci e Castagne

Chickpea Chowder with Chestnuts (Abruzzi)

INGREDIENTS for 4:

1 cup dried chickpeas

1 celery rib / 1 carrot

2 bay leaves / Pinch baking soda

10–11 oz chestnuts (about 2 cups)

1 onion / ¼ bunch oregano

1–2 oz pancetta (or smoked bacon)

2–3 Tbsp olive oil

1 cup canned pureed tomatoes

Salt and freshly ground pepper

Chili powder (to taste)

PREPARATION TIME: 45 minutes
SOAKING TIME: Overnight
COOKING TIME: 1¼ hours
PER PORTION: about 435 calories

1 Cover the chickpeas with plenty of water. Set aside to soak overnight.

2 Drain the chickpeas. Trim the celery and peel the carrot; dice the vegetables. Combine the veg-etables, bay leaves, baking soda, and chickpeas in 6 cups of water. Simmer for 1 hour or until the chickpeas have softened. As the chickpeas cook, add water if necessary.

3 Cut an X into the curved part of the chestnuts. Bring a pot of water to a boil and cook the chestnuts for 20 minutes. Rinse, peel, and chop the chestnuts.

4 Peel and mince the onion. Rinse and pat dry the oregano; mince the leaves. Chop the pancetta. Heat 2 tablespoons of oil in a large saucepan. Sauté the onion, oregano, and pancetta. Add the chestnuts and continue sautéing; add the chickpeas, veg-etables, and their water, and the tomatoes. Season with salt, pep-per, and with chili powder; cook for 15 more minutes. Drizzle with the remaining olive oil and serve.

Purea di Fave

Lima Bean Puree with Vegetables (Apulia)

INGREDIENTS for 4:

1 lb dried peeled lima beans (see Tip)

2 lbs cooking greens (such as Swiss chard, dandelion greens, broccoli rabe, or kale)

2 dried peperoncini (chili peppers)

Salt and freshly ground pepper

1½ cups olive oil

3–4 Tbsp pitted green olives

PREPARATION TIME: 25 minutes
COOKING TIME: 1½ hours
PER PORTION: about 540 calories

1 Put the lima beans in a pot and add water to cover them by about 1 inch. Bring to a simmer and cook the lima beans, partially covered, for about 1 hour or until they fall apart.

2 Rinse and trim the greens and cut them into bite-sized pieces. Crush the peperoncini. Bring a large pot of salted water to a boil. Add the peperoncini and vegetables. Cook, covered, for about 6 minutes.

3 Meanwhile, mash the cooked lima beans to a smooth puree with a large wooden spoon or with a hand mixer. If you like, use a potato ricer. Season with salt and pepper and add 2 table-spoons of the olive oil. Keep the puree warm.

4 Heat 1 cup of olive oil in a skillet. Pat dry the olives and fry them in the hot oil for 2 minutes. With a slotted spoon, remove them from the oil and set them aside to drain on paper towels.

5 Add the remaining oil and olives to the vegetables; season with salt.

Polpette Cacio e Uova al Sugo

Egg—Cheese "Meatballs" in Tomato Sauce (Abruzzi)

6 Distribute the puree in soup bowls and top with the sautéed vegetables. Drizzle with some additional olive oil and serve.

Tip: The original specialty is made with *catalogna*, an old type of dandelion. The vegetable topping makes the bean puree even more interesting. If you can find only beans in the shells, soak these overnight; squeeze the beans out of their shells and cook the beans as described.

INGREDIENTS for 4:

For the meatballs:

4–5 slices stale white bread

3–4 arugula leaves

4 eggs

1 lb freshly grated pecorino Romano cheese

Salt and freshly ground pepper

2 cups olive oil

For the tomato sauce:

6 medium tomatoes

2 red peperoncini (chili peppers)

1 onion

2 garlic cloves

1 organic lemon

2 Tbsp olive oil

Salt

1 Tbsp tomato paste

$\frac{1}{2}$ tsp honey

PREPARATION TIME: 1 hour
REFRIGERATING TIME: 4 hours
PER PORTION: about 625 calories

1 For the "meatballs," trim the crusts from the bread and soak the bread in water for about 10 minutes. Drain the bread, squeeze it well, and tear it in small pieces.

2 Rinse, trim, and pat dry the arugula; mince the leaves. Mix the bread, arugula, eggs, and cheese; season with salt and pepper. Cover and refrigerate for about 4 hours.

3 For the tomato sauce, bring a large pot of water to a boil. Blanch the tomatoes; rinse under cold water. Core, peel, and dice them. Rinse the peperoncini and cut off the stems. Mince the peperoncini with the seeds. Peel and chop the onion and garlic. Scrub the lemon under hot water. With a zester or grater, remove the lemon zest.

4 Heat the olive oil in a saucepan. Sauté the onion, garlic, peperoncini, and half of the lemon zest. Add the tomatoes, season with salt and pepper, and simmer for about 20 minutes.

5 Meanwhile, form the cheese mixture into balls using your hands. Heat the olive oil in a saucepan or deep skillet. Fry the cheese balls in batches for about 3–4 minutes or until they are golden brown and crispy. Remove with a slotted spoon and set them aside to drain on a layer of paper towels.

6 Stir the tomato paste into the tomato sauce; season with salt and stir in the honey. Place the fried cheese balls in the sauce and set them aside for about 5 minutes. Serve the dish sprinkled with the remaining lemon zest.

Calamari in Salsa con Frittelle di Fagioli

Squid in Tomato Sauce with Bean Fritters (Apulia)

INGREDIENTS for 4:

For the fritters:

$1\frac{1}{4}$ cups dried white beans (see Tip)

2 bay leaves

Pinch baking soda

1 bunch arugula

2 red peperoncini (chili peppers)

2 garlic cloves

1 spring onion

Grated zest of $\frac{1}{2}$ organic lemon

1 egg white

2 cups olive oil

Flour, for shaping

For the squid:

2 lbs small cleaned squid

1 carrot

1 small onion

2 garlic cloves

1 celery rib

$\frac{1}{2}$ bunch parsley

4–5 medium tomatoes

2 Tbsp olive oil

About $\frac{1}{2}$ cup dry white wine

2 tsp tomato paste

Salt and freshly ground pepper

PREPARATION TIME: $1\frac{1}{4}$ hours
SOAKING TIME: Overnight
COOKING TIME: 3–$3\frac{1}{2}$ hours
PER PORTION: about 470 calories

Tip: Speed preparation by using canned beans or chickpeas; you'll need about $2\frac{1}{2}$ cups, or a little less than two 15-oz cans. Choose canned legumes that are seasoned only with salt.

Recommended Wine:
Rosé or red from the Salento area.

Over many decades, the poor inhabitants of Apulia received most of their protein intake by way of legumes. What was the product of necessity in the past has now become custom, and legumes are widely used in soups, together with pasta, mashed or prepared in small bullets that are served either as antipasti or combined, as in this case, with tender squid.

In addition, this dish is also delicious when the squid is spiced with peperoncini (chili peppers) and herbs with garlic are added to the legume bullets.

1 Cover the beans with plenty of water and set them aside to soak overnight. The next day, drain them and combine with the bay leaves, baking soda, and water to cover them by about 1 inch. Cook for about 1–$1\frac{1}{2}$ hours or until they are tender. Drain the beans and set them aside to cool.

2 Meanwhile, rinse and drain the squid. Peel and mince the carrot, onion, and garlic. Trim and mince the celery. Rinse and pat dry the parsley; mince the leaves. Combine the minced ingredients.

3 Bring a large pot of water to a boil. Blanch the tomatoes; rinse under cold water. Core, peel, and finely chop the tomatoes; you should obtain almost a puree.

4 Heat the oil in a large saucepan. Sauté the minced vegetables. Add the squid and sauté briefly. Stir in the wine, tomato paste, and chopped tomatoes; season with salt and pepper. Simmer, covered, for about 45 minutes or until the squid is tender.

5 Meanwhile, rinse and pat dry the arugula; mince the leaves. Rinse the peperoncini and remove the stems; mince the peperoncini with the seeds. Peel and crush the garlic. Trim and mince the spring onion with the green top. Puree the beans.

6 Combine the arugula, peperoncini, garlic, spring onion, and lemon zest in a mixing bowl. Add the egg white and salt and mix thoroughly. With two tablespoons or with a melon baller, form into ovals about 2 inches long and set them on a work surface.

7 Heat the olive oil in a large saucepan or frying pan; with floured hands, smooth the ovals and drop them in the hot oil; fry the fritters for about 4 minutes or until they are golden. Remove with the slotted spoon and set them aside to drain on layers of paper towels. Serve the fritters with the squid.

Tonno in Crosta di Farro

Tuna in a Spelt Crust (Abruzzi)

INGREDIENTS for 4:
1 lb green beans
Salt and freshly ground pepper
1 lb new potatoes
8 Tbsp olive oil
2 garlic cloves
1 bunch parsley
1 cup canned tomatoes
1 cup fish or chicken broth
Zest of 1 organic lemon
4 Tbsp crushed spelt kernels
4 tuna steaks (about ½-inch thick and 6 oz each)

PREPARATION TIME: 45 minutes
PER PORTION: about 800 calories

1 Trim, rinse, and cut the green beans into 2-inch long pieces. Cook the green beans in salted water for about 5 minutes; drain well.

2 Scrub the potatoes and cut into ½-inch cubes. Heat 4 table-spoons of olive oil in a large skillet. Sauté the potatoes for about 10 minutes.

3 Peel and mince the garlic. Rinse and pat dry the parsley; mince the leaves. Add the green beans, tomatoes, garlic, broth, and half of the parsley to the potatoes. Cook, covered, for about 15 minutes. Season with salt and pepper.

4 Combine the lemon zest, the remaining parsley, and the spelt on a large plate. Season the tuna with salt and pepper and coat each steak with the spelt mixture, making sure to press the tuna into the spelt to help the coating adhere evenly and firmly. Heat the remaining 4 tablespoons of oil in a large skillet; sauté the tuna over medium-high heat for about 2–3 minutes each side, turning carefully. Serve with the vegetables.

Cozze con Verdure

Mussels with Vegetables (Apulia)

INGREDIENTS for 4:
1 red bell pepper
1 yellow bell pepper
2 small zucchini
1 large tomato
4 garlic cloves
1 red onion
1 bunch basil
4 lb mussels
12 Tbsp olive oil
1 tsp fennel seeds
2 Tbsp nonpareil capers
½ cup dry white or rosé wine
Salt and freshly ground pepper
About ⅓ cup plain breadcrumbs

PREPARATION TIME: 50 minutes
COOKING TIME: 25 minutes
BAKING TIME: 10 minutes
PER PORTION: about 530 calories

1 Trim, seed, and dice the peppers; trim and cube the zucchini. Core and chop the tomatoes. Peel and thinly slice the garlic. Peel and slice the onion. Rinse and pat dry the basil; tear the leaves into small pieces.

2 Rinse and brush the mussels under fresh running water. Discard any mussels that are already open or broken.

3 Heat 2 tablespoons of olive oil in a large saucepan. Sauté the peppers, zucchini, garlic, onion, and fennel seeds over medium heat for about 2–3 minutes. Add the tomatoes, half of the basil, and the capers; stir in the wine and season with salt and pepper.

4 Add the mussels to the vegetables; cover and simmer for about 15 minutes or until the mussels have entirely opened. Shake the pot occasionally so the mussels cook evenly.

222

Pesce Spada al Forno

Spicy Baked Swordfish with Vegetables (Abruzzi)

5 Preheat the oven to 425° F (if convection oven 400° F). Remove the mussels and vegetables from the liquid and place them in a heat-resistant serving dish; discard any mussels that have not opened. Mix the breadcrumbs with the remaining olive oil and sprinkle over the mussels. Bake for 10 minutes on the middle oven rack until the crumbs have become crispy. Sprinkle the mussels with the remaining basil. Serve hot, accompanied with crusty white bread and a mixed salad.

Mussels are cultivated in Apulia in the Lagoons of Varano and Taranto. The water is fairly shallow there and warm, so the mussels grow especially well.

INGREDIENTS for 4:

1 red bell pepper

1 yellow bell pepper

1 small eggplant (about 1 lb)

1 red onion

2 garlic cloves

$\frac{1}{2}$ bunch basil

1 organic lemon

8 Tbsp olive oil

Salt and freshly ground pepper

4 swordfish steaks (about $\frac{1}{2}$-inch thick and about 6 oz each)

7 oz cherry tomatoes

3 oz large capers or caperberries

PREPARATION TIME: 55 minutes
COOKING TIME: 20 minutes
PER PORTION: about 445 calories

1 Preheat the oven to 475° F (if convection oven 425° F). Cut the peppers into halves; remove the stems and seeds. With a fork, pierce the eggplant skin all around. Line a baking sheet with parchment paper. Place the eggplant, the onion, and peppers, cut-side down, on the paper. Roast the vegetables on the middle oven rack for about 15 minutes or until the pepper skins darken and blister.

2 Meanwhile, peel and crush the garlic through a press. Rinse and pat dry the basil; mince the leaves. Scrub the lemon under hot water. With a zester or grater remove the zest from half the lemon; extract the juice from half. In a blender or food processor, puree the garlic, basil, 2 tablespoons of lemon juice, and 4 tablespoons of olive oil; season with the lemon zest, salt, and pepper. Brush this mixture over the swordfish steaks.

3 Remove the vegetables from the oven and set them aside to cool. Reduce the oven temperature 375° F (if convection oven 350° F). Peel and slice the onion. Cut open the eggplant, scoop out the pulp, and cube. Peel the peppers and cut them into strips. Trim the tomatoes and cut them into quarters. If necessary, remove the stems from the capers. Mix these vegetables with the remaining 4 tablespoons of oil and season with salt and pepper. Layer with the vegetables in a baking dish; top with the fish.

4 Bake the fish on the middle oven rack for about 20 minutes; serve the fish and vegetables with fresh white bread.

Tip: These vegetables make an ideal antipasto; serve them warm or cold.

223

Pampanella
Spicy Pork (Molise)

INGREDIENTS for 4:
1½ lb boneless pork shoulder
8 garlic cloves
8 peperoncini (chili peppers)
2 thyme sprigs
4 sage leaves
2 Tbsp white wine vinegar
6 Tbsp olive oil
Salt and freshly ground pepper
1 lb fresh porcini, chanterelle, or
  cremini mushrooms
1 organic orange

PREPARATION TIME: 25 minutes
COOKING TIME: 1¼ –1½ hours
PER PORTION: about 380 calories

1 Preheat the oven to 350° F (if convection oven 325° F). Trim the pork, removing all fatty and sinewy parts; cut the meat into ½–1-inch cubes. Peel the garlic; rinse the peperoncini and remove the stems. Rinse and pat dry the thyme. Mince the garlic, thyme

leaves, peperoncini, and sage. In a baking dish or Dutch oven, combine these ingredients with the pork, vinegar, oil, salt, and pepper. Roast on the middle oven rack for about 1 hour, stirring occasionally.

2 Trim and clean the mushrooms; slice or cut the larger ones into quarters. Scrub the orange under hot water. With a zester or grater, remove the zest.

3 Stir the mushrooms and orange zest into the meat. Continue to roast for 15–30 more minutes or until the meat is tender.

Most recipes for pampanella have shorter cooking times than this recipe. However, this version, with its greater variety of flavors, needs more time to allow the aromas to intensify and the flavors to develop.

Coniglio allo Zafferano
Rabbit with Saffron (Abruzzi)

INGREDIENTS for 4:
2 garlic cloves
4 oregano sprigs
1 organic orange
6 Tbsp olive oil
1 rabbit (about 3 lbs; cut into 12
  pieces)
Salt and freshly ground pepper
1 envelope saffron (or a pinch)
½–¾ cup dry white wine
1 each red, yellow, and green bell
  pepper
2 small zucchini
8–9 oz cherry tomatoes
½ bunch basil

PREPARATION TIME: 1 hour
PER PORTION: about 655 calories

1 Peel the garlic and crush with a garlic press. Rinse and pat dry the oregano; mince the leaves.

2 Scrub the orange under hot water. With a zester or grater,

remove the zest. Mix 2 tablespoons of oil, garlic, and oregano; coat the rabbit pieces with the mixture. Season the rabbit with salt and pepper.

3 Crumble and dissolve the saffron in the wine.

4 Heat 2 more tablespoons of oil in a Dutch oven. Working in batches, brown the rabbit pieces on both sides over high heat. When all the pieces are golden brown, return them to the Dutch oven and add about half of the saffron wine; simmer, covered, for about 20 minutes.

5 Meanwhile, core, seed, and cut the peppers into thin strips. Trim and slice the zucchini ½-inch thick. Stem the tomatoes. Heat the remaining olive oil in a skillet. Sauté the peppers and zucchini

224

Capretto agli Agrumi
Baby Goat in Citrus Fruit Sauce (Apulia)

for about 5 minutes; season with salt and pepper.

6   Add the peppers, zucchini, and tomatoes to the rabbit; stir in the remaining saffron wine and cook for 15 more minutes or until the rabbit is tender. Rinse and pat dry the basil; shred the leaves. Sprinkle the basil over the rabbit before serving.

Saffron loses flavor as it cooks; for this reason, add half early in the cooking to infuse the meat, and the remaining half during the last 10–20 minutes of cooking to make the most of its flavor.

INGREDIENTS for 8:

½ trimmed baby goat (about 7 lbs; cut into 4 pieces)

Salt and freshly ground pepper

3–4 oz pancetta (or smoked bacon)

2 garlic cloves

4 rosemary sprigs

6 Tbsp olive oil

½–¾ cup dry white wine

2 organic oranges

1 organic lemon

1 tsp sugar

PREPARATION TIME: 15 minutes
COOKING TIME: 1½ hours
PER PORTION: about 580 calories

1   Preheat the oven to 325° F (if convection oven 275° F). Rub the goat on all sides with salt and pepper; place the meat in a roasting pan. Chop the pancetta. Peel and mince the garlic. Rinse and pat dry the rosemary; mince the leaves. Combine the pancetta, garlic, rosemary, and olive oil; drizzle over the meat. Pour in the wine.

2   Chop finely the pancetta bacon. Peel and mince the garlic. Rinse and pat dry the rosemary; tear the needles from the stems. Combine the chopped pancetta with garlic, rosemary, and olive oil and rub with the mixture the entire surface of the baby goat. Moisten with the white wine.

3   Roast the goat on the middle oven rack for about 1 hour, turning the pieces over occasionally.

4   Rinse the oranges and lemon under hot water. With a zester or grater, remove the citrus zest. Extract the juice from all the citrus fruits. Mix the citrus zest, juice, and sugar; pour over the goat. Bake for 30 more minutes, basting occasionally with the pan juices. Cut the pieces of goat in half and serve.

Tip: Capretto is kid, or baby goat; it is prepared as lamb is, but it is served much less often. It is usually available only if custom ordered from butcher shops.

Saffron—Abruzzi's Red Gold

The precious ingredient thrives around the mountain village of Navelli

Saffron was already used 1,500 years before Christ's birth; however, at that time it was used either for coloring or medicinal purposes. Arabs brought the flowers to Spain, and from there they found their way to Europe. The bulbs of the crocus variety (*crocus sativus*) were probably first planted in Abruzzi's soil around the thirteenth century; most likely, a friar brought them from Spain. Shortly after, the inhabitants of this poor region discovered the treasure introduced by the Christian Brother.

Ideal Growing Place. The soil of the mountainous Navelli plateau is perfect for cultivating the crocus plants that yield saffron. The flower not only grows well here but it also develops an especially intense aroma. Every August, the bulbs are carefully removed from the ground. After a cleaning process, the bulbs are replanted—but not in the same field. Saffron is a plant that requires lots of ground nutrients; therefore the fields need to be periodically allowed to regenerate. The bulbs are planted in fields that for about five years had been used for growing other plants such as vegetables, or in fields that were used as grazing pasture. Saffron grows elsewhere in Italy besides Abruzzi. The plant grows in Tuscany, but the renowned areas of cultivation are few.

Precious Harvest. Saffron is harvested around October (the time varies from year to year). How rich the harvest will be depends on the weather; the springtime should not have been too rainy, the summer should not have been too dry—and the boars should have been kept from damaging the fields. The harvest is also unpredictable because gathering the flowers is difficult. Attempts at harvesting mechanically have so far failed, and only a few farmers are left in Abruzzi to do this work by hand; those who are left harvest for sake of tradition or due to their individual passion. The blossoms are picked; the pistils removed and dried. Harvesting is best done very early in the morning, when the crocus blossoms are not yet opened or those that are just in the process of opening have much more intense aroma. Each flower has usually three pistils; it takes more than 14,000 pistels to make one ounce of saffron. This is why saffron is so costly—but fortunately, a little bit of saffron goes a very long way.

In the Kitchen. The color and the aroma of saffron require liquid to develop fully; the filaments need to be soaked. It is best to crumble them between your fingers as you add them and to soak them for at least 10 minutes in water or wine; the longer the filaments soak in liquid the stronger the saffron color will be in the dish. It is wise to buy saffron in envelopes—this size is enough to season recipes for 4 servings. Whenever possible, buy the filaments; these keep the flavor and the aroma longer than powdered saffron. Keep in mind that saffron, like other spices, loses flavor with cooking. Use some at the beginning of cooking and some 10–20 minutes before the end of cooking time.

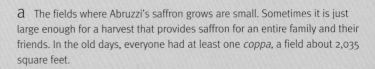

a The fields where Abruzzi's saffron grows are small. Sometimes it is just large enough for a harvest that provides saffron for an entire family and their friends. In the old days, everyone had at least one *coppa*, a field about 2,035 square feet.

b The pickers begin their work very early in the morning, when the dew still covers the fields and the flowers are still closed.   c The beautiful purple flower is picked before opening or just when it is in process of opening. The harvest lasts about two weeks, since the flowers open at different times.
d The bright orange filaments are removed from the picked flowers and placed on a very fine-meshed sieve.   e Even though the saffron harvest is labor intense, meeting for the work is still a good opportunity to chat, to exchange the latest news, and gossip.   f The very thin filaments are briefly heated over charcoal that is not too hot. The filaments shrink a little; they become darker, dry, and ready for long term storage—if they are packed well they can last up to three years.

Scamorza e Verdure alla Griglia
Grilled Scamorza Cheese and Vegetables (Abruzzi)

INGREDIENTS for 4:

2 large bell peppers (any color)

2 small zucchini

1 small eggplant

2 small fennel bulbs

4 small artichokes

4 spring onions

$1/2$ bunch parsley

Finely grated zest of $1/2$ organic lemon

6 Tbsp olive oil

Salt and freshly ground pepper

$1^1/_2$ lbs scamorza cheese (see Tip)

2 Tbsp shelled walnuts

2 tsps fennel seeds

PREPARATION TIME: 1 hour
PER PORTION: about 625 calories

Scamorza—a kneaded and shaped cheese very similar in texture to mozzarella—is often served as an entrée in Abruzzi, not just as an antipasto. Sometimes the cheese is even featured under its own special category on menus; for example, it is featured as a dish prepared grilled or with sausages or with porcini mushrooms or with ham.

That isn't to say scamorza isn't used as an antipasto. The cheese is often used to make crostini. For this specialty, bread is dipped in milk and placed in baking pans; it is then covered with slices of scamorza and baked until the cheese has melted.

Tip: Good scamorza is usually available in Italian specialty stores; when you ask for it, ask for one that is not too old.

Recommended Wine:
A white wine from the region; preferably a Trebbiano d' Abruzzo.

1   Cut the peppers in halves; core them and remove the seeds. Cut each half lengthwise into 3 slices. Trim and slice the zucchini and eggplant into $1/2$-inch slices. Trim the fennel and cut lengthwise into four pieces. With a sharp paring knife, remove the core. Trim the artichokes and cut each in four pieces. Peel the onions and cut them in half.

2   Rinse and pat dry the parsley; mince the leaves. Combine them with the lemon zest and olive oil; toss the vegetables with the herbed oil and season everything with salt and pepper.

3 Remove the rind from the scamorza and slice the cheese ½-inch thick. Break the walnuts into smaller pieces and mix these with the fennel seeds.

4 Prepare the grill or preheat the broiler. Grill or broil the vegetables on both sides until each piece is a nice golden brown. Times will vary according to the vegetables, but you may need about 8–12 minutes. Keep everything warm on a large serving platter.

5 Place the slices of cheese on the grill (line the grill with foil) or on a baking sheet (line with parchment paper). Grill or broil about 5 inches away from the heat for about 3 minutes. Turn the cheese over and sprinkle with the walnuts; continue grilling for 2–3 more minutes or until the cheese begins to brown and melt. Serve the cheese with the vegetables.

Sponsali al Forno
Baked Spring Onions (Apulia)

INGREDIENTS for 4:

1 lb spring onions

1 lb cherry tomatoes

1 red peperoncino (optional)

½ bunch oregano

2 Tbsp capers (preserved in salt)

6 Tbsp olive oil

Salt

½ bunch basil

PREPARATION TIME: 25 minutes
COOKING TIME: 45 minutes
PER PORTION: about 205 calories

1 Preheat the oven to 350° F (if convection oven 325° F). Trim the spring onions; cut the onions into 2–3-inch long pieces; cut the wider onions lengthwise in half.

2 Trim the tomatoes and cut into halves. Remove the stem from the peperoncino (if using); slice with the seeds. Rinse and pat dry the oregano; mince the leaves. Rinse the capers under water and mince or chop.

3 Combine the spring onions, tomatoes, peperoncino, oregano, capers, and oil in a baking dish, tossing to coat; season with salt. Bake for about 45 minutes or until the onions are tender and golden brown. Rinse and pat dry the basil; shred the leaves. Serve, sprinkled with shredded basil leaves.

Sponsali is the dialect name of Apulia's spring onions. They can enhance the flavor of a frittata; they are sliced thin and added fresh to salads; they are also stewed with meat. The best flavor of these onions comes forth when they are prepared with their green tops. The onions can also be served cold on an appetizer menu as finger food.

Melanzane al Coppo
Clay-Pot Eggplants (Abruzzi)

INGREDIENTS for 4:

2 small eggplants (about 1½ lbs)

1 each red, green, and yellow bell pepper

2 white or red onions

4 garlic cloves

1 bunch parsley

1 dried peperoncino (chili pepper)

2 Tbsp red wine vinegar

6 Tbsp olive oil

Salt

¼ bunch basil

PREPARATION TIME: 20 minutes
COOKING TIME: 45-50 minutes
PER PORTION: about 230 calories

1 Trim and cube the eggplants. Trim, seed, and slice the peppers into 1-inch wide slices . Peel and slice the onions.

2 Peel the garlic. Rinse and pat dry the parsley. Mince the parsley leaves with the garlic and peperoncino.

3 Soak a *coppo* or clay pot (see Tip). Combine the vegetables with the garlic mixture, vinegar, and oil in the clay pot; season with salt. (You can also use a small, heavy pot and cook the vegetables on the stove.)

4 Place the clay pot in a cold oven on the lowest rack and turn the oven to 400° F (if convection oven 350° F); bake the vegetables for about 50 minutes (or cook them over medium heat on the stove for about 45 minutes). While the vegetables cook, stir once or twice.

Tiella di Patate e Catalogna

Baked Potatoes and Dandelion Greens (Apulia)

5 Rinse and pat dry the basil; shred the leaves. Sprinkle the basil over the vegetables, then season with salt. This is delicious cold or warm or at room temperature.

Tip: A coppo is a clay pot that is used in Abruzzi and Molise to simmer foods directly over the fire. Whether potatoes or other vegetables, everything goes in the pot, which is sealed and cooked at high heat for a comparatively short time. Aromatics and seasonings may be added, too. The result: A savory, speedy dish.

INGREDIENTS for 4:

1 lb catalogna or dandelion greens (substitute with Swiss chard)
Salt
3 spring onions
2 medium tomatoes
6 Tbsp olive oil
2 dried peperoncini (chili peppers)
1/3 cup dry white wine
3 Tbsp plain breadcrumbs
4 garlic cloves
1 bunch parsley
1 lb red potatoes
3–4 oz freshly grated pecorino or caciocavallo cheese

PREPARATION TIME: 45 minutes
COOKING TIME: 1¼ hours
PER PORTION: about 425 calories

1 Rinse and clean well the greens; trim the tough stems. Cut the leaves 1–2 inches wide. Bring a pot of salted water to a boil and cook the greens for about 1 minute or until they begin to wilt. Drain in a colander and let cool.

2 Trim and slice the spring onions with their tops into 1-inch rings. Core tomatoes and cut them in eighths. Heat 2 tablespoons of oil in a skillet. Sauté the spring onions; add the tomatoes. Crush the peperoncini and add to the vegetables. Stir in the wine; season with salt and cook over medium heat, uncovered, for about 15 minutes.

3 Meanwhile, toast the breadcrumbs in a skillet until golden brown. Transfer them to a mixing bowl. Peel and mince the garlic. Rinse and pat dry the parsley; mince the leaves. Add the parsley and garlic to the breadcrumbs.

4 Preheat the oven to 350° F (if convection oven 325° F). Scrub and peel the potatoes; slice them thin. Mix the greens with the tomatoes.

5 In a baking dish, arrange layers of the potato and sautéed vegetables. Sprinkle each layer with some of the breadcrumbs and grated cheese. Top the last layer with the remaining cheese and drizzle this last layer with the remaining olive oil. Bake for about 1¼ hours or until the potatoes are soft and tender. Cover with foil, if necessary, to prevent the vegetables from becoming too dark. Remove from the oven and let cool slightly before serving.

Vegetables—Lesser known varieties

When it comes to vegetables, southern Italy offers many choices

At farmers' markets in L'Aquila, Lecce, or Otranto, or in Palermo, Naples, or Matera, shoppers find mountains of fat red peppers, juicy and tender salad greens, asparagus, varieties of cabbages, artichokes, and cardoons. These vegetables thrive in the south while providing the locals with lots of flavor. Many of these vegetables have found their way into our markets.

Catalogna. A member of the chicory family, this large plant has leaves similar to dandelion; the leaves are much longer and can be either dark or light green. The late plants are blanched like endive to allow the leaves to remain pale green. *Catalogna* is available in spring and in summer; it is usually chopped and cooked with fava beans and served as a side dish, often with lamb.

Cime di rapa. This vegetable is related to the broccoli family and is sometimes called rapini or broccoli rabe. The flavorful vegetable evolved from local wild greens. The dark green leaves with the long stems and the small florets that look like young broccoli taste slightly bitter. The greens are often braised and served either as a side dish or served with a piece of cheese and toasted bread as a small meal. Cime di rapa are readily available in most produce departments; if they are out of season, substituted with the bok choy.

Fave. These large beans are also called broad beans, english beans, Windsor beans, or horse beans. In springtime and in early summer, they are often found in Middle Eastern, Italian, or Greek markets in their long, thick pods. If these beans are fresh, they can be stewed or boiled after being shelled. Older beans must be removed from their thick, leathery skins; the skins slip off easily after the beans are blanched. In Italy, fave are not only used fresh but also dry. Young fava beans are delicious raw; old fava beans must be cooked; they are drizzled with olive oil or mixed with other vegetables.

Cardi. The cardoon is also called cardoni or weed artichoke, and is considered the parent plant of the artichoke. Cardi's flavor is pronounced; it is slightly nutty and bitter; the lightly furred ribs, harvested in fall and in winter, look like celery and taste like artichokes. The ribs should be trimmed of all leafy and stringy parts, peeled, and cut into pieces. They are best cooked in water before being used in recipes. In southern Italy, they are served with tomato sauce or may be fried or baked. The young shoots are also tasty served raw as a salad.

Carciofi. Italian artichokes tend to be oblong and are a favorite ingredient during late winter and throughout spring. The delicate young varieties are eaten raw or grilled or fried after they are cleaned and trimmed (the outer leaves are removed until those that remain behind are tender to the bite; the pointy leaves that remain are cut short). The larger varieties are braised or stuffed. Thorny artichokes come from the south of Italy. Pay attention when you handle these!

a   Stewed Catalogna: Rinse, clean, and chop about 1½ lbs of catalogna. Peel and mince 2 red onions and 2 garlic cloves; sauté these in 2 tablespoons of olive oil. Add the catalogna; season it with 1–2 dried crushed peperoncini and salt. Moisten the vegetables with about ½ cup of water and cook for about 10 minutes. Finally, add 2 tablespoons of pitted black olives and stir. Drizzle everything with 2 tablespoons of olive oil.

b Cauliflower is a favorite in Italy; whether it is used raw in *pinzimonio* (raw vegetables dipped in olive oil) or cooked in a soup or baked. In the south, a very flavorful purple cauliflower is available.   c A favorite in Tuscany: cavolo nero, also called black kale, which is a member of the cabbage family. Remove the leaves, slice, and steam or braise.   d During springtime gourmets hunt the wild asparagus that is especially flavorful. Green asparagus requires only very little cooking.   e An incredible bounty of vegetables are routinely available at the local farmers' markets.   f After removing by hand the outside leaves of the artichokes, the remaining leaves are trimmed with scissors.   g Very young artichokes have not yet developed a hairy choke; the choke should be removed from older ones before cooking.

Crema al Limone
Lemon Cream (Abruzzi)

Semifreddo alla Nocciola
Hazelnut Semi-Iced Cream (Apulia)

INGREDIENTS for 4:

1 large organic lemon

About 3–4 Tbsp candied lemon slices

About 3 Tbsp slivered almonds

About 4 Tbsp softened butter

$\frac{1}{3}$ cup sugar

1 egg, at room temperature

3 egg yolks, at room temperature

1 cup heavy cream

Confectioners' sugar, for dusting

PREPARATION TIME: 35 minutes
PER PORTION: about 580 calories

egg and egg yolks; fold in the lemon juice and mix well. Beat in the top of a double boiler until the cream thickens. Remove the bowl from over the hot water and place it in very cold water; continue beating until the cream has cooled.

3 Beat the heavy cream until stiff peaks form. Fold it into the lemon cream with the candied lemon pieces.

4 Distribute the lemon cream in small flan cups; garnish with the slivered almonds and dust with the confectioners' sugar. Serve immediately.

1 Scrub the lemon under hot water. With a zester or grater, remove the zest. Extract the juice. Chop the candied lemon slices. Toast the almonds in a dry skillet.

2 Cream the sugar and butter in a mixing bowl (preferably made of metal). While mixing, add the

INGREDIENTS for 6:

4 egg yolks

5 Tbsp sugar

$\frac{1}{3}$ cup milk

3 Tbsp crushed nut brittle

3 Tbsp hazelnuts

2 organic oranges

About 1 cup of heavy cream

Confectioners' sugar, for dusting

PREPARATION TIME: 35 minutes
FREEZING TIME: 3-4 hours
PER PORTION: about 370 calories

1 Cream the sugar and egg yolks in a mixing bowl (preferably made of metal). Add the milk. Beat over hot water or in the top of a double boiler until the cream thickens. Remove the bowl from over the hot water and place it in very cold water; continue beating until the cream has cooled.

2 Soften the nut brittle over the hot water. Chop the hazelnuts. Scrub the oranges under hot water and use a swivel peeler to remove just the zest. Cut the orange peel into thin strips.

3 Fold the brittle, hazelnuts, and the strips of orange peel into the cream. Beat the heavy cream until stiff peaks form. Add the whipped cream to the nut cream. Distribute the mixture among 6 small flan cups and freeze for about 3–4 hours.

4 Peel the oranges to remove the white membrane. Cut the orange in wedges and remove the strings. Briefly dip the flan cups in hot water and turn them over on serving plates. Garnish with the orange wedges and dust everything with confectioners' sugar.

Ricotta Fritta con Composta di Fichi

Fried Ricotta with Stewed Figs (Apulia)

The fertile Apulia region is one of Italy's grain baskets. For this reason, it is not only Apulia's bread and pasta that are famous but also grains that are used for other culinary purposes. Grano cotto—whole grain kernels cooked in wine and flavored with sugar and spices—is a favorite dessert, especially with creamy and cold desserts.

INGREDIENTS for 6:

For the figs:

1 lb ripe fresh figs

About 3 Tbsp sugar

Juice of 1 lemon

$\frac{1}{2}$ cup dry white wine

For the ricotta:

2 eggs

About 3 Tbsp flour

1 lb ricotta cheese

2 cups olive oil

Confectioners' sugar, for dusting

PREPARATION TIME: 45 minutes
PER PORTION: about 425 calories

1 Rinse the figs and remove the stems. Cube the figs and place them in a saucepan with the sugar, lemon juice, and wine. Bring to a boil; reduce the heat and simmer for about 20 minutes or until the syrup has thickened slightly. Stir occasionally to prevent burning.

2 Transfer the figs to a bowl and let cool. Later, taste and add more sugar or lemon juice if necessary.

3 Beat the eggs in a dish. Put the flour in another dish. Form the ricotta into bite-sized pieces.

4 Heat the oil in a skillet. Coat each piece of ricotta with flour; then dip each piece in the beaten eggs to coat on both sides. Fry the ricotta balls in batches for 1–3 minutes or until they are golden brown, turning them over occasionally. Remove the ricotta pieces with a slotted spoon and place them on layers of paper towels to drain.

5 Before serving, place the figs on a plate and top with the ricotta balls. Dust with confectioners' sugar.

Figs grow everywhere in the south of Italy. The fruits are used in many recipes: stewed, as in this case, or prepared as jams; dried and dipped in chocolate (as in Calabria); they are also pickled and served with cheese, roasted or broiled or folded into pasta and cheese—the array of specialties is vast.

Basilicata and Calabria

The South: burning sun, rugged hills, and the most tantalizing cuisine

The Region and Its Products

Diverse and fresh fish and shellfish, hard wheat for pasta, and pigs for sausages

If we imagine Italy as a boot, Calabria could be considered the toe and Basilicata the ankle. Calabria is surrounded by the sea; Basilicata, once known as Lucania, is mountainous and rugged, with only a few miles of coast. Fish is predominant in the former; wheat, livestock, and vegetables in the latter.

Primitive mountain world.
Most of Basilicata's terrain consists in steep mountains. On small fields, the locals grow rounded eggplants, beans, tomatoes, and peppers—especially the very fiery peperoncini. Inland, on the fertile soil at the foot of the inactive volcano Monte Vulture, thrive wheat, Aglianico vines, olives, vegetables, and fruits; in the north, chestnuts are in season in fall. What the people can't grow in their gardens, they gather. Mushrooms, from porcini and chanterelles, to *cardoncelli* (a type of oyster mushroom) and *ovuli* (edible Italian type of Caesar's mushrooms of the Amanita family) are popular. Wild chicory, wild asparagus, and cime di rapa (also called broccoli rabe), as well as the small wild *lampascioni* onions, are also favorites. The semidomesticated and famous Podolica cattle that graze throughout the provinces of Potenza and Matera feed on wild herbs, grass, and wild berries. Their milk is used to make the best *caciocavallo* cheese. Other cheeses are made from the milk of goats and sheep; their meat may also become Sunday's meal. In Basilicata and Calabria, pigs are the major source of meat; especially for sausage products such as the *luganega* (or lucanica), a traditional sausage that is occasionally seasoned with wild herbs that was already a favorite during ancient Roman times.

A long coast.
There is plenty of sea around Calabria; as in Sicily, located at a shot's distance, tuna and swordfish are great favorites. But all sorts of sea creatures have their fans, from sea urchins to the very young, almost larvae-sized fish called *rosamarina*. Around Tropea and throughout Capo Vaticano large red onions are cultivated; they are so mild that they can be eaten raw. Eggplants grow especially well and are the basis of many local specialties. In this cuisine, vegetables play a more important role than meat; fava beans, picked fresh from the nearby garden and shelled, are a delicacy that is offered among friends with a glass of wine. Olives yield an especially fruity and distinctive oil, with an aroma reminiscent of the wild fennel that grows here. And what would Calabria be without the hard wheat that with its gluten content can make dough that holds together even without eggs? Fruits of the region grow in abundance. Citrus groves are a common sight, as are the figs from the hills of Cosentino, which are either dried in the sun, or baked in the oven, or grilled.

The ancient breed of Podolica cattle is raised in Basilicata throughout the provinces of Potenza and Matera. It has been said that they originated in Turkey. The animals live almost wild throughout the flat plateaus of the Apennines and feed on grass, wild herbs, and berries. Their milk is especially flavorful and is used to make the best cheese in the region, the *caciocavallo podolico*, a cheese that is similar to the provolone.

The red onions that hang in front of a grocery store in Tropea are one of the principal crops of Calabria. They are particularly mild and are used not only in stews and sautés but are also eaten raw.

Whey that is left over from the cheese production is used to make "cooked" ricotta; the whey is mixed with new whole milk and reheated. In this way, a moist type of fresh cottage cheese is made.

As in nearby Sicily, swordfish is among the favorite fish in Calabria. Smoked swordfish is used like bacon, to flavor specialties.

Steep and rocky coastlines and bays with wonderfully fine and sandy beaches—Capo Vaticano is among the preferred vacation spots in Calabria. In the backcountry, red onions, wheat, and flavorful vegetables like eggplants and tomatoes and potatoes are cultivated.

Basilicata is a vacation spot for the individualists. This small region is difficult to get to, but travelers are rewarded with a fascinating landscape and delightful small villages such as Maratea Superiore, which has a lot to offer from a culinary point of view.

The Cuisine

The art of creating a special cuisine from very simple ingredients

Fish is always available along the endless coastlines of Calabria, but legumes—whether red beans (fagioli rossi) or chickpeas (ceci) or fava beans (fave) that are usually preferred fresh and raw—are popular favorites throughout the region and in Basilicata as well. Eggplants, tomatoes, red onions, and above all very spicy peperoncini are the basis of the simple but flavorful way of cooking that is winning fans around the globe for its modern yet classic style.

Red and fiery. In the *mezzogiorno*, as Italian south is also called, there are almost no dishes without peperoncini; whether fresh or dried, or whole or ground to powder, the red pods are everywhere. One ingredient without which Calabria's cuisine seems not to be able to subsist is *n'duja*, a hellishly fiery type of spreadable sausage made from pork meat ground with garlic and coriander before it is smoked. *N'duja* is spread on bread, stirred into sauces, or used for stews or specialties made with legumes.

Overabundance of vegetables. Perhaps nowhere else in Italy besides Calabria and Basilicata are there a wider array of recipes that call for eggplant, even though this vegetable has only recently become popular. This cuisine also uses artichokes, fennels, sweet and hot peppers, wild greens, and mushrooms. Vegetables are used in a variety of dishes, especially sauces that complement homemade pasta.

Pork is indispensable. Meat specialties are a favorite throughout Basilicata, which has very little coastline. Pork is a major ingredient in ragùs. Sheep and lamb may be stewed with vegetables and flavored with wild herbs. Fresh sheep or goat cheese is served with homemade jams, puff pastry, or freshly picked berries from the woods.

The exotic fruit from South America, the tomato, found an ideal climate in the south of Italy, but it took a few hundred years to be adopted into the cuisine. To have it available throughout the year, it is cut into halves, sprinkled with salt, and sun-dried. If these pomodori secchi are soaked briefly and marinated in olive oil, they make a good antipasto or can be used to flavor sauces, breads, and pizzas.

Eggplants are Calabria's vegetables—versatile and very much adaptable. The fat round species with white-striped skins are the ultimate favorites. Because the original species tasted somewhat bitter, eggplants were discovered culinarily only about 100 years ago. When cooks learned to lessen their bitterness with salting and draining, they found their culinary triumph as melanzane.

From the sea into the frying pan—this is the way fish is served in the modest beach restaurants around Capo Vaticano. A small swordfish (*spatola*), various breams (*mormore*, *occhiate*), and bass (*spigola*) are among the preferred fish.

What looks like a sea of flowers are the blossoms of the red onions that grow throughout huge fields around Tropea and Capo Vaticano on the western coast of Calabria. Since the onions are very mild, they are a favorite raw food; however, they are also stewed as a vegetable dish.

The daily ritual includes the visit to the market. Recipes are exchanged and daily news is discussed as locals shop for onions, eggplants, tomatoes, peppers, fennel bulbs, celery, and potatoes from the mountainous plateau of the Sila, as well as preserved vegetables, olives, and peperoncini.

Onions are cleaned right in the fields as they are harvested. Despite the hard work, it is also an opportunity for the women to socialize. The men have the task of keeping the knives sharp to keep the onions from being damaged during the cleaning and trimming process. Here the round *tonda* onions are harvested; there is also another, more oblong variety, which is called *lunga*. Both onions are deliciously sweet and flavorful; they are purple outside and white inside.

The Wines

With the rediscovery of ancient vine varieties there is new activity along the volcano

Basilicata is home to some superlative vineyards: the soil around the inactive volcano Vulture brings forth excellent reds. Calabria was long renowned for its Cirò, a basic wine that is available as red, rosé, and white (rosso, rosato, and bianco). Cirò's reputation has suffered of late, but efforts by involved winemakers indicate that new respect might soon be due to this ancient wine.

Aglianico del Vulture.
A match made in heaven: the old volcano Vulture and the red grape variety Aglianico. These grapes ripen late, are sensitive to too much rain, and require lots of sun. This is the only DOC zone in Basilicata, and although the grapes can be used for sparkling wines, the still wines are the ones that earn renown. The Aglianico del Vulture is a full-bodied aromatic wine that goes well with dark meats and with flavorful spicy vegetables specialties typical of the South. These wines tend to be robust to the point of roughness when young, but they can become smooth and very well balanced as they age.

Cirò and Co.
In the old days, Calabria was known as a fringe area on the wine-making map; although conditions seem favorable because of the cool mountain valleys and mild weather, wines from Calabria have never been held in high regard. Cirò is perhaps the best known wine. It is made from Gaglioppo grapes and is usually bottled as a red wine but it is available also as rosé and white. The red Savuto, also made from Gaglioppo grapes, and other regional varieties such as Greco nero, Nerello Cappuccio and others, are less known. The same applies to the Melissa and the Scavigna, which are both available as reds and whites.

With great expectations for the future, the focus has shifted to the DOC region Lamezia. Reds from such grapes as Nerello Mascalese, Cappuccio, Gaglioppo, and Magliocco, and whites from Greco bianco, Trebbiano, and Malvasia, have already earned quality awards.

The Moscato di Saracena, which has been produced since ancient times, still remains a secret. Only recently rediscovered, this has a scent of citrus fruits and herbs, and is made with Malvasia and Guarnaccia grapes and sun-dried Moscatello di Saracena grapes.

Left: Greco bianco grapes, mixed with Trebbiano and Malvasia grapes, result in white Lamezia wines.
Above: Famous samples of the region (from left to right) – Vignali, Efesto, Aglianico del Vulture, Venosa.

Regional Recipes
New variations of rediscovered culinary treasures

The *mezzogiorno* is a treasure trove for Italy's most beloved ingredients. Fresh, sun-ripened vegetables and fruits, aromatic herbs, and culinary methods combine to enhance the flavor of ingredients; add the spiciness of *peperoncini* to give the dishes a fiery kick.

Cianfotta Primavera
Vegetable Medley (Basilicata)

INGREDIENTS for 4–6:

2 small eggplants

2 zucchini

2 onions

4 garlic cloves

2 celery ribs

1 lb fava beans in their shells
(10–11 oz shelled; substitute
with lima beans)

10–11 oz asparagus

6–7 medium tomatoes

6 Tbsp olive oil

$\frac{1}{2}$ cup dry red wine

1 sprig each oregano, rosemary,
and thyme

2 sage leaves

2 dried peperoncini (chili peppers)

Salt and freshly ground pepper

$\frac{1}{2}$ tsp cayenne pepper

2–3 parsley sprigs

PREPARATION TIME: 40 minutes
COOKING TIME: 20 minutes
**PER PORTION (WITH 6
SERVINGS):** about 325 calories

A vegetable stew made with eggplants and tomatoes is prepared not only in Basilicata but also in Calabria; there the dish is called ciambotta. It is hard not to notice how similar the dish is to the ratatouille of Provence. Cianfotta's flavor is mainly determined by the vegetables used to prepare it, and has fewer herbs and spices than ratatouille does.

According to purists, cianfotta should include broad green beans, zucchini, onions, potatoes, tomatoes, and should be stewed; to season it only sea salt, high-quality olive oil, and a little peperoncino are used—and no celery is included. With this dish the flavor of vegetables lends the main character to the whole. Be sure to use only impeccably fresh ingredients.

Recommended Wine:
a dry white wine such as
Moscato from Basilicata.

1 Trim the eggplants and zucchini into 2-inch long pieces. Peel and mince the onions and the garlic. Trim and chop celery.

2 Shell the fava beans and remove the leathery skin (open the skin with the thumb and squeeze out or peel the bean). Trim the asparagus, cutting off the lower parts if necessary. Cut the asparagus into 1-inch long pieces.

3 Bring a large pot of water to a boil. Blanch the tomatoes; rinse under cold water. Core, peel, seed, and chop coarsely. Heat the oil in a large skillet. Brown the eggplant over high heat for about 5 minutes or until they are golden brown; remove them from the skillet and place them to drain on a layer of paper towels.

4 In the same skillet, sauté the zucchini; when they are done place these too on a layer of paper towels. Reduce the heat to medium-low and sauté the onions, garlic, and celery.

5 Add the beans and asparagus and cook them briefly; they should not become brown but only release their flavor. Stir in the tomatoes and cook until they have fallen apart. Stir in the red wine and simmer again.

6 Return the eggplants and zucchini to the skillet. Rinse and pat dry the oregano, thyme, and rosemary and add the sprigs with the sage leaves to the vegetable medley. Crumble the peperoncini over the vegetables; season with salt, pepper, and cayenne pepper.

7 Simmer the cianfotta over low heat, covered, for about 20 minutes. Remove the sprigs of herbs and the sage leaves. Rinse and pat dry the parsley; mince the leaves. Sprinkle the parsley over the vegetable medley and serve either warm or cold with fresh white bread.

Uova con Crema di Tonno

Eggs with Creamed Tuna (Calabria)

INGREDIENTS for 4:

1 can water-packed tuna (5–6 oz)
1 Tbsp capers (preserved in salt)
1 very fresh egg yolk
1 Tbsp lemon juice
4–5 Tbsp olive oil
1 tsp white wine vinegar
1–3 Tbsp dry white wine
Salt and freshly ground pepper
4–5 oz arugula
4 hard-boiled eggs

PREPARATION TIME: 30 minutes
PER PORTION: about 315 calories

1 Drain and flake the tuna. Rinse the capers. Puree the tuna in the food processor. With the machine running, add the egg yolk and lemon juice, then add the oil in a thin stream. Add the vinegar and wine until the mixture is smooth and creamy. Add the capers and continue processing. Season with salt and pepper and refrigerate until ready to serve.

2 Select the best leaves of arugula; rinse and pat dry. Peel the eggs and slice them thin. Distribute the egg slices on small plates and top with the creamed tuna. Garnish with some arugula. Serve with fresh white bread.

This cream is also often prepared with poached sea bass—then it is called *tartaro di branzino*.

Funghi Impanati
Breaded Oyster Mushrooms (Basilicata)

INGREDIENTS for 4:

5–6 medium tomatoes
2 garlic cloves
6 Tbsp olive oil
Salt and freshly ground pepper
Pinch sugar
Small pinch powdered peperoncino (you may substitute with cayenne pepper)
2–3 basil sprigs
$1/2$ lb oyster mushrooms
1 egg
2–3 Tbsp flour
2–3 Tbsp breadcrumbs
Lemon wedges, to garnish

PREPARATION TIME: 45 minutes
PER PORTION: about 260 calories

1 Bring a large pot of water to a boil. Blanch the tomatoes; rinse them under cold water. Core, peel, seed, and cube them. Peel and mince the garlic.

2 Heat 2 tablespoons of olive oil in a large skillet. Sauté the garlic until golden; add the tomatoes and simmer for about 20 minutes, stirring occasionally. Season the sauce with salt, pepper, and peperoncino. Rinse and pat dry the basil; chop the leaves and sprinkle them over the sauce.

3 Meanwhile, clean and trim the mushrooms; cut off the woody stems and slice the larger pieces lengthwise. Season the mushrooms with salt and pepper. Whisk the egg. First dust the mushrooms with flour, then drop them in the egg, and finally coat them, one by one, in breadcrumbs.

4 Heat the remaining oil in a frying pan. Fry the mushrooms, in batches if necessary, for about 5 minutes on each side or until they are nice and golden brown. Serve immediately with the sauce and the lemon wedges.

246

Involtini di Melanzane
Eggplant Rollups (Calabria)

INGREDIENTS for 4:

2 small eggplants (about 1½ lbs)

Salt and freshly ground pepper

6–7 medium tomatoes

1 onion

About 8 Tbsp olive oil

1 dried peperoncino (chili pepper)

1–2 oz thinly sliced ham

1–2 oz shaved pecorino or parmesan cheese

2–3 oz shaved provola cheese (round made either from buffalo or cow's milk; substitute with sliced provolone)

PREPARATION TIME: 45 minutes
BAKING TIME: 15 minutes
PER PORTION: about 335 calories

New cardoon sprouts (*cardoncelli*), usually not available in this country, are gathered for this specialty in the Basilicata region.

1 Trim the eggplants and cut them horizontally as thin as possible. Sprinkle them with salt and set them aside to drain.

2 Meanwhile, bring a large pot of water to a boil. Blanch the tomatoes, rinse them under cold water. Core, peel, seed, and chop them. Peel and chop the onion. Heat 2 tablespoons of olive oil in a large skillet. Sauté the onion over low heat until translucent. Crumble in the peperoncino and stir in the tomatoes. Simmer for about 20 minutes.

3 Set out the shaved ham and the shaved pecorino or parmesan cheese.

4 Rinse the eggplant slices with fresh cold water and pat them dry with paper towels. Arrange them in a single layer in a large hot skillet with some olive oil and cook them until they are limp.

5 Arrange the eggplant slices on a work surface; line each slice with shaved pecorino or parmesan and with shaved ham; roll up the eggplant slices and spear the rolls with toothpicks.

6 Preheat the oven to 400°F. Season the tomato sauce with salt and pepper. Oil a baking pan and line it with the tomato sauce. Place the rollups on the sauce and top them with shaved provola; bake for about 15 minutes or until the cheese has melted. Serve lukewarm or cold.

Treasures Preserved in Olive Oil

Vegetables preserved in oil are especially a favorite as antipasti

Preserving summer's bounty for those months when vegetables do not grow or are scarce has always been one of the Italians' creative talents. The favorite method, especially in the south, has always been to preserve the foods in cold-pressed olive oil. The finished product is called *sott'olio*, which translates to "under oil"—which in this case of course means olive oil.

Fast antipasti.

Every gardener is familiar with this scenario: a harvest of a particular vegetable that is far too abundant to be used right away. The solution: canning or freezing. In Italy, the preferred method is to can with olive oil; the advantage being that preserved foods can be served as they are, right out of the container. For example, if they are needed for antipasti they are simply taken out of the jar. The rich gifts of summer are thus available year-round, with minimal labor or special equipment. The primary requirement: ripe, aromatic vegetables at their peak, ready to be processed right after the harvest to prevent loss of flavor.

Vinegar and Salt.

The vegetables need to be cleaned first and then cut decoratively into smaller pieces; their appeal goes not only to the palate but also to the eye. A brief bath in boiling-hot salted water with lemon juice or vinegar follows; this helps to set the color, as well as the quality and flavor. It should not be long enough to overcook the food, though. The vegetables are then placed in well-ventilated areas to dry; they dry until they have lost enough moisture that even when placed under oil there is no molding or spoilage. To know when the right time has come to place the vegetables in oil comes in large part with experience.

The best olive oil.

Some vegetables such as tomatoes and peperoncini can be dried without such preparation. Tomatoes that are left to dry with a thick coating of salt can be canned in oil without loss of flavor after simply being dipped briefly in a refreshing bath of vinegar water. Other vegetables are canned decoratively in glasses with spices and herbs and covered with local extra virgin oil. The cold-pressed olive oil's purpose is to seal from the air; its antioxidants have such a preserving quality that the *sott'olio* can last several months as long as the glasses are stored cool and dark.

Regional Delicacies.

For the *involtini di melanzane* in Calabria, eggplants are marinated raw, rolled around a filling of dried tomatoes and cheese, and placed under oil. Small delicate artichokes—cleaned, quartered, and blanched—are placed in oil and are called *carciofini*. Peperoni *sott'olio* from Tuscany are red and yellow peppers that have been peeled and dried with garlic, sage, rosemary, and filled in glasses with oil. In the Maremma and in the Abruzzi regions green asparagus is blanched, cut into pieces, and preserved in oil with herbs. *Funghi muschio*, a specialty from Tuscany and Calabria, are dark and light mushrooms that are first blanched in vinegar water then dried and placed under olive oil. And finally the peperoncini *ripieni* from Sicily that are cherry shaped chili peppers stuffed with anchovies and capers and preserved in olive oil.

a

a For *pomodori secchi sott'olio*, wash about 3 oz of sun-dried tomatoes. Pour over the tomatoes 4 cups of water and 4–5 tablespoons of vinegar and let them soak for about 20 minutes or until they have softened. Drain them and set them on a clean dishcloth to dry at room temperature for about 2 hours. Layer the tomatoes in sterilized glass jars with chopped garlic and crumbled peperoncino and cover with olive oil. Set aside for a week before using it. Once the jar is opened the tomatoes will last about 1 week.

b Vegetables are preserved for antipasti and for use in other recipes throughout the south and in the central parts of Italy. Usually it is done by small family businesses that later sell their wares. If you purchase these edible treasures, keep them in a cool and dark place, but not in the refrigerator as the olive oil congeals. Once you open the jar, use it soon. c Tomatoes must first dry well to concentrate flavor; Only then are they placed in oil. Pureed tomatoes that under the southern sun turn easily into tomato paste are another important winter staple. d Vegetables such as zucchini and eggplants are especially suited for preservation once sliced, blanched in salted vinegar-water, and dried.

Friselle
Bread Rings (Calabria)

INGREDIENTS for 4 bread rings:
4 cups bread flour
flour, for kneading
1 envelope active dry yeast (or ½ cube of fresh yeast)
1½ tsp salt

PREPARATION TIME: 20 minutes
RESTING TIME: 6¾ hours
BAKING TIME: 70 minutes
PER BREAD RING: about 465 calories

1 Put the flour in a mixing bowl forming a well in the center. Combine the yeast with about 1 cup of lukewarm water and set aside till foamy. Pour the yeast sponge into the well. Season with salt and knead to make a smooth dough. Set the dough aside, covered, to rest and rise for about 4–6 hours.

2 On a floured work surface, knead the dough and shape it into 4 flattened balls about 7 inches in diameter. Cut a hole (about 1–2 inches in diameter) in the middle of each. Line a baking sheet with parchment paper, place the bread rings on the paper and cover them with a slightly damp dish cloth; let the bread rise again for 45 minutes.

3 Preheat the oven to 425°F (if convection oven 400°F) and place a heat-resistant bowl filled with water on the bottom of the oven. Brush the bread rings with water and bake them on the middle oven rack for 25 minutes or until they are golden brown. Remove the bread rings and place them on a cooling rack. Reduce the oven temperature to 400°F.

4 Slice the bread rings horizontally and bake for about 45 minutes. Cool the bread rings on the rack completely. Keep these bread rings well aired and dry.

Friselle al Pomodoro
Bread Rings with Tomatoes (Basilicata)

INGREDIENTS for 4:
4 small tomatoes
1 garlic clove
Salt and freshly ground pepper
3 Tbsp olive oil
2 Tbsp white wine vinegar
4 Friselle halves

PREPARATION TIME: 20 minutes
PER PORTION: about 295 calories

1 Bring a large pot of water to a boil. Blanch the tomatoes; rinse them under cold water. Core, peel, and chop the tomatoes. Place in a bowl. Peel and mince the garlic. Stir the garlic, salt, pepper, and 1 tablespoon of olive oil into the tomatoes.

2 In a second bowl, mix 1 cup of water with the vinegar. Break the Friselle into cracker-sized pieces and dip into the water vinegar; drain them and place them on a small serving plate. Distribute the dressed tomatoes evenly among the Friselle and drizzle with the remaining olive oil.

Friselle are the favorite appetizer in Basilicata, Calabria, and Apulia. Since they are very hard, soak them briefly before serving them; they will almost taste as if they were freshly baked. Friselle are often rubbed with garlic and lots of fresh sliced tomatoes before being topped with ham, cheese, or sardines. They also are topped with *n'duja* (see opposite).

N'duja
Spicy Pork Spread (Calabria)

INGREDIENTS for 6 (about 8 oz):

About 4 oz air-dried, salted smoked bacon

6–8 red peperoncini (about 4 oz)

1½ garlic bulbs

½ tsp ground coriander

PREPARATION TIME: 30 minutes
PER PORTION: about 120 calories

1 Chop the bacon and if necessary remove any rind or gristle. Rinse the peperoncini and cut off the stems. Slice open the pods and scrape out the seeds. Mince the pods. Peel and mince the garlic.

2 Pass all the ingredients through a fine meat grinder or chop together in a food processor. Season with the coriander

(salt is not necessary since the bacon is already salty). Use this as a spread or place in a jar and refrigerate for no more than 3 days.

N'duja is a major seasoning ingredient and condiment in Calabria's cuisine; it is usually prepared with fat and salted pork mixed with lots of peperoncini and garlic, and then smoked. This simplified version is also tasty.

Cipolle in Agrodolce
Sweet-and-Sour Red Onions (Calabria)

INGREDIENTS for 4:

1 lb large red onions (preferably mild, like those growing around Capo Vaticano)

Salt and freshly ground pepper

2 tsp sugar

2 Tbsp white wine vinegar

4 mint sprigs

PREPARATION TIME: 25 minutes
PER PORTION: about 35 calories

1 Peel and slice the onions. Place them in a skillet and add about 4–5 tablespoons of water; season with the salt, pepper, sugar, and vinegar.

2 Rinse the mint and add them to the onions. Simmer over low

heat until the onions are soft and tender. Serve the onions in small bowls; they go well with other appetizers or side dishes, or as an accompaniment to Friselle (see left).

The onions that grow around Capo Vaticano are large, deep red, and extremely mild in flavor. Those that grow around Tropea look the same but have a stronger flavor. Sweet onions such as Vidalias are similar in size and flavor, but not in color.

Filei alla Ricotta Casalinga
Pasta Rollups Filled with Ricotta (Calabria)

INGREDIENTS for 6:

For the ricotta:

2 cups organic whey (available at natural food stores)

4 cups whole milk

Salt and freshly ground pepper

For the noodles:

2½ cups bread flour + flour, for dusting

1 cup semolina flour

2 eggs

Salt

For serving:

3–4 oz grated or shaved smoked cheese (such as Provola or Scamorza)

PREPARATION TIME: 45 minutes
RESTING TIME: 4 hours
PER PORTION: about 465 calories

Recommended Wine:
mild, not-too-acidic white wine such as a Cirò.

This is an ancient, almost forgotten recipe from Calabria. The whey that is left over after the production of cheese (typically from sheep's milk) is combined with fresh milk and heated. As the mixture curdles, it is filtered through a cloth and drained well. The result is true ricotta, or cheese that is "cooked twice." The remaining whey is not discarded but is used to cook the noodles. They are tossed with fresh ricotta and seasoned only with salt and pepper—a very frugal but delicious specialty.

Filei or *fileia* are similar to maccheroni and are made in various shapes and lengths. If they are served with sauce, they will be longer; if they are served with legumes (especially red beans) they will be shorter.

The use of eggs to prepare these noodles is a modern update. Originally these noodles were prepared from gluten-rich hard wheat flour made from mountain wheat; besides flour, only water and salt were needed.

1 For the ricotta, pour the whey into a saucepan and heat to 190° F (use a candy thermometer). Pour in the milk and wait until the mixture begins curdling (make sure the mixture does not boil). Remove the saucepan from the stove and set it aside for 1 hour.

2 Place a fine-meshed colander over a large pot. Line the colander with a clean damp dishcloth or cheesecloth. Carefully pour the whey mixture into the colander and gather and tie the cloth around the ricotta. Hang it up to facilitate the draining of the liquid. Let the ricotta drain for about 3 hours.

3 Meanwhile, for the noodles, mix the flour and semolina. Add 4–6 tablespoons of water and 1 teaspoon of salt (if you work with a pasta machine you may need a little less water); knead everything well, wrap in plastic wrap and let the dough rest for about 1 hour.

4 Knead the dough and dust it and a work surface with flour. Roll out the dough into very thin sheets (if you work with the pasta machine use the lowest number of thickness). Cut the dough into 3–4 inch wide pieces. Layer these pieces near each other on a clean dishcloth and cover them with a slightly damp one.

5 One at a time, roll the pieces of dough around a very thin stick or skewer (such as a thin knitting needle). Roll the pasta sheet for 1½ rotations, cut the remaining sheet, and slide the pasta off the stick. Roll up the pasta piece by piece until you have no pasta sheets left; place the noodle rolls on a dishcloth dusted with flour.

6 Place the ricotta in a mixing bowl and season it with salt and pepper. Add about 4 cups of water and some salt to the whey; bring to a boil. Drop the noddles into the boiling water and cook them for about 6–7 minutes or until al dente; while the noodles cook, scoop out about 1 cup of the cooking water.

7 Drain the noodles. Fold them into the fresh ricotta and if necessary moisten everything with some cooking water. Distribute among serving plates and serve with shaved or shredded cheese.

Linguine al Paparul Crusc
Linguine with Dried Peppers (Basilicata)

INGREDIENTS for 4:

4 large sun-dried red peppers (see Tip; substitute with mild peper-oncini)

6 garlic cloves

1 lb linguine or other narrow and flat noodles

Salt and freshly ground pepper

1 bunch parsley

¼ cup olive oil

PREPARATION TIME: 30 minutes
PER PORTION: about 515 calories

1 Remove the seeds and stems from the peppers and crumble them. Grind the peppers in a spice mill to a medium-fine powder.

2 Peel the garlic and slice each clove lengthwise into 4 pieces. Bring a large pot of salted water to a boil. Cook the pasta according to package directions or until al dente. Rinse and pat dry the parsley; mince the leaves.

3 Drain the pasta, reserving 1 cup of cooking water. In the same pot, heat the olive oil and sauté the garlic over medium heat for about 5 minutes or until it has become golden brown.

4 Add the pepper powder and continue sautéing. Pour in the pasta water and add the noodles. Briefly stir the noodles into the pepper mixture. Season with salt and pepper and sprinkle with the parsley; toss all ingredients and distribute the pasta in the serving plates. Serve immediately.

Tip: This recipe is very similar to Abruzzi's spaghetti aglio e olio, but this version is less spicy. Also, no cheese goes with this dish! If you can't find the dried peppers called *paparul* in the Italian specialty markets, look for similar peppers in the Latin section of your supermarket; dried chiles such as red mulato, or red New Mexico, or pasilla peppers are similar. Or you can try to dry peppers yourself in the oven at 200° F; use whole red Anaheim or Hungarian cherry peppers and roast until the seeds rattle when you shake the pods. If the pods do not taste spicy enough (a certain spiciness is part of the specialty) you may increase the heat with cayenne pepper.

Recommended Wine: a fruity light red wine such as the Basilicata Rosso.

Fusilli con Alici
Fusilli with Anchovies and Shredded Bread Rings (Basilicata)

INGREDIENTS for 4:

1 oz anchovies (preserved in salt)

2 Friselle bread rings (page 250)

1 lb fusilli pasta

Salt and freshly ground pepper

4 Tbsp olive oil

2 garlic cloves

2–3 parsley sprigs

PREPARATION TIME: 30 minutes

PER PORTION: about 705 calories

1 Rinse the anchovies under cold water; pat them dry with paper towels and if necessary remove and scrape off any bones. Chop the anchovies.

2 Break the Friselle into pieces and process them into large crumbs in a food processor.

3 For the pasta, bring a large pot of salted water to a boil. Cook the fustilli according to package directions or until al dente.

4 Heat 2 tablespoons of olive oil in a large skillet or saucepan. Peel the garlic and crush it with the garlic press. Sauté until fragrant. Stir in the anchovies and sauté until the anchovies fall apart.

5 Heat the remaining oil in a small skillet and toast the Friselle crumbs over medium heat for about 5 minutes until golden but not brown. Rinse and pat dry the parsley; mince the leaves.

6 When the pasta is done, scoop 1 cup of the cooking water into the anchovies. Drain the pasta and toss it into the anchovy mixture. Season with salt and enough freshly ground pepper.

7 Distribute the noodles in serving plates and top them with the Friselle crumbs. Sprinkle the pasta with the parsley. Serve immediately.

This very flavorful pasta dish is traditionally served on St. Joseph's Day, March 19th.

Recommended Wine: a hearty, full-bodied white wine such as a Chardonnay from Basilicata.

Small Red Chili Devils

The more southern and hotter the land, the spicier the seasoning

In Italy, the spicy, almost hellishly hot chili pods, are called peperoncini; often they are also called endearingly diavoletti, or little devils. Whether fresh or dried, they lend their fiery character to countless recipes. In the southern regions especially they are more frequently used than pepper.

Spicy Safety. There is a practical reason that explains why people in hot regions like eating spicier than those in cooler regions. Harmful bacteria that can cause food to spoil and lead to stomach and intestinal problems multiply faster when it is hot. Spicy seasonings have compounds that create the conditions that inhibit the action of those microorganisms that allow foods to spoil. These substances are found in high concentrations in garlic, onions, and peperoncini.

Instead of pepper. It was Christopher Columbus who brought peperoncini from South America to Europe and to Italy. Italians were not at first overly enthusiastic about the spicy pods; in fact peppercorns, imported at great expense from India, had been most valued since the times of the ancient Romans. However, with pepper prices constantly on the rise, the less expensive peperoncini became more popular over time, in no small part because they could be grown locally. The plants grew easily from seeds and thrived in hot climates. In fact, the hotter the climate, the spicier these fruits became for people who at first considered them almost hellishly spicy.

From green to red. Peperoncini's berrylike fruits, also called pods or capsules, are first green and turn bright red or dark red when entirely mature. However, they can be used during all stages of maturity and their color does not determine whether the pod is spicy or mild. The heat level depends upon the amount of capsaicin the pepper contains—which can vary within one same plant from pod to pod. In Italy, medium-hot varieties seem to be preferred; the short *veneti* that are either canned green or served broiled as antipasti or the longer and slender *lombardi* that are suitable for canning and that when red and ripe are used for drying and as a staple seasoning for long storing purposes.

A Calabrian specialty is *paparul crusch* or *paparul crusc*, dark red pepper pods that are sun-dried in autumn and fried whole and served as an appetizer; they are also ground to a fine powder (as is done in Turkey to prepare *pulbiber*). For seasoning purposes, the pods are also crushed and sautéed in olive oil or added to dishes. They are medium-hot and their flavor is very similar to paprika.

Sweet Fire. Italians' love for peperoncini even extends into the realm of sweets. Fiery pods are used to spice up chocolate and candies; there are also jams made with peperoncini, that are served with cheese or are spread over crumbly pies (crostate).

a

a For an infernally hot peperoncini oil (in Abruzzi called olio santo, or holy oil), put 5–6 very hot dried peppers in 1 cup of olive oil in a glass jar. Leave at room temperature for about 2 weeks, periodically shaking them. Only a few drops of this oil are enough to season and give spice to salads, pasta, pizza, beans, or stews with meat.

b When peperoncini are ripe and red but not yet dried they are lined up on strings and hung up to dry. In this way, they also decorate the southern Italian vegetable stands. When they are thoroughly dried the pods can supply spiciness until the next harvest since they maintain their heat and flavor even when dried.   c Chocolate flavored with dried peperoncini is a specialty that is popular in other countries.   d To clean the pods, it helps to have patience as well as a leathery skin. Wear gloves—and take care not to handle the peppers and later rub your eyes!   e Peperoncini don't only hang for decoration outside the homes; they are a fiery ingredient for almost all the dishes, for spicy pasta sauces, and for stew specialties.

Brodetto di Pesce

Fish Chowder (Calabria)

INGREDIENTS for 4:

7–8 medium tomatoes

2 onions

5 garlic cloves

3 sprigs fennel greens

1 peperoncino (chili pepper)

5 Tbsp olive oil

2 lbs fresh mixed fish, cleaned and ready-to-cook (such as grouper, eel, monkfish, mullet, stone bass, and sea bream)

$\frac{1}{2}$ lb unpeeled jumbo shrimp

Salt and freshly ground pepper

8 small slices of white bread

3–4 parsley sprigs

1 thyme sprig

PREPARATION TIME: 20 minutes
COOKING TIME: 1 hour and 10 minutes
PER PORTION: about 400 calories

Recommended Wine:
A full-bodied refreshing white wine such as Calabria's Scavigna Bianco.

Fish specialties are prepared throughout the coastal areas of Italy, and the ingredients are similar.—Don't use pretty or delicately flavored fish in this dish, but instead use the less expensive varieties (that might not be sold to restaurants and thus have lower demand). These fish lend a definite flavor to the broth; the ugly grouper (be careful, as some species can have fins that sting and are poisonous!), small breams, or monkfish (which lend to the broth a richer consistency with its cartilaginous body) or any whitefish. The only fish not well suited for this dish are fatty fish such as herring and mackerel that would give an oily flavor to the chowder.

1   Bring a large pot of water to a boil. Blanch the tomatoes; rinse them under cold water. Core, peel, and chop them. Peel and mince the garlic and the onion. Rinse and chop the fennel greens. Trim the peperoncino; remove the stem and seeds and mince the pod.

2   Heat 3 tablespoons of oil in a large saucepan. Sauté the onions and garlic until golden brown. Add the tomatoes and fennel and stir in 1 cup of water; simmer, covered, for about 30 minutes.

3   Rinse the fish under running water (especially the insides). With a knife or a fish scaler, scrape off the dark scales from the fish; they would lend the broth a bitter taste. Rinse the shrimp.

4 Add 4 cups of water to the tomatoes; season with salt and pepper and bring everything to a boil over high heat. Reduce the heat; add the fish (but not yet the shrimp) and cook everything over low heat for about 15–20 minutes. Preheat the oven to 165°F (if convection oven 140°F) and heat the serving bowls.

5 Remove the fish from the broth; remove the skin and bones from the fish, leaving the fillets as intact as possible. Keep the fillets warm. Replace the bones and the fish heads in the broth and simmer for 15 more minutes. Heat the remaining oil in a skillet. Toast the bread slices until they are golden.

6 Rinse and pat dry the herbs; mince the leaves. Pour the fish broth through a fine-meshed colander and return it to the saucepan. Heat the broth and season it. Cook the shrimp in the broth for 5 minutes. Place the toasted bread slices in the bowls; top these with fish fillets. Remove the shrimp from the broth and add them to the bowls. Pour in enough fish broth to cover the fish. Sprinkle the fish chowder with the minced herbs. Serve immediately.

Baccalà alla Molinara

Dried Cod with Olives and Capers (Calabria)

INGREDIENTS for 4:

1 lb baccalà (dried and salted cod fish)

1 bay leaf

1 large tomato

1 lb red potatoes

3 celery ribs (with the green tops)

3 red onions

1 Tbsp capers (preserved in salt)

5 Tbsp olive oil

Flour, for dusting

$1/4$ cup pitted black olives

Salt and freshly ground pepper

Pinch crushed peperoncino or cayenne pepper

$1/2$ cup dry white wine

2–3 parsley sprigs

1–2 tsp lemon juice

PREPARATION TIME: $1^1/_2$ hours
SOAKING TIME: Overnight
PER PORTION: about 730 calories

1   Soak the baccalà in cold water to cover overnight; change the water periodically.

2   Bring a large pot of water to a boil and add the bay leaf. Boil the baccalà for about 3 minutes. Remove the fish (keep the water boiling) and cut it into 1–2-inch large pieces; while you cut the fish, discard the skin and the bones.

3   Blanch the tomatoes; rinse under cold water. Core, peel, seed, and cube them. Scrub and peel the potatoes; cut them into quarters. Trim and slice the celery; mince the green tops. Peel and mince the onions. Rinse the capers and let them drain.

4   Heat the olive oil in a large saucepan. Dust the fish pieces with flour and fry them on both sides over medium heat; remove

them from the pan. Add the onions and sauté until they are golden. Add the potatoes, celery, olives, capers, and 1 cup of water. Season with salt, pepper, and peperoncino; cover and simmer for about 15 minutes.

5   Add the wine and cook over high heat for 5 minutes or until the liquid has reduced. Add the fish pieces and tomatoes and simmer for about 5–7 minutes. Rinse and pat dry the parsley; mince the leaves.

6   Season the stew with salt, pepper, and lemon juice. Sprinkle with the parsley and serve with white bread.

Sarde in Padella

Fried Sardines (Calabria)

INGREDIENTS for 4:

1½ lbs fresh sardines

Salt and freshly ground pepper

4 garlic cloves

2 oregano sprigs (substitute with 2 teaspoons dried oregano)

1 peperoncino (chili pepper)

¼ cup olive oil

Flour, for dusting

2 bay leaves

½ cup dry white wine

2 Tbsp white wine vinegar

PREPARATION TIME: 45 minutes
COOKING TIME: 15 minutes
PER PORTION: about 400 calories

1 Rinse each sardine and cut open the belly. With your thumb, carefully spread open and lift the central bone and the intestines. Free the bone and carefully pull it toward the head of the fish; with scissors, cut the central bone from the tail to the head, making sure that the smaller bones are removed. Cut off the heads.

2 Rinse the sardines inside and out; pat them dry and season them with salt and pepper. Press the fish closed. Peel and mince the garlic. Rinse and pat dry the oregano; remove the leaves from the stems. Rinse the peperoncino; remove the stem and seeds, and mince it.

3 Heat the olive oil in a large skillet. Sauté the garlic and peperoncino over low heat until everything is translucent. Dust the sardines with flour and fry them,

in batches if necessary, on both sides. Season with salt and pepper and sprinkle with half of the oregano; add the bay leaves.

4 Stir in the wine and vinegar; simmer, covered, over low heat for about 10–15 minutes, periodically shaking the skillet. Serve these with salted boiled potatoes or with fresh white bread.

261

Lepre alla Cacciatora e Maiotica
Stewed Hare with Elderberry Blossoms (Calabria)

INGREDIENTS for 4:

For the ragù:

2 lbs hare meat with the bone (cut into pieces)

1 rosemary sprig

3 Tbsp white wine vinegar

¾ cup dry red wine

¼ cup olive oil

2 red onions

4 garlic cloves

3 celery ribs

2 carrots

11 oz cherry tomatoes

1 bay leaf

Salt and freshly ground pepper

2–3 parsley sprigs

For the elderberry blossoms:

½ cube fresh yeast (0.7 oz)

1¾ cups all-purpose flour

Salt

1 egg

8 elderberry blossoms

about 1 cup oil to fry

PREPARATION TIME: 45 minutes
MARINATING TIME: Overnight
COOKING TIME: 2 hours
PER PORTION: About 730 calories

1   Trim the meat and remove all fatty or sinewy parts; rinse the meat, pat it dry and place it in a dish. Rinse the rosemary and add it to the meat. Add the vinegar and wine; cover and refrigerate overnight.

2   The next day, remove the meat from the marinade and pat it dry (keep the marinade). Heat the oil in a large saucepan. Brown the meat on all sides over medium heat for about 10 minutes. Meanwhile, peel and chop the onions and garlic, and add them to the meat. Cook 10 more minutes.

3   Peel and trim the carrots and celery; cube the vegetables. Add the carrots and celery to the meat and cook 5 more minutes. Stem the tomatoes and cut into halves; add to the hare.

4   Stir in the marinade, including rosemary, and add the bay leaf; season with salt and pepper. Simmer, covered, over low heat for about 2 hours.

5   Meanwhile, crumble the yeast and mix it with about 1½ cups of lukewarm water. Make a batter by adding the flour, salt, and egg; set the batter aside for about 30 minutes. Clean the elderberry blossoms very carefully (don't rinse them).

6   Rinse and pat dry the parsley; mince the leaves. Heat the oil in a deep skillet. The oil will be ready for frying when small bubbles show around a wooden spoon dipped in the oil. Dip the elderberry blossoms in the batter and fry them in the hot oil for about 2–3 minutes or until crispy and golden. With a slotted spoon, remove the fried blossoms and place them to drain on a layer of paper towels.

7   Season the meat with salt and pepper. Sprinkle with the minced parsley and serve with the fried elderberry blossoms.

Hare alla cacciatora, or hunter's-style, is prepared in many regions of Italy, but only in Calabria is it served with elderberry blossoms.

Maiale alla Cirotana
Meatballs in Pork Ragù (Calabria)

INGREDIENTS for 4:

For the ragù:

$1\frac{1}{2}$ lbs lean pork meat (such as leg or tenderloin)

2 red onions

4 garlic cloves

1–2 oz bacon

$\frac{3}{4}$ cup dry white wine

1 rosemary sprig

1 bay leaf

$\frac{1}{2}$ tsp ground fennel seeds

Salt and freshly ground pepper

5–6 plum tomatoes

1 Tbsp lemon juice

1–2 basil sprigs

For the meatballs:

9 oz lean veal cutlets

1 small white onion

1 slice stale white bread

1 egg

Salt and freshly ground pepper

$\frac{1}{2}$ tsp grated lemon zest

PREPARATION TIME: 30 minutes
COOKING TIME: 1 hour and 10 minutes

PER PORTION: about 1150 calories

1   For the ragù, pat dry the pork and cut into 1-inch cubes. Peel and mince the onions and garlic.

2   Chop the bacon and sauté it in a large saucepan until the fat has rendered and the bacon bits are golden and crispy. Remove the bacon bits and brown the pork on all sides over medium heat. Add the onions and garlic and sauté until golden brown.

3   Stir in the wine. Rinse the rosemary and add to the meat with the bay leaf; season with the fennel, salt, and pepper. Simmer the ragù, covered, over low heat for about 30 minutes.

4   Meanwhile, bring a large pot of water to a boil. Blanch the tomatoes; rinse them under cold water. Core, peel, seed, and chop them. Add the tomatoes to the ragù and if necessary add a little water; simmer for 20 more minutes.

5   For the meatballs, pat dry the veal and cube it. Peel and coarsely chop the onion. Remove the crust from the bread and cube it. Process everything in the food processor. Pulse in the egg and season everything with salt, pepper, and lemon zest. With your hands, form into small meatballs and add these to the ragù. Simmer 20 more minutes.

6   Remove the rosemary and the bay leaf from the ragù. Season the sauce with lemon juice, salt, and pepper. Rinse and pat dry the basil; mince the leaves and sprinkle over the ragù. Serve immediately.

This ragù, prepared with smaller chunks of meat and tiny meatballs, is often served over cavatelli pasta.

263

Lombo d'Agnello con Olivi

Leg of Lamb with Olives (Basilicata)

INGREDIENTS for 4:

1 lb leg of lamb (cut into 4 pieces and deboned)

Salt and freshly ground pepper

1 Tbsp dried and ground hot peppers (for example *paparul crusc* or crushed red peperoncini)

4 rosemary sprigs

1–2 oz sun-dried tomatoes (not preserved in oil)

5–6 oz chanterelle mushrooms (substitute with shiitake mushrooms)

$\frac{1}{4}$ cup small pitted black olives

1 onion

2 garlic cloves

2 Tbsp olive oil

About 1 cup dry red wine (for example Aglianico del Vulture)

2 oregano sprigs

PREPARATION TIME: 1 hour
PER PORTION: about 665 calories

People in the region of Basilicata love lamb almost as much as they love pork. The choice pieces of this meat are usually grilled or sautéed in a skillet; less tender cuts are roasted in the oven with vegetables, mushrooms, and herbs.

Italians would most likely use *ovuli* mushrooms in this dish. However, they are very hard to find outside of Italy. A similar variety grows wild in this country; however, they are also very rare and should be treated cautiously. To substitute for *ovuli* mushrooms, you may use chanterelles, shiitake mushrooms, white, or cremini mushrooms.

Herbs such as rosemary, thyme, sage, oregano, and wild mint are always added to this dish. Of course, dried and ground *paparul crusc* (see page 256) are mandatory as well. For spiciness, you may add dried and crushed peperoncini or chili peppers. Add sparingly—peppers vary in spiciness—and taste before adding more. Another possibility could be using pure *pulbiber* that is sometimes available in Middle Eastern markets.

Recommended Wine:
an aromatic berry-scented red wine such as Basilicata's Aglianico del Vulture.

1   Trim the lamb, removing any fatty or sinewy parts. Pat the meat dry with paper towels and rub them with salt and crushed pepper. Rinse and pat dry the rosemary; place a sprig on each piece of meat and tie the meat and the rosemary together with the kitchen twine.

2   Soak the tomatoes in a little hot water and set them aside to soften. Clean the mushrooms with a brush or a clean dishcloth; do not rinse them, otherwise they soak up water. Leave the small mushrooms whole and cut the larger ones in halves.

3   Slice the olives. Peel and mince the onion and garlic. Preheat the oven to 165°F (if convection oven 140°F) and heat the serving plates.

4 Chop the tomatoes. Heat the olive oil in a skillet. Brown the lamb on both sides over medium heat for about 4–5 minutes. Transfer the meat to a roasting pan and place it on the middle oven rack for about 15 minutes.

5 Add the onion and the garlic to the skillet and sauté for about 3–4 minutes until they are golden brown. Add the mushrooms and simmer them until the moistness has visibly reduced. Add the tomatoes and olives and simmer briefly. Stir in the wine and simmer, uncovered, for about 10 more minutes.

6 Rinse and pat dry the oregano; mince the leaves. Season the sauce with salt and pepper. Remove the meat from the oven and discard the kitchen twine and rosemary. Slice the meat ½-inch thick against the grain. Place the meat on the heated plates and pour over the mushroom gravy; sprinkle with the oregano.

Pomodori alla Lucani

Stuffed Tomatoes (Basilicata)

INGREDIENTS for 4:
8 firm tomatoes
Salt and freshly ground pepper
1–2 oz anchovies (preserved in salt)
3–4 slices stale white bread
2 garlic cloves
2–3 parsley sprigs
4 Tbsp olive oil + oil for the baking pan
1/3 cup raisins
1/4 cup pine nuts

PREPARATION TIME: 20 minutes
COOKING TIME: 20–25 minutes
PER PORTION: about 270 calories

1 Rinse the tomatoes and cut off the tops; set the tops aside. Scoop out the tomato pulp and set aside. Season the insides of the tomatoes with salt and turn them upside-down on a layer of paper towels in order to drain as much juice as possible. Rinse the anchovies, pat them dry, and mince them. Preheat the oven to 375°F (if convection oven 350°F). Remove the crust from the bread and crumble into a food processor. Process the bread to make coarse crumbs.

2 Peel and mince the garlic. Rinse and pat dry the parsley; mince the leaves. Heat the oil in a skillet. Sauté the garlic and bread crumbs over medium heat until brown. Add the raisins and pine nuts. Stir in the anchovies and parsley. Season with salt and pepper; stuff the tomatoes with the mixture.

3 Oil a baking dish and place the tomatoes in it. Spoon the tomato pulp over the filling, cover with the tomato tops, and moisten everything with about 1/3 cup of water. Bake the tomatoes on the middle oven rack for about 20–25 minutes.

Romanesco con Alici

Green Cauliflower with Anchovies (Calabria)

INGREDIENTS for 4:
1 green cauliflower (about 1 1/2 lbs)
Salt and freshly ground pepper
4 anchovies (preserved in salt)
1 ball buffalo mozzarella (4–6 oz)
1 red peperoncino (chili pepper)
2 hard-boiled eggs
2 garlic cloves
1/4 cup olive oil
8 small pitted olives
3–4 Tbsp lemon juice

PREPARATION TIME: 30 minutes
PER PORTION: about 270 calories

1 Rinse and trim the cauliflower; break into florets. Bring a large pot of salted water to a boil and cook the cauliflower for about 7 minutes or until firm to the bite.

2 Meanwhile, rinse, pat dry, and mince the anchovies. Cube the mozzarella. Trim, seed, and mince the peperoncino. Peel and chop the egg. Peel and thinly slice the garlic. Heat the olive oil in a skillet and sauté the garlic until it is translucent.

3 Drain the cauliflower and rinse it under cold water; drain the florets and distribute them among serving plates or on one large serving plate; season with salt and pepper. Sprinkle the cauliflower with the olives, anchovies, mozzarella, peperoncino, and eggs. Drizzle with the garlic oil and some lemon juice. Serve at room temperature.

Surijaca

Borlotti Beans with N'duja and Onions (Calabria)

INGREDIENTS for 4:

1³⁄₄–2 cups dry borlotti beans (substitute with red kidney beans or pinto beans)

2 garlic cloves

2 bay leaves

2 tsp crushed pepper flakes (or to taste)

Salt and freshly ground pepper

3 oz bacon (Calabrians use lard instead)

2 Tbsp flour

2 large red mild onions

5–6 oz N'duja (page 251)

PREPARATION TIME: 20 minutes
SOAKING TIME: Overnight
COOKING TIME: 1½ hours
PER PORTION: about 495 calories

1 Rinse the beans and discard the bad ones. Soak the beans in cold water to cover overnight.

2 The next day, drain the beans. Bring the beans and about 6 cups fresh water to a boil. Cook the beans periodically skimming off the foam with a fine-meshed skimmer. Peel the garlic and drop it whole in the simmering beans with the bay leaves and the pepper flakes; simmer over low heat for about 1–1½ hours; when the beans are almost done season with salt and pepper.

3 Chop or mince the bacon. Sauté the bacon in a skillet over medium heat until the fat has rendered and the bacon bits are golden brown. Remove the bacon bits and stir the flour into the bacon fat; make a golden brown roux. Moisten the roux with a little bean water and cook until it bubbles. Fold the beans into the thickened roux and cook the beans for 5 more minutes in the roux.

4 Peel and cut the onions into quarters. Distribute the beans in small bowls (preferably clay bowls) and top them with a scoop of N'duja and some onion wedges. Before eating, stir the N'duja into the beans, and use the onion wedges like spoons. Serve together with fresh white bread or Friselle (see page 250). After using the onion "spoons" they are usually eaten.

This simple farmers' specialty from Capo Vaticano was originally flavored with wild herbs, such as the wild chicory that grows easily along country paths and throughout meadows; they can be used before their light blue flowers show up.

Recommended Wine: A full-bodied red wine such as a Cirò Classico Superiore Riserva.

267

Fichi alla Griglia

Grilled Figs (Calabria)

INGREDIENTS for 4:

¹/₄–¹/₂ cup almonds

8 oz dried figs (choose soft ones)

1 tsp fennel seeds

1 cup semisweet chocolate

Oil, for grilling

PREPARATION TIME: 45 minutes
PER PORTION: about 430 calories

1 Soak wooden or bamboo skewers in water. Toast the almonds in a dry skillet to bring out their aroma. Cut open the figs horizontally and place 2 almonds and a few fennel seeds in each fig. Press the figs shut and thread them on the skewers.

2 Light a grill and bring it to medium heat. Oil a roasting pan and set the grill rack approxi-

mately 5 inches from the heat. Put the figs in the pan and grill for about 10 minutes. Set them aside to cool.

3 Chop the chocolate and melt it in the top of a double boiler. Dip the figs on both sides into the chocolate, leaving the center part of the figs uncoated. Place the skewers on a cooling rack and allow the chocolate to harden.

Mustazzuoli

Honey Fritters (Calabria)

INGREDIENTS for 60 fritters:

¹/₄–¹/₂ cup almonds

¹/₂ tsp groung cloves

6–8 Tbsp sugar

1 organic orange

10–11 oz wild honey

4 cups all-purpose flour + flour, for rolling

2 eggs

PREPARATION TIME: 30 minutes
BAKING TIME (PER BAKING SHEET): 10–15 minutes
PER PIECE: about 55 calories

1 Chop the almonds and toast them in a dry skillet; set them aside to cool. Mix the cloves with the sugar. Scrub the orange under hot water. With a zester or grater, remove about 1 tablespoon of the zest.

2 In a mixer with a kneading hook, mix the honey and flour; add the eggs, almonds, sugar mixture, and orange zest; mix and knead all the ingredients to make a smooth dough.

3 Heat the oven to 425°F (if convection oven 400°F). On a floured work surface, roll out the dough and cut it into rectangles (about 1 × 2 inches). Line a baking sheet with parchment paper and place the rectangles on the sheet; bake on the middle oven rack for about 10–15 minutes. Place the baked mustazzuoli on a cooling rack.

In Calabria, these honey cookies are served with the white dessert wine *Greco di Bianco.*

Sorbetto di Mandarino

Mandarin Sorbet (Basilicata)

INGREDIENTS for 4:

4 large mandarins (preferably organic; substitute with clementines)

¾ cup sugar

2 very fresh egg whites

Confectioners' sugar, for dusting

PREPARATION TIME: 30 minutes
FREEZING TIME: 3 hours
PER PORTION: about 170 calories

1   Scrub the mandarins under hot water and cut off the tops; set the tops aside. Working over a bowl to catch the juice, use a melon baller or sharp grapefruit knife to cut out the mandarin pulp, making sure not to damage the peels.

2   Gather the fruit pulp in a cheesecloth or a clean dishcloth and squeeze out the juice over the bowl. Place the mandarin shells and tops into the freezer.

3   Combine 1½ cups water and ⅓ cup of the sugar in a saucepan. Bring to a boil. Let the liquid cook down over high heat for 5 minutes; add the mandarin juice and simmer for 5 more minutes. Set the mandarin syrup aside to cool, then pour it through a fine-meshed sieve. Pour the liquid in a flat pan and freeze for 1 hour.

4   Beat the egg whites with the remaining sugar until stiff peaks form and fold it into the partially frozen mandarin juice. Freeze for 2 more hours, stirring with a fork every 30 minutes.

5   To serve, scoop out the mandarin sorbetto and puree with a hand mixer to break up the ice crystals. Fill the frozen mandarin shells with the sorbetto; cover with the mandarin lids, if desired. Set the mandarins on plates or on one large serving plate and dust them with confectioners' sugar. Garnish, if you like, with mandarin leaves or blossoms.

Refreshing sorbetti made from the juice of citrus fruits are a favorite throughout the entire south of Italy. Sometimes they are scooped into sparkling wine, liqueur, or Prosecco as an aperitivo.

Sicily

Island world: A hot wind from Africa, hardy sheep, and seafood

The Region and Its Products
Sicily—A bridge between Italy and Africa, surrounded by islands and seas

The largest island of the Mediterranean Sea also borders the Ionian and Tyrrhenian Seas. Scattered in the nearby seas are three groups of islands: to the north, the Eolian Islands, with Lipari as the largest; to the west, the Egadi Islands with Favignana as the largest, and in the south, the Pelagos Islands with Lampedusa as the largest. At the western end of the island is the island of Pantelleria, also called the Black Pearl. Sicily's most amazing sight is Mount Etna, or Monte Etna, the highest of Europe's active volcanoes, which reaches above the sea more than 11,000 feet.

A Hooded Smoking Giant. Its peak hidden above the clouds, Mount Etna, like all volcanoes, carries the threat of unspeakable damage and destruction. Paradoxically, however, lava flows have also brought fertility to the land. Hard wheat, various types of citrus fruits, almond and pistachio trees, as well as innumerable fruits, vegetables, and grapes for wine grow in the rich soil around the volcano.

Wheat, olives, and almonds are the traditional crops grown in Sicily. Vegetables and greens—especially eggplants, tomatoes, zucchini, and fennel—are planted everywhere in small, carefully tended gardens. Even the inhabitants of the coastal areas tend their plots with love and care. Pigs are raised for their meat, and sheep provide milk, meat, and lamb. Game animals as well as mushrooms that thrive from June to November are hunted throughout the oak forests. Meadow mushrooms and porcini are even known to children here; recently, cultivated cremini and oyster mushrooms have become favorites. To flavor and season there are diverse herbs, and of course garlic is used often and with dedication.

Fish and Seafood are the Markers of this Coastal Cuisine. Even though the local fishing yield has decreased compared to the days when the Mediterranean Sea was still a truly rich source of fish, seafood is still one of the main foods for the island inhabitants; swordfish and red tuna, which moves to spawn in the warm water that surrounds Sicily are especially popular. Other popular fish are sardines and anchovies, which are sold fresh by the local fishmongers and are ready to cook. Seafood like squid (calamari), octopus (pulpo), mussels (*cozze*), clams (*vongole*), and rock limpets (*patelle*) abound. *Gamberetti di nassa* (nassa is the basket used to catch them) are a type of shrimp found only around Sicily. These creatures have a very delicate orange shell and carry a bright blue roe. These shrimp spoil very quickly and are only offered around the coastal areas.

Walking around the open market of Catania can be sheer joy. Among the treasures for sale are the most aromatic tomatoes; Sicily boasts plenty of sun to provide flavor and color to them. San Marzano tomatoes grow well in the mineral-rich soil around Mount Etna. They are often canned to stretch the tomato season from one harvest to the next. The bright red tomatoes are especially suited for sauces; the firm, irregularly shaped green and yellow tomatoes are not unripe but of a special variety. These are better to use raw in salads or to prepare stuffed. Flavorful oranges are used in Sicily for an interesting and refreshing salad dish with onions.

Sicilians prefer to buy their fish directly off the boat. At the mouth of the river at the port of Mazzara del Vallo, fishermen auction their catch, which cooks in the frying pan shortly thereafter.

When the almond trees begin to bloom around the end of January the city of Agrigento celebrates with a blossom festival. Almonds are ultimately a very important ingredient for sauces and cookies, as well as for the famous marzipan called *pasta reale* (royal paste).

The Sicilian sun makes it possible: when seawater evaporates in shallow basins what remains behind is coarse sea salt. Between Marsala and Trapani, salt is still produced in this traditional way.

A little time for a little chat is a must. The daily trip to the small neighborhood grocery store is also a good opportunity for keeping up with the latest news from around town.

According to legend, In the Benedictine cloister of Palermo founded by Eloisa Martorana, the first fruit-shaped marzipan was made. Called frutta di martorana, this sweet can be bought today in every *pasticceria* (pastry shop), though it was traditional to make them on All Soul's Day.

The Cuisine

Several cultures have left their mark on this truly remarkable cuisine

Sicily is a true melting pot—its cuisine, and the cuisine of neighboring islands—reflects the island's central location and its history. For millennia, traders, merchants, and conquerors left their traces and their recipes. Greek, Roman, French, Spanish, and Arabian influences are readily discernable. North African cuisine can be seen as well in the preference for sweet-and-sour combinations and cous cous, the steamed wheat dish, made from tiny pieces of semolina.

Daily Pasta. Arabs occupied Sicily for about 200 years, and their culinary legacy is seen in the maccheroni prepared from a dough kneaded with wheat flour, egg white, and rose water. The thin strips were curled around an iron thread. Pasta is still a daily meal, often tossed simply with ricotta, seafood or fish, or tomatoes. Peperoncini, tomatoes, eggplants, and potatoes were brought to Italy from the new world and introduced here by Sicilian seamen. Rice. however, is not very popular here; if used at all, it is used for arancini, the small stuffed rice balls that are served as appetizers at the bars.

Tuna, swordfish, and small sardines and anchovies are the favorite on the island. The simplest way to prepare them is still the best: with pure olive oil, fresh herbs, and seasonal vegetables. The *sardea beccafico* (stuffed sardines) reflects very much the Arab influence and is so popular that virtually every restaurant along the coast offers its own version.

In the old days, beef was so tough that it was most often ground. Even today, recipes with ground meat are more popular than are grilled steaks. Sicilians love pork, especially the definite flavor of the meat of the black pigs.

If any vegetable could be singled out as the "typical" Sicilian vegetable it would have to be eggplant also called *milinciani*. Eggplants have always found their way into myriad dishes: Marinated or grilled, fried in slices or cubes, filled with noodles or savory mixtures and baked, stewed with tomatoes and raisins as in caponata, or layered with cheese and vegetables in parmigiana.

Frozen desserts like sorbetto and granita also show the influence of Arabs (sorbetto is from the Arab word *sciarbat*). Originally made with snow from Mount Etna and flavored with flowers and fruits, today these are prepared with sugar syrup and flavored with citrus fruits, watermelon or mulberry juice, as well as with jasmine flowers. Pan di Spagna, or Spanish bread, dates back to Spanish domination. It is a sweet cake that is the basis of tiramisù. *Cassata* made from ricotta and candied fruits, gets its name from the Arabic word *qas'at*, meaning round bowl.

a

b

c

d

a Eggplants and peppers are indispensable to Sicilian cuisine; they are used in countless ways.

b In Palermo's market's, vegetables and fruits are sold fresh, but also—as here at the mercato della Vucciria—cooked as a snack or light meal so that no one goes hungry.

c The fearsome swordfish and tuna are popular foods on the island. Whether stewed, grilled, or sautéed, their meat is somewhat reminiscent of beef or veal. One clear benefit to these fish: no pesky fish bones!

d Tiny bright orange shrimp with blue roe, called *gamberetti di nassa*, can be eaten raw or sautéed and combined with zucchini blossom over pasta.

e Granita, a grainy crushed-ice dessert flavored with the juices of lemons, blood oranges or berries, is the specialty of Sicily and the Lipari Islands.

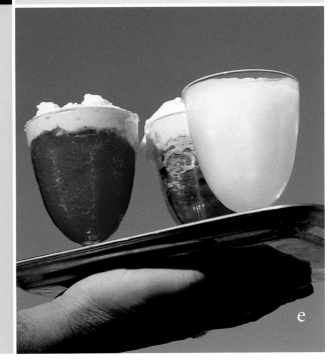

e

The Wines
Ancient vines and rising wine stars

It is hard to believe that a small island should offer so many varieties of wine, but Sicily boasts more vineyards and produces more wine than any other region in Italy. Nero d'Avola and Cataratto are, respectively, the most commonly planted red and white grapes. Even Cabernet Sauvignon or Chardonnay grapes grow here to a remarkable quality.

Wines from the Volcano.
Sicily's landscape is overshadowed by the presence of the volcano Etna. This very fertile region is blessed with a peculiar climate: the grape vines, which grow as high as 3,280 feet, thrive with shifts in temperature between day and night; exposure to the hot summer sun and cool—even cold—nights helps to develop aroma and flavor. The mineral-rich volcanic soil provides the grapes with an abundance of nutrients. A few wineries produce excellent red wines from the grape varieties Nerello and Cappuccio, as well as apple-scented white wines.

Red South.
The most important areas that grow Nero d'Avola, the indigenous grape found in almost all the red and rosé wines of Sicily, are located in the south, in the province of Agrigento and around the town of Vittoria. Until a few years ago this vine was still almost unknown; today it has become almost a status symbol. With well-tended vines and storage in small barrels, the wine is earning a reputation of fine quality. It has a slightly bitter and fruity aroma and has all the elements for a long aging maturation. Vines such as Cabernet Sauvignon and Syrah have found a suitable home in this region. Other authentic Sicilian wines are characterized by a delicate aroma of candied oranges. The white grape varieties of the island such as the Cataratto, Trebbiano, Grillo, and Inzolia sometimes produce pure variety wines and sometimes mixed mild and fruity wines.

New in the West.
Marsala is Sicily's most famous wine region. Most closely associated with the fortified wine of the same name—which isn't necessarily a good thing—the area nevertheless produces some excellent aged fortified wines. The grape variety Grillo is used not only to produce strong dessert wines but also to make sparkling white wines. Throughout the area of Trapani, full bodied aromatic reds are produced from Nero d'Avola grapes. Two other dessert wines create serious competition for Marsala wines: the Malvasia delle Lipari Passito, made from sun-dried Malvasia grapes that have a scent of lemon and orange blossoms, and the Passito di Pantelleria made from Zibibbo grapes with a scent of orange and apricot.

Left: Grape cultures in Sicily – the vines are trained along bamboo frames.
Above: Famous regional samples (from left to right)—the reds Nero d'Avola and Monreale Syrah; the whites Grillo Parlante and Don Pietro.

Regional Recipes
Sicily's cuisine lives off the freshness and the aroma of its ingredients

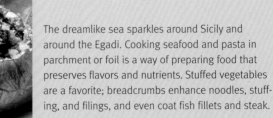

The dreamlike sea sparkles around Sicily and around the Egadi. Cooking seafood and pasta in parchment or foil is a way of preparing food that preserves flavors and nutrients. Stuffed vegetables are a favorite; breadcrumbs enhance noodles, stuffing, and filings, and even coat fish fillets and steak.

Sfincione di Caltanisetta
Small Pizzas with Tomatoes and Cheese (Sicily)

INGREDIENTS for 4:

For the dough:

2 cups all-purpose flour

½ cup semolina flour

1 tsp salt

¼ cube fresh yeast (about 0.3 oz)

Oil, for baking sheet

For the topping:

½ lb plum tomatoes

1 small onion

2 Tbsp olive oil

1–2 basil sprigs

Salt and freshly ground pepper

Pinch freshly ground peperoncino

2 garlic cloves

3 anchovies (preserved in salt)

12 pitted green olives

3 oz fresh goat or sheep cheese
   (substitute with cottage cheese)

3 Tbsp aged pecorino cheese

PREPARATION TIME: 30 minutes
RESTING TIME: 2 hours
BAKING TIME: 20 minutes
PER PORTION: about 415 calories

Sicilians use lard to obtain a smoother dough. You may substitute the water in the recipe with milk, which will also make a softer dough.

These small and thick-crusted pizzas are often topped with olives, anchovies, and two varieties of cheese, and are available not in pizza places but in bakeries and eateries found everywhere in Palermo. In the old days they were prepared on Friday, which was commonly known as bread-baking day. Cooks took advantage of the hot ovens and baked small pieces of dough after the large loaves; the smaller breads were eaten still warm with olives, cheese, and olive oil.

1 Mix the flour and semolina in a bowl. Crumble the yeast into ⅔–¾ cup of lukewarm water and let stand until foamy. Add it to the flour and knead vigorously to make a springy dough. Cover the dough with a clean dish towel and let it rise for about 2 hours.

2 For the topping, bring a large pot of water to a boil. Blanch the tomatoes; rinse them under cold water. Core, peel, seed, and cube them. Peel and thinly slice the onion. Heat ½ Tbsp of olive oil in a large skillet. Sauté the onion until translucent. Add the tomatoes and simmer for about 15 minutes.

3 Rinse and pat dry the basil; mince the leaves. Season the tomato sauce with salt, pepper, peperoncino, and basil. Let the sauce cool a bit. Peel and chop the garlic. Rinse the anchovies and remove any bones from them; chop the anchovies.

4 When the dough has doubled in size, preheat the oven to 425°F (if convection oven 400°F). Oil a baking sheet. Cut the dough into 4 pieces and knead and shape each piece to a thick wheel about 5 inches in diameter. Place on the baking sheet and brush them with olive oil.

5 With your fingers, make small indentations all over the surface of the dough. Push a piece of garlic, a piece of anchovy, or an olive into each major indentation.

6 Crumble and spread the fresh cheese over the dough, then spoon on the tomato sauce.

7 Coarsely grate the pecorino over the tomato sauce and drizzle with the remaining olive oil. Bake the pizzas on the middle oven rack for about 20 minutes or until they are golden brown. Serve these either warm or cold.

Muffuliette

Fennel Rolls (Sicily)

INGREDIENTS for 4:
4 cups all-purpose flour + flour, for kneading
2 tsp salt
2 tsp fennel seeds
½ cube fresh yeast (about 0.7 oz)

PREPARATION TIME: 15 minutes
RESTING TIME: 4 hours
BAKING TIME: 15–20 minutes
PER PORTION: about 455 calories

1 Mix the flour, salt. and fennel seeds in a bowl. Crumble the yeast in about 1 cup of lukewarm water and let it stand until foamy. Add it to the flour and combine and knead all ingredients.

2 Knead the mixture to make a smooth dough and dust the dough with a little flour. Cover the dough with a clean dish towel and let it rise for about 3 hours or until it has visibly doubled in size.

3 Punch down the dough and knead it again; cut the dough into 4 pieces and knead and shape these pieces into rolls. Line a baking sheet with parchment paper and set the rolls on the baking sheet. Cover the rolls with a clean damp dishcloth and let them rise 1 hour more.

4 Preheat the oven to 475°F (if convection oven 450°F). With a small sharp knife, cut crosses into the surface of each roll. Bake the rolls on the middle oven rack for about 15–20 minutes or until they are light brown. Just before the rolls are done, brush them with hot water to give them sheen. Let the rolls cool off on a cooling rack.

Muffuliette are a Sicilian specialty; they are traditionally baked on Saint Martin's Day and are stuffed with either cheese or sausage and served with local young wines.

Pomodori nel Panino

Tomato Subs (Sicily)

INGREDIENTS for 4:
2 medium fresh firm tomatoes
1 small cucumber
Salt and freshly ground pepper
1 mild white onion
1 red peperoncino (chili pepper)
3 basil sprigs
2 Tbsp white wine vinegar
3 Tbsp olive oil
4 large oblong or round sandwich rolls

PREPARATION TIME: 35 minutes
PER PORTION: about 245 calories

1 Core the tomatoes and cut them into thin wedges. Rinse, trim, and cube the cucumber. Season the cucumbers and tomatoes with salt and place them into a colander to drain for about 15 minutes.

2 Peel and chop the onion. Trim the peperoncino; cut stem, seed, and mince it. Rinse and pat dry the basil; slice the leaves.

3 Mix the tomatoes, cucumber, onion, peperoncino, and basil; toss with the pepper, vinegar, and olive oil; taste and if necessary season with salt.

4 Cut off a horizontal "lid" from each of the rolls; remove the soft insides of each roll and fill the cavities with the tomato-cucumber salad. Replace the lids and serve immediately.

These salad-filled sandwiches were originally taken to the field where workers ate them during Vesper time. Use this method of scooping out rolls and filling them to make other sandwiches.

Tonno con l'Insalata di Patate
Tuna on Potatoes and Onions with Mint (Sicily)

INGREDIENTS for 4:

1 lb thin-sliced tuna steaks

2 garlic cloves

Salt and freshly ground pepper

$\frac{1}{4}$ cup dry white wine

4–5 medium boiling potatoes

2 organic lemons

2 large red onions

4 mint sprigs

6 Tbsp olive oil

PREPARATION TIME: 1 hour
PER PORTION: about 470 calories

1 With paper towels, pat dry the tuna steaks and place them in a shallow dish. Peel the garlic and crush it with a pinch of salt in a mortar; stir in the white wine and drizzle this mixture over the tuna steaks. Cover the tuna with plastic wrap and refrigerate for about 30 minutes.

2 Scrub the potatoes and place them in salted water; cook them, covered, for about 25–35 minutes or until tender.

3 Scrub the lemons under hot water. Slice one thinly and set aside for garnish. Juice the other lemon. Peel and chop the onions. Rinse and pat dry the mint; tear off the top leaves and set them aside. Slice the remaining mint leaves.

4 Remove the potatoes from the boiling water and let them cool slightly; peel and cube them while they are still warm. Toss the potatoes with the onions, sliced mint, lemon juice, and 4 tablespoons of olive oil; season them well with salt and pepper. Let cool to room temperature.

5 Remove the tuna steaks from the marinade and pat them dry with paper towels. Heat the remaining oil in a skillet and fry the steaks over medium heat for about 1 minute on each side. Remove the skillet from the heat and let the tuna cool slightly.

6 Distribute the potato salad among serving plates and top each portion with a tuna steak. Garnish with the lemon slices and mint. Serve with fresh white bread.

Recommended Wine:
A refreshing and smooth white wine, as a Cataratto from Sicily, will go best with this. This type of wine is clean tasting and not acidic but fruity.

Carciofi Gratinati
Baked Artichokes (Sicily)

INGREDIENTS for 4:

6 small artichokes (see Tip)

1 Tbsp lemon juice

Salt and freshly ground pepper

6 Tbsp freshly grated pecorino cheese (substitute with parmesan cheese)

5 Tbsp plain white breadcrumbs

6 Tbsp heavy cream

1 garlic clove

3 Tbsp butter + butter for the baking pan

2 oregano sprigs (substitute with 1 tsp dried oregano)

2 Tbsp Marsala wine (fortified dessert wine)

$1\frac{1}{4}$ cups tomato puree

2 small dried peperoncini (chili peppers)

$\frac{1}{2}$ bay leaf

PREPARATION TIME: 45 minutes
BAKING TIME: 15 minutes
PER PORTION: about 265 calories

Recipes like this one were originally not eaten throughout the day like an antipasto but, like Spanish tapas, with a glass of wine in the evening. They were also served as a contorno after the first course or instead of a main course of fish or meat.

Today antipasti such as this are sold ready-to-eat in small eateries to take out or to eat in.

Tip: You may substitute the artichokes with zucchini, cutting them lengthwise 3–4 inches long. With a melon baller or a sharp knife, scoop out the inside of the zucchini and bake them as you would the artichokes.

1 Rinse the artichokes. With sharp scissors, cut off the top leaves until you reach the tender heart. Trim the stem and peel the pieces that were cut off. Fill a pot with cold water and the lemon juice.

2 Cut the artichokes in half lengthwise along the stem and remove the choke. Drop the artichoke halves in the lemon water to prevent them from becoming brown; when all artichokes are trimmed and prepared, season the water with salt and bring the whole pot to a boil.

3 Cook the artichokes, covered, for about 15–20 minutes. Preheat the oven to 425°F (if convection oven 400°F). Mix the pecorino cheese with the breadcrumbs and heavy cream. Peel the garlic and crush with a garlic press; add to the mixture and season with salt and pepper.

4 Remove the artichokes from the water and set them aside to drain. Fill them with the cheese mixture and place them in a buttered baking pan. Sprinkle them with the breadcrumbs and top with thin slices of butter.

5 Rinse and pat dry the oregano; mince the leaves. Mix with the Marsala and tomato puree. Crush the peperoncini and bay leaf in a mortar. Season with salt and pepper and top the artichokes with the mixture.

6 Bake the artichokes on the top oven rack for about 15 minutes or until the buttered breadcrumbs begin to brown. Serve the artichokes while still hot, with fresh white bread on the side.

Versatile and Boneless—Cephalopods

The fine difference between squid, cuttlefish, and octopus

The popularity of squid and its relatives has something to do with the way they are built—they have no shells, no scales, and no bones. On top of this, they are inexpensive and are culinarily very versatile, not to mention delicious.

Clouds of Ink. Though they are sometimes categorized as "shellfish," these members of the mollusk family are more similar to snails. Their tentacles are placed around their heads; for this reason they are also called cephalopods. These creatures all have an ink sac, which they use to defend themselves. When the creatures feel threatened they eject this ink and disappear in the dark cloud. This ink is very valued; cooks use it to color and flavor pastas and risotto, and artists use it for special ink drawings. For this reason it is rare to find squid with their ink sacs in most markets; the ink sacs themselves are usually only available at the fishmonger if ordered ahead of time.

Fat and round. Cuttlefish is more common in Europe than in the United States. Called *seppie* in Italy, it has a round fat head with eight short "arms" and two longer tentacles. It differs from squid in that it has a hard calcareous inner shell. Its body is about 3 inches long and about 1–2 inches wide and lends itself to being stuffed and stewed. The tentacles are often minced and added to the stuffing. If you don't find them ready-to-cook in the market, just cut off the tentacles above the eye part. Cut around the body at the darker part and carefully remove the hard shell. Behind the shell you will find the ink sac; remove this too. Then peel the body by slipping a finger under the skin; pull the skin and discard the unwanted parts. Finally rinse and clean well the part you wish to use.

Small fry. The very small cuttlefish, called *seppiola* or *seppiolina*, are not baby ones but are actually a variety that are rarely exported but are found almost exclusively throughout the Mediterranean Sea. In our supermarkets these are usually available only frozen since they spoil very easily.

Long and slender. If your definition of calamari begins and ends with the fried appetizer, it's time to expand your horizons. Calamari, or squid, can be stuffed, stewed, baked, or tossed into salads. If they are available fresh they are usually handled like seppie; frozen squid are often already cleaned and headless. A smaller variety of these are called calamaretti and are usually prepared in salads or stewed in tomato and pasta sauces.

Eight legs and arms. Last but not least is the octopus (called polpo in Italian), with eight tentacles that have each very visible suction cups along these extremities. Among the cephalopods, the octopuses have the toughest flesh; before being cooked they should be either pounded or, as was once common, thrown on stones to tenderize them. When they are purchased frozen this procedure is not necessary; the freezing has already had the same tenderizing effect. Nevertheless, an octopus requires about 1 to 2 cooking hours. *Moscardini* are small octopus that require only about 30 to 45 minutes cooking time.

a For polpo insalata, bring to a boil a 1-pound octopus in 3 cups of water, 1 cup of white wine, and 2 teaspoons of sea salt; simmer over low heat, covered, for about 45 minutes. Remove the pot from the heat and allow the octopus to cool in the water. Drain it in a colander and cut it into bite-sized pieces. Dress it with 4 tablespoons of white wine vinegar, 5 tablespoons of olive oil, and plenty of minced or chopped parsley; season it with salt and pepper and mix. Set it aside for the flavors to blend before serving it cold.

4 Heat the oil in a large skillet. Sauté the garlic. Add the parsley and wine and allow to cook down over high heat for about 5 minutes. Add the tomatoes and peperoncino and simmer for about 10 minutes.

5 Cook the linguine according to package directions until firm to the bite. Add the seafood to the sauce, stir, and simmer for 5 more minutes or until the mussels and clams have opened. Discard any unopened clams or mussels. Season the sauce with salt and pepper. Brush 4 sheets of foil with oil. Drain the noodles and fold them into the sauce.

6 Divide the pasta and seafood among the foil sheets. Seal the foil like a bag, making sure that all the ends are tightly twisted shut. Place the foil bags on the middle oven rack and bake them for about 10 minutes or until all ingredients have gained in flavor.

7 Place each bag on a serving plate and allow each person to open the bag at the table (do this carefully as steam will escape) and enjoy the aroma and flavor of the specialty. No cheese with seafood pasta!

Sarde a Beccafico

Baked Sardine Rolls (Lipari)

INGREDIENTS for 4:

16 small fresh sardines (about 6 inches long each; about 1 1/2 lbs total)

2 Tbsp raisins

2 anchovies (preserved in salt)

2 Tbsp pine nuts

2–3 parsley sprigs

1 cup plain white breadcrumbs

6 Tbsp olive oil + oil for baking dish

1 Tbsp limoncello (lemon liqueur; substitute with Cointreau)

Salt and freshly ground pepper

$\frac{1}{2}$ tsp ground cinnamon

4 large bay leaves

2 large organic lemons

2 tsp sugar

PREPARATION TIME: 1$\frac{1}{4}$ hours
COOKING TIME: 22–25 minutes
PER PORTION: about 445 calories

1 Rinse the sardines, removing the scales, under running water. Cut from the head to the tail and along the back cut open each sardine. Carefully remove the head and the entrails. Rinse the sardines once more, especially their insides; cut off the central fish bone up to the tail. Cut off the fins but leave the tails. Pat the sardines dry with paper towels.

2 Soak the raisins in warm water. Rinse and pat dry the anchovies; chop them with the pine nuts. Drain and chop the raisins. Rinse and pat dry the parsley; mince the leaves.

3 Heat 3 Tbsp of oil in a small skillet. Add half of the breadcrumbs and brown over medium heat. Put into a mixing bowl; add the anchovies, pine nuts, raisins, parsley, and limoncello and mix.

Season with the salt, pepper, and cinnamon. Preheat the oven to 425°F (if convection oven 400°F).

4 Brush a baking dish (about 10 inches in diameter) with oil. Season the sardines with salt and pepper. Place a little breadcrumb mixture on each of the butterflied sardines, rolling up each fish from the head to the tail. Set them in the baking dish close together, leaving the tail parts exposed. Cut each bay leaf in half lengthwise, placing one piece between the sardine rolls. Sprinkle with the remaining bread crumbs; drizzle with the remaining olive oil. Bake the sardines on the middle oven rack for about 15 minutes.

5 Meanwhile, scrub 1 lemon under hot water and slice it thin.

Extract the juice from the remaining lemon; whisk the lemon juice and the sugar together. Drizzle the lemon sugar mixture over the fish and bake 7–10 more minutes. Serve in the baking dish and garnish with lemon slices.

Beccafico is the name of a small warbler bird that likes to eat ripe fallen figs. The sardine rolls not only look like small fat birds but taste also very good.

Tonno alla Messinese

Tuna Messina-Style (Sicily)

INGREDIENTS for 4:

4 tuna steaks (about 4–5 oz each)

1 Tbsp lemon juice

3 large tomatoes

1 onion

2 garlic cloves

2 Tbsp nonpareil capers (pre-served in salt)

2–3 parsley sprigs

3 Tbsp olive oil

$\frac{1}{2}$ cup pitted green olives

Salt and freshly ground pepper

PREPARATION TIME: 20 minutes
COOKING TIME: 20 – 25 minutes
PER PORTION: about 395 calories

1   Pat dry the tuna with paper towels and drizzle with the lemon juice.

2   Bring a large pot of water to a boil. Blanch the tomatoes; rinse under cold water. Core, peel, seed, and chop the tomatoes. Peel the onion and garlic; slice the onion and mince the garlic. Rinse and drain the capers. Rinse and pat dry the parsley; mince the leaves.

3   Heat the olive oil in a large skillet. Sauté the onion over medium heat; add the garlic, tomatoes, capers, and olives. Season with salt and pepper and simmer, covered, over low heat for about 15 minutes.

4   Place the tuna steaks in the tomato sauce and simmer, covered, for about 5–10 minutes. Season the sauce with salt and pepper; sprinkle with the parsley. Serve immediately with fresh bread.

The Italian word for tuna is tonno, but Sicilians called tuna tunnu. Throughout Italy, this fish is as popular as swordfish. The fish have similar textures and can be used interchangeably in most recipes—including this one. No matter which you use, take care not to overcook as both have a tendency to dry out easily. Like beef, tuna can be cooked to different donenesses. For this recipe, the inside of the steaks should still be pink.

Bistecche alla Palermitana

Rib-Eye Steaks, Palermo-Style (Sicily)

INGREDIENTS for 4:

4 rib-eye steaks (about 6 oz each)

4 Tbsp olive oil

1 lb cherry tomatoes

2 thyme sprigs

Salt and freshly ground pepper

2 anchovies (preserved in salt)

2 Tbsp capers (preserved in salt)

2 Tbsp plain white breadcrumbs

2 Tbsp freshly grated pecorino or parmesan cheese

2 garlic cloves

1/4 cup dry white wine

PREPARATION TIME: 30 minutes
COOKING TIME: 20 minutes
PER PORTION: about 405 calories

Sicilians love to grill their meats; besides steaks, they grill lamb, pork, rabbit, quail, and spicy and hearty sausages. Cooking steaks on a grill pan means you can enjoy this recipe even on the coldest winter evening, and finishing them in the oven provides a delicious sauce and also a side dish.

We recommend purchasing steaks from a good butcher; ask for evenly marbled steaks, which will be more tender.

Recommended Wine: a full-bodied red wine with a scent of berries, such as a Cabernet Sauvignon from Sicily.

1 Pat dry the steaks with paper towels; trim the fat and make sharp cuts around the edges of steaks. Brush the steaks with 1 tablespoon of olive oil and massage the oil into the meat. Cover the steaks and set aside at room temperature.

2 Preheat the oven to 450°F (if convection oven 400°F). Brush a roasting pan with oil. Stem the tomatoes and cut them into halves. Rinse and pat dry the thyme. Layer the tomatoes and thyme leaves in the roasting pan.

3 Season the tomatoes with salt and pepper. Rinse the anchovies and capers and pat them dry. Chop both and place them in a bowl.

4 Add the breadcrumbs to the anchovies and capers. Peel the garlic and crush it using a garlic press; stir in the remaining olive oil; season with salt and pepper.

5 Drizzle the white wine over the tomatoes; braise on the middle oven rack for about 10 minutes. Meanwhile, heat a grill pan or griddle over very high heat until very hot; do not add any fat. Sear the steaks for 1 minute on each side. Season the meat with salt and pepper, then transfer the steaks to the roasting pan.

6 Sprinkle the breadcrumb mixture over the steaks and return the roasting pan to the oven. Roast everything for 10 more minutes or until the breadcrumbs have all turned golden brown. Serve immediately.

Spiedini di Carne

Meatball Kebabs (Sicily)

INGREDIENTS for 4:

1 lb ground pork
1 bunch parsley
1 basil sprig
Salt and freshly ground pepper
4 thick slices stale white bread
8 oz mozzarella balls (*bocconcini*)
2 eggs
About ¼ cup breadcrumbs
1–2 cups olive oil

PREPARATION TIME: 45 minutes
PER PORTION: about 580 calories

1 Put the pork in a large mixing bowl. Rinse and pat dry the parsley and basil; mince the parsley leaves and slice the basil leaves. Add to the pork and season with salt and pepper; mix well. With a melon baller or your hands, make small meatballs (about 1 inch in diameter).

2 Cut the crusts from the bread and cube the bread. Oil 4 metal skewers and thread them alternately with the meatballs, mozzarella balls, and bread cubes.

3 Whisk the eggs with a little salt in one shallow bowl; put the breadcrumbs in another. Pour olive oil (about 1 inch deep) in a frying pan and heat.

4 Dip the skewers first into the egg wash, then in the breadcrumbs, coating them thoroughly. Fry the skewers in the hot oil for about 2–3 minutes on all sides until crispy. Remove the skewers from the oil and place them on a layer of paper towels to drain. Serve immediately.

Pollo alla Liparota

Chicken with Onion Gravy (Lipari)

INGREDIENTS for 4:

4 chicken legs (about 7 oz each)
2 large onions
4 garlic cloves
1 celery rib
2 Tbsp nonpareil capers (preserved in salt)
¼ cup olive oil
Salt and freshly ground pepper
1 Tbsp flour
1 Tbsp sugar
1⅓ cups dry white wine
1 Tbsp white wine vinegar
2 parsley sprigs

PREPARATION TIME: 30 minutes
COOKING TIME: 30 minutes
PER PORTION: about 465 calories

1 Rinse and pat dry the chicken legs. Peel the onions and garlic; slice the onions and chop the garlic. Trim and chop the celery. Rinse and drain the capers.

2 Heat the oil in a Dutch oven. Season the chicken legs with salt and pepper and dust them with flour. Brown the chicken legs over medium heat for about 5 minutes on each side. Remove the chicken legs.

3 Sauté the onions and celery in the pan drippings until both are translucent. Add the garlic and sprinkle with the sugar; cook until the ingredients are almost caramelized. Pour in the wine and vinegar and bring to a boil; simmer to allow the liquid to cook down.

4 Return the chicken legs to the pan; add the capers and simmer over low heat for about 30

Fegato di Vitello su Caponata
Veal Liver over Caponata (Sicily)

minutes. Rinse and pat dry the parsley; mince the leaves.

5 Season the sauce with salt and pepper. Transfer the chicken legs to serving plates and spoon the onion gravy over them. Sprinkle the chicken with the parsley and serve with fresh white bread.

Recommended Wine:
A fruity, somewhat sparkling white wine such as Bianco Alcamo from western Sicily.

INGREDIENTS for 4:

1 small eggplant (about 12–13 oz)

Salt and freshly ground pepper

1 Tbsp raisins

2 Tbsp brandy

5 medium tomatoes

2 shallots

2 garlic cloves

¼–½ cup pitted purple or black olives

1 Tbsp capers (preserved in salt)

1 small rosemary sprig

4 slices calf's liver (about 3–4 oz each)

6 Tbsp olive oil

1 dried peperoncino (chili pepper)

2 Tbsp pine nuts

1 tsp white wine vinegar

PREPARATION TIME: 45 minutes
PER PORTION: about 400 calories

1 Trim and cube the eggplant. Place the cubes in a colander; season them liberally with salt and set them aside to drain for about 20 minutes.

2 Meanwhile, soak the raisins in brandy. Bring a large pot of water to a boil. Blanch the tomatoes; rinse under cold water. Core, peel, and cut into eighths. Peel and chop the shallots and the garlic. Slice the olives. Rinse the capers and set them aside to drain. Rinse and pat dry the rosemary; mince the leaves. Pat dry the liver and brush with 2 tablespoons of olive oil.

3 Heat the remaining olive oil in a Dutch oven. Pat dry the eggplant cubes and sauté them over medium heat, stirring occasionally for about 7–10 minutes. Add the shallots and garlic and sauté

them briefly. Add the raisins and brandy, the tomatoes, olives, and capers; crumble in the peperoncino. Simmer over low heat for about 10 minutes. Toast the pine nuts in a small skillet until they are golden brown.

4 Set a large skillet or a frying pan over high heat. When hot, sear each piece of liver on both sides for about 2–3 minutes. Season with salt, pepper, and rosemary.

5 Adjust the flavor of the caponata by seasoning, if necessary, with salt and pepper; stir in the wine vinegar. Spoon the caponata onto plates and top with a slice of liver; sprinkle with the pine nuts and serve immediately. As a side dish, serve either boiled and salted potatoes or fresh white bread.

295

Capers—Precious Flower Buds

The fine capers are from the island of Pantelleria, but those from Salina and Lipari are also excellent.

The thorny low-growing bushes can be found throughout the Mediterranean, but their flower buds, capers, are mainly harvested and preserved in Italy, especially on the islands surrounding Sicily. They are dried in the sun, preserved in salt, and aged for two months.

Beautiful blossoms. The blooming plant is beautiful,
but farmers hate to see the blossoms. They show that buds were missed during the harvest. They will have to wait until new pear-shaped buds, similar to capers but called *cucunci*, grow out of the old blossoms. These are not as tasty or as tender as capers, but they can be preserved in vinegar and served with antipasti, and harvesting them means the buds are not wasted. Capers are not the fruits of the shrub but the tightly shut buds. The round buds can be harvested throughout the entire summer. Every three or four days, the farmer goes out to the field and harvests capers—which is actually not a simple thing, since the plants protect themselves with thorns that threaten everyone that comes too near. In addition, goats love the flavorful leaves of these bushes, and where there are many goats there tend to be very few caper bushes.

The smaller the better. The smaller the buds are the better—and
more expensive and precious—they are. They have better flavor, and many more are needed to fill a jar. Each size has its own term: the smaller capers are called *puntina* (they are typically labeled and sold under the French term *nonpareil*, however, so that is what we call for in these recipes); the medium sized are called *capperi*, and the larger ones *capperoni*. Up to 11 lbs of capers per year can be harvested from a fully grown plant. However, after 15 years the plants need to be pulled and renewed, otherwise the harvest output declines.

It is the salt. Fresh green buds have an intense, almost bitter taste.
To remove the bitterness, they are placed in salt, or they may be preserved in sea salt. The salt draws out the water and at the same time the bitterness; after 8 days the buds are drained and salted again. This procedure is repeated once or twice and after that their flavor and aroma have settled. The typical aroma of the capers originates from oils that develop only with an enzyme that occurs as the capers cure. Capers can be packed in salt or in a vinegar brine after they are cured. Gourmets prefer the salt-packed capers for their firmer texture and purer flavor.

Watered only briefly. Whether they are packed in brine or salt,
capers should be rinsed before they are used in recipes. For the removing of salt crystals they don't need much rinsing and draining. The very tiny capers from the Sicilian islands have a mild flavor and don't need much rinsing; they also should not be cooked too long, since this mutes and dissipates their delicate flavor.

a The caper salad made on the island of Lipari is fiery and spicy: Rinse and drain 1 handful of capers (preserved in salt). Rinse 1 handful of red peperoncini; cut off their stems, seed them, and mince them. Peel and mince 1 handful of garlic cloves. Dress everything with 3 tablespoons of white wine vinegar and 6 tablespoons of olive oil. Mix and set aside at room temperature for a few hours; season with salt. Toss again before serving with antipasti.

b The pink and white blossoms of the caper bush look fragile and delicate; each blossom indicates that one more caper has been missed. c For the production of capers only the small, firmly closed buds are harvested; the farmer passes and checks several times per week to check on the plants, since each branch has buds that are at different stages of maturation. d One day's harvest is on a clean cloth, waiting to be preserved in salt. e The low-growing caper bush requires the same soil and climate conditions as the Malvasia grapes that grow on the island of Salina. f The best capers are the smallest, the *puntina*; the medium-sized are called *capperi*, and the large ones are *capperoni*. g Caperberries, called *cucunci*, are usually preserved in vinegar and used to garnish antipasti.

Melanzane Ripiene
Stuffed Eggplants (Sicily)

INGREDIENTS for 4:

4 small round eggplants (about 7 oz each)

Salt and freshly ground pepper

1½ lbs plum tomatoes

1 large onion

½ bunch parsley

4 Tbsp olive oil

2 garlic cloves

1 cup plain breadcrumbs

1 egg

¼ cup freshly grated pecorino cheese (preferably Sicilian pecorino; substitute with parmesan cheese)

2 Tbsp Marsala wine (Italian dessert wine; substitute with white wine)

Pinch salt

Pinch freshly ground peperoncino

PREPARATION TIME: 30 minutes
COOKING TIME: 30–45 minutes
PER PORTION: about 270 calories

Because these stuffed eggplants look like small tobacco pouches; Sicilians sometimes call them *tabacchiere*. Unfortunately, round, light purplish eggplants that are the most suitable for this specialty may be difficult to find; look for them in specialty grocers or farmers' markets. You only need the eggplant shells for this dish; rather than waste the flesh, use it in other recipes such as caponata or pasta sauces.

Recommended Wine:
A light, cherry-scented rosé wine such as Rosato di Sicilia made from Nero d' Avola grapes; served chilled.

1   Rinse the eggplants and cut them almost in half, so that the end closer to the stem is the smaller; reserve the stem sections for another use. Put the eggplant halves in a pot of water and simmer over low heat, covered, for about 15 minutes.

2   Meanwhile, bring another large pot of water to a boil. Blanch the tomatoes; rinse them under cold water. Core, peel, seed, and chop them. Peel the onion and cut it in half. Slice one half and mince the other.

3   Rinse and pat dry the parsley; mince the leaves. Heat 3 tablespoons of olive oil in a large saucepan. Sauté the minced onion for 5 minutes or until translucent. Peel the garlic and crush through a garlic press into the pan. Remove the saucepan from the heat, stir in the breadcrumbs and set aside to cool.

4 Stir the egg, parsley, and cheese into the breadcrumb mixture; season with salt and pepper. Set it aside for a few minutes. Drain the eggplants and use a small paring knife or a melon baller to cut or scoop out the eggplant pulp, leaving a shell no thicker than ¼-inch.

5 Reserve the eggplant flesh for another use. Fill the eggplant shells with the breadcrumb mixture; press the stuffing down and flatten the surfaces.

6 Heat the remaining olive oil in a large saucepan. Brown the onion slices; add the tomatoes and simmer over low heat for about 10 minutes or until they have fallen apart. Stir in the Marsala; season with the salt, pepper, sugar, and peperoncino.

7 Place the stuffed eggplants in the sauce and simmer, covered, over low heat for about 30–45 minutes or until they are soft. Season the eggplants, if necessary, and serve them with the sauce. Fresh white bread makes an ideal accompaniment.

Insalata di Pane

Bread Salad (Lipari)

INGREDIENTS for 4:

1 small head Romaine lettuce
(about 7 oz)

8–9 oz cherry tomatoes

2 small red onions

2 Tbsp nonpareil capers
(preserved in salt)

$1/2$ cup pitted black olives

2 Friselle (page 250; substitute
with plain bagel chips)

2 Tbsp white wine vinegar

Salt and freshly ground pepper

$1/2$ cup olive oil

PREPARATION TIME: 30 minutes
PER PORTION: about 355 calories

1 Rinse and clean the lettuce;
slice the leaves $1/2$-inch wide.
Stem the tomatoes and cut them
in quarters. Peel and slice the
onions. Briefly rinse the capers
and drain them. Put everything in
a mixing bowl and add the olives.

2 Break the Friselle in small
pieces and soak them briefly in
cold water; remove the pieces
from the water, drain them and
add them to the salad in the
bowl.

3 Whisk together the vinegar,
salt, and pepper. Gradually whisk
in the olive oil to make a creamy
dressing. Pour the dressing over
the salad and toss in carefully.
Serve the salad right away while
the Friselle is still crispy.

On the island of Lipari, cooks
fold into the salad cold, cubed,
boiled potatoes instead of
Friselle.

Bietole con Uva Secca

Swiss Chard with Raisins (Sicily)

INGREDIENTS for 4:

$1/2$ lbs Swiss chard

Salt and freshly ground pepper

3 Tbsp olive oil

2 garlic cloves

3 Tbsp raisins

2 Tbsp white wine vinegar

PREPARATION TIME: 30 minutes
PER PORTION: about 150 calories

1 Rinse and pat dry the Swiss
chard. Trim the stems and cut
everything, including the stems,
into 1–2 inch long pieces. Bring a
large pot of salted water to a boil.
Blanch the chard for about 3–5
minutes or until the stems are still
firm to the bite. Drain, rinse under
ice water, and set aside in a
colander.

2 Heat $1/2$ tablespoons of olive
oil in a skillet. Peel the garlic and
crush through a garlic press into
the oil. Add the raisins and sauté
over medium heat until the raisins
appear to be puffed. Add the
Swiss chard and sauté briefly until
it is hot; season with salt and
pepper.

3 Place the Swiss chard on a
serving plate; drizzle with the
remaining olive oil and the vinegar. Serve hot or lukewarm.

In Sicily, this recipe is also used
to prepare the peeled stems of
cardoons, a thistlelike vegetable
that tastes like artichokes.

Involtini di Peperoni

Pepper Rolls (Sicily/Lipari)

INGREDIENTS for 4:

6 red bell peppers

1½ cups plain breadcrumbs

4 Tbsp butter

2 garlic cloves

½ bunch mixed herbs (preferably including wild fennel greens, dill, and parsley)

⅓ cup freshly grated pecorino cheese (substitute with parmesan)

1 egg

3–4 Tbsp dry white wine

Salt and freshly ground pepper

3–4 Tbsp olive oil

PREPARATION TIME: 20 minutes
COOKING TIME: 42–50 minutes
PER PORTION: about 435 calories

1 Preheat the broiler. Stem the peppers, cut them in half, and seed them. Place the peppers, cut-side down, on an oiled baking sheet and press them down a little. Broil them on the upper oven rack about 7–10 minutes until their skins have become charcoal black and look burned. (You can also bake them on the highest oven temperature for 10–15 minutes.) Reduce the oven temperature to 325°F (if convection oven 300°F).

2 Set the peppers aside to cool. Peel them and cut them into halves and flatten the strips on a work surface.

3 Heat 1 Tbsp of butter in a small skillet. Toast the breadcrumbs for about 3 minutes or until they are golden. Peel the garlic and crush through a garlic press into the breadcrumbs. Remove from the heat and set aside to cool. Rinse and pat dry the herbs; mince the leaves.

4 Mix the breadcrumbs with half of the grated cheese, the remaining butter, and the minced herbs. Add the egg and stir in the wine, 1 tablespoon at a time, until you have a soft but not runny stuffing. Season with salt and pepper.

5 Oil a shallow baking dish. Place a small amount of stuffing on each pepper strip, roll up the strips, and place them in the baking dish, one near the other, with the seam sides down.

6 Sprinkle the pepper rolls with the remaining cheese and drizzle with the olive oil. Bake on the middle oven rack for about 35 minutes or until the cheese has lightly browned; serve either warm or cold with fresh white bread.

Recommended Wine:
A fruity but not too tannic red wine with a berry aroma and a slightly smoky flavor, such as the red Corvo from Sicily.

301

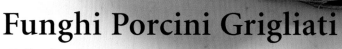

Funghi Porcini Grigliati
Grilled Porcini Mushrooms

INGREDIENTS for 4:

2–3 parsley sprigs

2 oregano sprigs (substitute with 1 tsp dried oregano)

4–6 small sprigs lemon verbena (substitute with lemon balm)

2 garlic cloves

Salt and freshly ground pepper

2 Tbsp lemon juice

8 Tbsp olive oil

1 lb fresh porcini mushrooms (substitute with cremini mushrooms)

PREPARATION TIME: 30 minutes
PER PORTION: about 240 calories

1 Rinse and pat dry the herbs; mince the parsley and oregano leaves, and slice the verbena leaves. Peel the garlic and crush it through a garlic press over a mix-ing bowl. Add the parsley and oregano; season with salt, pepper, and lemon juice. Combine all ingredients well, making sure that there are no chunks of salt. Stir in 4 tablespoons of olive oil to make a somewhat creamy sauce.

2 Wipe the mushrooms clean with a clean dishcloth and slice them about ½-inch thick. Heat the remaining oil in a large skillet. Sauté the mushrooms on both sides for about 5–7 minutes; season them with salt and pepper. When you turn the mushrooms over, slip a verbena leaf under each mushroom.

3 Distribute the mushrooms and the verbena leaves among serving plates; sprinkle or drizzle with the herb mixture and serve warm.

Patate al Forno
Oven-Roasted Potatoes (Sicily)

INGREDIENTS for 4:

1½ lbs red potatoes

1 red peperoncino (chili pepper)

1 large onion

2 Tbsp capers (preserved in salt)

½ cup pitted green olives

¼ cup olive oil

Salt and freshly ground pepper

1⅓ cups beef or vegetable broth

PREPARATION TIME: 25 minutes
COOKING TIME: 30–35 minutes
PER PORTION: about 250 calories

1 Scrub, peel, and cut the pota-toes into 1-inch cubes. Stem, seed, and mince the peperoncino. Peel and chop the onion. Rinse and drain the capers. Cut the olives into halves.

2 Preheat the oven to 425°F (if convection oven 400°F). Heat the olive oil in a skillet. Sauté the onion and potatoes until the onion is golden and translucent. Add the peperoncino, capers, and olives. Mix everything and season with salt and pepper (taste before seasoning, as the olives and capers are salty and the peper-oncino is hot).

3 Place the vegetables in a shallow baking dish and moisten everything with ⅓ cup of the broth. Bake on the middle oven rack for about 30–35 minutes or until the potatoes are tender, moistening occasionally with more broth; the dish should be dry before serving. Serve along-side fish or squid.

Scarola Ripiena

Stuffed Lettuce or Escarole (Lipari)

INGREDIENTS for 4:

4 small hearts of Romaine (see Tip)

Salt and freshly ground pepper

4 anchovies (preserved in salt)

1 Tbsp nonpareil capers (preserved in salt)

4 garlic cloves

3 Tbsp pitted green olives

2–3 parsley sprigs

⅓ cup olive oil

About 4 Tbsp plain breadcrumbs

PREPARATION TIME: 30 minutes
COOKING TIME: 30 minutes
PER PORTION: about 245 calories

1 Rinse, clean, and trim the lettuce, leaving the heads intact (the best way to do this is to immerse them in cold water). Bring a large pot of salted water to a boil. Blanch the lettuce for about 4–5 minutes or until the leaves have softened a little. Immerse the lettuce in ice water and set them aside to drain well.

2 Rinse and pat dry the anchovies. With a sharp paring knife scrape off any visible bones. Rinse, drain, and mince the capers. Peel and mince the garlic. Chop the olives. Rinse and pat dry the parsley; mince the leaves. Preheat the oven to 350°F (if convection oven 325°F).

3 Heat about 4 tablespoons of olive oil in a skillet. Sauté the garlic over medium heat. Add the anchovies, half of the breadcrumbs, the capers, olives, and parsley and sauté briefly. Remove the skillet from the heat and season with salt and pepper.

4 Carefully open the hearts of lettuce and stuff them with the breadcrumb mixture; press down to shut the leaves once they are stuffed. Oil a shallow baking dish and place the stuffed lettuce in the dish. Sprinkle with the remaining breadcrumbs and drizzle with the remaining olive oil.

5 Cover the baking dish with foil and bake on the middle oven rack for about 20 minutes. Remove the foil and bake for about 10 more minutes or until the breadcrumbs have become golden brown. Remove the baking dish from the oven and set aside to cool slightly. Serve lukewarm.

Tip: Scarola means escarole, and if you can find this green by all means use it in this dish. Hearts of Romaine are an ideal substitute, or try Belgian endive, radicchio, or large Swiss chard leaves.

Babà all' Amaretto

Raised Yeast Muffins with Amaretto Syrup (Sicily)

INGREDIENTS for 4:

For the dough:

2½ cups all-purpose flour + flour for the molds

½ cube fresh yeast (substitute with ½ envelope active dry yeast)

⅓ cup milk

1 Tbsp sugar

6–8 Tbsp butter, softened + butter for the molds

2 eggs

Pinch salt

3 Tbsp apricot jam

For the syrup:

About ¾ cup sugar

¼ cup Amaretto (almond liqueur)

To garnish:

1 handful fresh mixed berries (such as small wild strawberries, blueberries, raspberries, or red currants)

1 Tbsp sugar

⅓ cup heavy cream

2 tsp vanilla sugar

Pinch of ground cinnamon

PREPARATION TIME: 35 minutes
RESTING TIME: 1¾–2¾ hours
BAKING TIME: 20–25 minutes
PER PORTION: about 860 calories

Recommended Wine:
A flavorful, orange blossom-scented dessert wine such as the Malvasia delle Lipari Passito.

These small puffy breads are available in many regions of Italy but appear to have originated in Sicily. The syrup with which they are moistened seems to indicate an Arabian influence, which is common in Sicilian cuisine.

Babàs are a delicious and impressive dessert that are deceptively easy to make.

1 To make the dough, place the flour in a mixing bowl, make a well in the center, and crumble in the yeast. Mix the milk and sugar and pour into the well; stir the mixture and set aside at room temperature, covered, to rest for about 15 minutes.

2 Add the eggs, salt, and softened butter to the flour mixture. Knead to make a smooth dough; cover the dough with a damp dishcloth and let rise for about 1–2 hours or until the dough has visibly doubled in size.

3 Grease a muffin tin with butter and dust with flour. Fill each cup about half full with dough and cover with the same cloth for about 30 minutes while they rise again. The dough is ready when it reaches the top border of the muffin pans.

4 Preheat the oven to 375°F (if convection oven 350°F). For the syrup, bring 1⅓ cups of water and the sugar to a rolling boil. Let the syrup boil vigorously over high heat for 2–3 minutes until it is clear. Remove it from the heat and let cool. Meanwhile, bake the babàs on the middle oven rack for about 20–25 minutes or until lightly browned. Set them aside to cool a bit.

5 Mix the sugar syrup with the Amaretto and gently place the babàs into the liquid; turn them over to coat them thoroughly with syrup. Set them on a cooling rack to drain and cool further. Meanwhile, heat the jam until it begins to melt. Using a pastry brush, brush the babàs with the jam.

6 To garnish, rinse and drain the berries; roll them in the sugar. Beat the cream and vanilla sugar until stiff peaks form. If you wish, spoon the whipped cream into a pastry bag. Pour a little syrup onto each of the serving plates.

7 Place the babàs over the syrup and garnish with the sugared berries. Pipe or spoon some whipped cream onto each serving and dust very lightly with ground cinnamon.

305

Macedonia
Mixed Fruit Salad (Sicily)

INGREDIENTS for 4:
½ lb small strawberries
½ lb sweet cherries
½ lb small apricots
1 large organic orange
¼ cup Marsala wine
3 Tbsp sugar
1 tsp vanilla extract
⅓ cup shelled pistachio nuts

PREPARATION TIME: 30 minutes
MARINATING TIME: 1 hour
PER PORTION: about 190 calories

1   Rinse and hull the strawberries; cut them in half. Remove the stems from the cherries; rinse and pit them. Rinse and pit the apricots; slice them into thin wedges. Combine the prepared fruits.

2   Scrub the orange under hot water. With a zester or grater, remove 1 teaspoon the zest. Extract the juice from the orange. Combine the orange juice, zest, Marsala, sugar, and vanilla, stirring until the sugar has dissolved.

3   Drizzle the Marsala mixture over the mixed fruits and mix everything gently. Set the fruit salad aside for 1 hour at room temperature.

4   Toast the pistachio nuts in a small skillet; sprinkle them over the fruit salad and serve.

Tortine di Pasta Frolla
Pie Dippers (Sicily)

INGREDIENTS for 6–8:
1¾ cups all-purpose flour + flour for dusting
⅔ cup sugar
1 tsp vanilla sugar
1 egg
1 Tbsp white wine
½ tsp baking powder
Pinch salt
7 Tbsp cold butter + softened butter for the pie plate
Confectioners' sugar, to dust

PREPARATION TIME: 20 minutes
BAKING TIME: 50 minutes
PER PORTION (FOR 8 SERVINGS): about 260 calories

1   Preheat the oven to 300°F (if convection oven 275°F). Put the flour on a work surface and make a well in the center. Add the sugar, vanilla sugar, egg, white wine, baking powder, and salt to the well and mix. Cut in the cold butter, kneading together to make a pie crust.

2   Brush a pie plate (about 9–10 inches in diameter) with softened butter; dust the pie plate with flour. Press the dough into the pie plate. Bake on the middle oven rack for about 50 minutes or until the dough has become crispy. Remove from the oven and set aside to cool.

3   Turn out the pie crust onto a plate and break it into pieces; dust the pieces with confectioners' sugar. Serve these pie dippers as a dessert together with grappa, a sweet dessert wine, or espresso. Everybody gets a piece of "pie" and dips it into a liquid.

Frittelle d'Arancia con Fichi d'India

Orange Fritters with Cactus Pears (Sicily)

INGREDIENTS for 4:

8–9 Tbsp flour

¼ cup carbonated mineral water

5 Tbsp sugar

2 eggs

Pinch salt

4 seedless oranges

1 tsp lemon juice

2 cactus pears (see Tip)

3 Tbsp butter

Lemon balm, to garnish

PREPARATION TIME: 45 minutes
PER PORTION: about 335 calories

1   Combine the flour, mineral water, 3 tablespoons of sugar, the eggs, and the salt in a mixing bowl to form a batter; cover and refrigerate for about 30 minutes.

2   Meanwhile, peel 2 oranges over a bowl, removing as much of the bitter white pith as possible.

Collect the juice that drips out of the orange while you peel it. Slice the oranges about ½-inch thick horizontally and place on paper towels to drain. Extract the juice from the 2 remaining oranges and add to the juice in the bowl. Stir in the lemon juice and strain through a very fine-meshed sieve or through a colander lined with cheese-cloth.

3   Sprinkle the remaining sugar in a small saucepan and drizzle with a few drops of water; let the sugar caramelize over very low heat. Add the orange juice (be very careful since it might spatter). Caramelize the orange sugar, stirring constantly; remove the saucepan from the heat.

4   Peel the cactus pears (be careful and wear gloves) and chop them. Add them to the orange syrup and set everything aside.

5   Melt the butter in a skillet. With a fork, spear the orange slices one at a time and dip them in the batter. Fry the orange fritters over medium heat on both sides for about 4–5 minutes or until they are golden brown.

6   Place the fritters on serving plates and drizzle with some of the orange syrup; garnish with fresh lemon balm leaves and serve.

Tip: Cactus pears (sometimes called prickly pears) grow on the fleshy leaves of wild cactuses; they are a popular dessert in Sicily, where they are called Indian figs. Look for them in the produce departments of supermarkets that have Latino customers. Their sweet, mild-flavored flesh is speckled with many tiny, edible seeds. When you peel them you need to be careful to avoid the tiny prickles that might have been left behind during packaging.

Citrus—Scented Blossoms and Flavorful Fruits

The flavors vary especially in the case of lemons and oranges

Green, yellow, or orange; sweet or bitter—the world of the citrus fruits is diverse and varied. The cultivation of oranges has an especially long tradition in Sicily. Originally the fruits that the Arabs brought and cultivated were bitter. In time, sweeter citrus has been bred, but those bitter varieties are still used and liked.

Yellow Lemons.
During early springtime the entire island of Sicily, as well as Calabria and Campania, is fragant with the wonderful scent of lemons. In fall, the trees may bloom again a second time if after a long dry season they are watered abundantly. And since different trees are in different stages of blooming and ripening throughout, lemons are typically available throughout the entire year. Lemons are called by different names according to their blooming and harvesting time. *Primofiori* are those lemons that come after the first blossoming and that can be harvested green around November. The fruits that mature between December and June are the *limoni*; these are yellow, thin-skinned, and very juicy. *Verdelli* are the green ones that mature after the second blooming; they are harvested green from June until September of the following year and kept refrigerated for a slower ripening process. Citron lemons have little juice and lots of peel; the juice they have is sweet and at the same time bitter. Their peel is used to flavor limoncello, the lemon liqueur, and in the production of candied citron.

Blond and red.
Oranges mature during the winter months until late springtime. It is almost impossible to classify all the colors and shapes of the existing varieties; they are labeled according to their peel and according to their fleshiness. They are subdivided into blond oranges (the navel oranges) and blood oranges (*sanguinello* and *moro* oranges). Blood oranges have a dark yellow and red peel and red fruit flesh. Their flavor is slightly bitter and stronger than the flavor of the blond oranges, which actually are not the favorites in Sicily. There are also bitter oranges used for jams and liqueurs, for orange products, and for *arancini,* the candied slices of the whole orange with its peel; they have a slightly bitter, seed-rich, not-very-juicy pulp and very flavorful peels. The peels are used to produce pomarance oil, and the blossoms are used to obtain neroli oil; both are used as essential oils in the perfume industry. Even the leaves are scented and are also used as flavoring agents. A type of bitter orange is the bergamot that is cultivated in Calabria. Its peel has scented oils that are used to flavor or aromatize liqueurs, desserts, and Earl Grey tea.

Small and sweet.
Mandarins and their cousins are smaller than the oranges and ripen sooner. They are identifiable by their flattened shape and fairly loose peel. They have a very sweet and aromatic flesh, but they are so full of seeds that even in Italy their popularity has diminished. The Clementine ripens a little sooner, is pleasantly mild and sweet, but has less flavor than the authentic mandarin. Tangelos are increasingly popular in the market; they are orange-sized and are easy to peel, juicy, refreshing, and sweet—and they have hardly any seeds.

a For making limoncello, the Sicilian lemon liqueur: Scrub 5 very large citrons under hot water; use a swivel peeler to remove the peel. Marinate the peel in 2 cups of pure alcohol (96% proof); set aside in a cool, dark place for about 14 days. Pour the liquid through a fine-meshed sieve or through a colander lined with cheesecloth. Bring 7 oz sugar and 3 cups of water to a rolling boil; set aside and let cool. Add it to the lemon-flavored alcohol and fill everything in clean bottles; seal and store in a cool, dark place. Serve ice cold in small frosted shot glasses.

b   Lemon trees are very stubborn and have unique requirements—besides bringing forth fruits, they also bloom constantly. Only throughout cultivated plantations when they are purposely watered are they unified in their blooming time.   c   At the *Costa dei Cedri*, the coastal area from Tortona to Paola, citrons grow that are used to make citronade.   d   Oranges such as these found in Calabria brighten up Sicilian markets and the landscape during spring-time. The *tarocco* is a blood orange hybrid with a light red flesh that is delicious to be eaten just as it is. Blood oranges of the *sanguinello* and *moro* varieties are mainly suited for extracting juice.   e   Along the Amalfi coast, various types of citrus fruits grow—for example the *sfusato* variety that with its peel is used for the production of limoncello.

Index from A to Z

Please note that page numbers in **bold-face** indicate that the entry is *not* a recipe.

Recipes from Appetizers to Dessert

Here you find listed the recipes from all regions according to a menu-related serving order: first all Italian titles and then all English titles, in alphabetical order.

Glossary

Abbacchio: baby lamb

Acciughe: anchovies; also called alici

Aceto: Vinegar

Aceto balsamico: dark and very aromatic balsamic vinegar from Modena

Aglio: garlic

Agnello: lamb

Al dente: noodles cooked firm to the bite; term used also for vegetables

Al forno: baked in the oven

Alici: anchovies; also called acciughe

Alla griglia: from the grill; grilled

Anguilla: eel

Anitra: duck

Anguria: watermelon; also called cocomero

Arrosto: roasted

Arancia: orange

Arista: pork loin

Asparagi: asparagus

Baccalà: dry salted cod fish or dish made from it

Barbabietola: red beet

Besciamella: white sauce

Bietola: Swiss chard

Biscotti: cookies

Bistecca: steak

Bollito: boiled meat

Brasato: stew

Branzino: sea bass

Brodetto: chowder or soup

Brodo: broth

Budino: pudding; custard

Burro: butter

Calamari: squid

Cantarelli: chanterelle mushrooms (also called finferli)

Capesante: scallops

Capperi: capers

Capra: goat; capretto: baby goat

Caprino: goat cheese

Capriolo: deer

Carciofi: artichokes

Cardo: cardoon

Carne: meat

Carote: carrots

Cartoccio: in the bag; food cooked in foil or parchment

Casalingo/a: homemade

Castagna: chestnut

Caviale: caviar

Cavolfiore: cauliflower

Cavolo: cabbage

Ceci: chickpeas or garbanzo beans

Cedronella: lemon balm

Cervo: Stag

Ciabatta: regional oblong bread (term used also for a slipper)

Cime di rapa: broccoli rabe

Cinghiale: boar

Cipolla: onion

Cocomero: watermelon; also called anguria

Coniglio: rabbit

Contadino: farmer

Cosciotto: leg

Costoletta: cutlet

Cotto: cooked

Cozze: mussels

Crudo: raw

Dente di leone: dandelion

Di magro: lean (without meat)

Erbe: herbs

Erba orsina: yarrow

Fagiano: pheasant

Fagioli: beans

Fagiolini: green beans

Faraona: guinea hen

Fave: fava beans (similar to lima beans)

Fegato: liver

Fichi: figs

Filetto di manzo: filet of beef

Finferli: chanterelle mushrooms (also cantarelli)

Finochhio: fennel

Formaggio: cheese

Fragole: strawberries

Frittata: savory pancake/omelet

Fritto: fried

Frutti di mare: seafood

Funghi: mushrooms

Gamberi, gamberoni, gamberetti: shrimp, jumbo shrimp, tiny shrimp

Gelato: ice cream

Gnocchi: dumplings made with potato dough

Gratinato: baked

In agro: sour

In agrodolce: sweet-sour

In brodo: in broth

In padella: in the skillet

In umido: stewed

Insalata: salad

Involtini: rolls

Lardo: lard

Latte: milk

Lenticchie: lentils

Lepre: hare

Limone: lemon

Lingua: tongue

Lombata: piece of loin

Lombo: loin

Maiale: pork; pig
Mandorle: almonds
Manzo: beef
Marrone: chestnut
Marinato: marinated
Mela: apple
Melanzane: eggplants
Melone: melon/cantaloupe
Merluzzo: cod
Miele: honey
Minestre: soups
Minestrina: light broth soup with small
   noodle pastina
Minestrone: chunky vegetable soup
Moscardini: tiny squid
Muggine: grey mullet
Murena: murry, moray

Nasello: pike
Noci: nuts

Olio: oil
Orata: gilt head bream
Ortolano: orchard farmer
Orzo: barley
Ostrica: oyster
Ovuli: white egg-shaped mushroom of
   the edible amanita family

Pan melato: honey cake
Pane: bread
Panini: rolls
Panna: heavy cream/whipped or liquid
Papavero: poppy
Parmigiano: parmesan cheese (also
   inhabitant of Parma)
Patate: potatoes
Pepato: peppered, spicy, sharp
Pepe: pepper
Peperoncini: spicy Italian peppers
Peperoni: sweet peppers
Pera: pear
Pernici: partridges
Pesce spada: swordfish
Pesci: fish
Pinocchi, pinoli: pine nuts or pinions
Piselli: peas
Pollame: poultry
Pollo: chicken
Polpi: octopus
Pomodori: tomatoes
Pomodorini: small tomatoes
Porchetta: baby pig on the spit
Porcini: cèpes; porcini mushrooms
Porro: leek
Prataioli: meadow mushrooms;
   champignons
Prezzemolo: parsley
Prosciutto: cold smoked ham

Quaglie: quail

Rafano: horseradish
Rapa: turnip
Ricotta: Italian type of raw cheese
Riso: rice
Rosmarino: rosemary

Salmerino: char
Salsiccia: sausage
Salvia: sage
Sarde: sardines
Scalogno: shallot
Scaloppini: thin boneless slices of meat
Scampi: prawn
Scorfano: grouper
Sebaste: red bass
Sedano: celery
Selvaggina: game; venison
Senape: mustard
Seppie: cuttlefish
Seppioline: small cuttlefish
Sgombri: mackerels
Sott'olio: canned under oil
Spinaci: spinach
Spugnoli: morel mushrooms
Strutto: lard (also called lardo)
Stufato: stewed; stewed roast

Tagliata: tenderloin (from the beef)
Tartufo: truffle
Teglia: saucepan
Timo: thyme
Tonno: tuna
Triglie: red mullets
Trifolato: prepared with garlic, oil,
   parsley, and salt
Trippa: tripe
Trote: trout

Uova: eggs

Verdure: vegetables
Vitello: veal
Vongole: striped Venus clams

Zafferano: Safran
Zucca: pumpkin

Photographs on the title pages: pages 2–3

Lake Aorta, San Giulio Island

Photographs used in the chapter opening sections:

Ligurian and Tuscan Coast:
Elba, weather station

Po Basin:
Canal in Venice

Alpine Regions:
Alpine High Mountain Refuge,
South Tirol

Tuscany, Umbria and Marche:
Wine, olives, cypresses around
Chianti Classico

Lazio, Campania, and Sardinia:
Campania/Procida, La Coricella

Abruzzi, Molise, and Apulia:
Trabocchi—The way they fish
around Abruzzi

Basilicata and Calabria:
Calabria, National Park of the
Aspromonte

Sicily:
Madonia, Piano Battaglioa

The Authors

Reinhardt Hess—is a prize-winning GU author and one of the authors of the classic work, *Regional Italian Cuisine*. By profession a food and wine journalist, he loves the cuisine of the islands and hidden mountain villages of southern Italy.

Cornelia Schinharl—is GU's specialist for Italian cuisine. Many of her books have been awarded culinary prizes. She often travels from Munich to beautiful Italy in search of gastronomic delights.

Sabine Salzer—has been developing many beautiful cookbooks at GU since 1988. Her first book was *Regional Italian Cuisine*, in 1990. In 1999 she published her best-seller *Basic Cooking* in collaboration with Sebastian Dickhaut.

The Photo Studio

Eising Foodphotography has studios in Munich as well as in Kennebunkport, Maine, and is internationally renowned in the field of food photography. Its clients include cookbook publishers and important marketing and advertising agencies. The photographs in this book were made by Martina Görlach, who has been at Eising for many years, and by her assistant, Sandra Eckhardt. In charge of food styling was Michael Koch, and Ulla Krause was in charge of quality control.

Eising would like to thank Barbara Butz (Bad Tölz) and Petra Fisher (Munich) for their beautiful stoneware.

Acknowledgment of support given during photographic work:

La Cantinetta in Munich (www.lacantinetta-shop.de)

Ingo Keul von Fisher + Trezza in Stuttgart

Wein Wolf Import in Bonn, Weinland Ariane Abayan in Hamburg

BioHof Salmsen in South Tyrol (www.salmsein-biohof.com)

Photo Credits

Cover Photograph (based on Martina Görlach's idea):
foodartfactory OHG
Klaus-Maria Einwanger,
Michael Pannewitz

Eising Foodphotography, Martina Görlach:
all photographs in the recipe sections; short recipes on page 16 right; 22, 50, right, 58, 92 right, 130 right, 136, 156, 168 right, 186, 208 right, 232, 242 right, 248, 256, 276 right

Photographs in the ingredients information:

Peter Amann: page 4 left, 5 right, 6 above right, center right, below left and right, 32, 69 below (2), 137 above, 162, 163, 165 above, 165 below left and in center (2), 166, 167, above right, 167 below left, 187 above left, 204 below, 205 below (3), 206 left, 207 above right, 233 above at the extreme left; 233 above right, 233 below left, 236/237, 238, 239 above center, 239 below (2), 241 above right, 249 above, 249 below right, 257 above, 257 below right, 270/271, 272, 273, 274, 275 above left and below right, 276 left, 285 above left and center, 285 above right, 309.

Michael Schinharl: page 2/3/4 right, 5 left, 6 above left, center left, 12, 13, below (3), 14, 15, 16, left, 23, 33 below center, 59, 68, 69, above, 88, 89, 90 right, 91 above (2), 99, 104, 105, 124/125, 126, 127, 128, 129, 130 left, 137 below (2), 142, 143, 165 below right, 174, 175, 187 above right, 187 below left and below center, 196, 197, 202/203, 204, above, 205 above, 207 above left, 207 below, 208 left, 212, 213, 226, 227, 233 above left center, 233 below center and below right.

Ulrich Sanberger: page 10/11, 44/45, 46, 47, 48, 49, 50, 257, below left, 284.

Klaus Neumann: page 6 below center, 13 above, 92 left, 187 below right, 206 right, 239 above right, 240 right, 249 below left, 285 below left

Reinhardt Hess: page 33 above, below left and right (2), 86, 87, 90 left, 91 below, 98, 164, 167 above left, 167 below right, 168 left, 239 above left, 240 left, 241 above left, 241 below (2), 242 left, 275 above right.

Tiziano Scaffai: page 78/79

Martin Hofbauer: page 257 below in the center, 285 below right.

Published originally under the title *Die neue echte italienische Küche*. © Copyright 2006 by Gräfe und Unzer Verlag GmbH, Munich **GU**

English translation © Copyright 2008 by Barron's Educational Series, Inc.

All inquiries should be addressed to:
Barron's Educational Series, Inc.
250 Wireless Boulevard
Hauppauge, NY 11788
http://www.barronseduc.com

ISBN-13: 978-0-7641-6068-4
ISBN-10: 0-7641-6068-0

Library of Congress Control Number: 2006939684

Printed in Germany
9 8 7 6 5 4 3 2 1